# The Historical Encyclopedia of
# COSTUME

## ALBERT RACINET

## INTRODUCTION BY DR AILEEN RIBEIRO

Head of Costume Department,
The Courtauld Institute

**STUDIO**
EDITIONS

This edition of *The Historical Encyclopedia of Costume*
first published in 1988 by Studio Editions Ltd,
Princess House, 50 Eastcastle Street,
London W1N 7AP, England

ISBN 1 85170 173 7

This book was edited, designed and produced for Studio Editions by
Morgan Samuel Editions, 4 Somerset Road, London W13 9PB

Typeset by Michael Mepham, Somerset
Originated by Scantrans, Singapore
Printed in Slovenia

The Historical Encyclopedia of
# COSTUME

# INTRODUCTION
## By Dr Aileen Ribeiro

WITH THE AIR OF SELF-CONFIDENCE so typical of late-19th-century Europe, Racinet declares that *Le Costume Historique* will cover dress *'dans tous les temps et chez tous les peuples'*. It is indeed a vast work which, while being thorough in its sources and comprehensive in its scope, is without the narrow specialization which marks the age of the 'expert' in our own century. Racinet's work embraces both the history *and* the geography of dress, not just in Europe but in the whole world opened up by exploration, trade and empire.

*Le Costume Historique* is heir to a long tradition of illustrated costume books, a genre that first appeared in the 1560s to satisfy a demand for information on the dress and manners both of Europe and of exotic lands. Such books also included some historical costume, in response to the Renaissance re-discovery of the classical world and a growing sense of the historic past particularly among artists and intellectuals. No doubt such costume books also provided practical help and inspiration for those engaged in staging the elaborate and lavish festivals that were an important part of court life in the Renaissance.

These early costume books were little more than collections of costume illustrations, chosen seemingly at random for fashionable appeal and novelty. By the 18th century a new element was introduced: that of antiquarian research inspired by the need for a more accurate knowledge of the past. Dom Bernard de Montfaucon's *Monuments de la Monarchie françoise* (1729-33) includes a considerable amount of information on costume in his impressive survey of medieval visual remains, but the first important work to concentrate on the history of dress, illustrated 'by Engravings taken from the most authentic Remains of Antiquity', was Joseph Strutt's *A Compleat View of the Manners, Customs, Arms, Habits, etc . . . of the People of England, from the Arrival of the Saxons . . . down to the Present Time* (1775-6); both these highly useful sources are listed in Racinet's extensive bibliography.

The 19th century, with its passion for facts, and with a new mass market to hand, produced a veritable flood of costume books. Some were re-issues of earlier works, such as the most famous 16th century costume book, Vecellio's *De gli Habiti antichi et moderni di Diverse Parti del Mondo* (Venice, 1590), which was published in a French edition in 1859 by Firmin-Didot who also produced *Le Costume Historique*. Others were more encyclopaedic in range, like Quicherat's *Histoire du Costume en France* and J. R. Planché's *A Cyclopaedia of Costume or Dictionary of Dress* (1876-9). Both these books — still worth reading for their wide-ranging sources and intelligent comment — rely on black and white illustrations; Racinet's work is the first large-scale costume book to take advantage of new reprographic techniques to produce the charming colour plates which are one of its most appealing features.

In the late 19th century the informed and intelligent reader would not only have an interest in the different cultures of the world outside, but would also have a keen sense of history, particularly that of his own country. In France it was probably the stirring events of the French Revolution that had helped to focus minds not just on the chronology of history but the reasons behind it. To many contemporaries the drama of 1789 and the following turbulent years reminded them of the heroic days of classical antiquity; during the Revolutionary period there were published a number of books on the costume of the ancient world in order that artists could accurately depict classical dress in history paintings that glorified the link between past and present.

By the late 19th century, the excitement of the French Revolution was also history; so, too, was the Second Empire, heir to the Napoleonic legend. Men and women, while admiring the technological achievements of Western Europe, felt at the same time that they were living in a drab, industrialized world; they felt in need of the imagined glamour of far-away civilizations and the remembrance of things past. Catering to this desire for the romance of the past were paintings (of glorious and sentimental episodes in history) and novels and plays with popular historical themes, ranging from the medieval (widely interpreted) to the 18th century. Historical accuracy in stage costume was increasingly *de rigueur*, part of the lavish spectacle expected by a sophisticated and visually aware audience. Costume historians played their part in this educative process; J. R. Planché, for example, first came to study the history of dress as a result of commissions to design the costumes for some of Shakespeare's history plays.

Other manifestations of the 19th-century love-affairs with the past were *tableaux vivants* and *bals costumés*. Against painted backdrops, Victorian families posed in imitation of famous works of art or dramatic events in history. Queen Victoria and Prince Albert loved fancy dress balls with historical themes; so too did the court under the Second Empire in France, where the 18th century was a favoured source of inspiration for masquerades. Even fashionable toilettes incorporated 'historical' features; comte Fleury (aide-de-camp to Napoleon III) noted how often one saw 'Renaissance sleeves, Louis XVI panniers, Grecian draperies, and those little basques formerly worn by ladies of the time of the Fronde'.

The great Parisian couture house established by Charles Frederick Worth was famous for its sumptuously detailed costumes inspired by the dress and paintings of the past, and in London Liberty's offered, from 1884, dresses to suit aesthetic tastes in the muted colours and flowing lines which were supposed to be 'medieval'. By the 1880s it was essential for the cultivated person to have an interest in and a knowledge of the history of dress. Artists and dress-reformers (particularly in England) also sought to escape from the boring uniformity of the masculine business suit of the late 19th century by promoting (unsuccessfully it must be said) the colourful costume of the past.

*Le Costume Historique* of 1888, six volumes containing a wide-ranging text and abundant illustration (500 plates), must have been welcomed at many levels, from that of the serious student of the history of dress, including the stage designer, to that of the fancy dress reveller. Racinet's previous publications included the illustrations for books on such diverse topics as prostitution, the history of shoes, various historical topographical subjects, and a work on polychrome ornament; he had the varied interests and magpie knowledge essential in the writing of a costume history that claims to cover all peoples and all times.

Not surprisingly Racinet's main interest is in the visual side of the subject and he relies on the existence of original coloured illustrations. Where these are difficult to come by – as in the period after the fall of Rome up until the beginning of the Middle Ages – he omits all but the most cursory discussion; where he is forced, *faute de mieux*, to use black and white woodcuts or engravings (for example from early costume books and fashion plates), he often gilds the lily by adding his own colour. Delightful though the colour plates are, they are not always accurate when compared to the original works of art; until the advent of high quality colour photography it was impossible to reproduce the colours of manuscripts and paintings with any degree of precision.

The selection of plates in this edition (as in the 1888 original) reflects Racinet's concentration on the dress of Europe, particularly its history. The coverage is somewhat uneven as the author dashes, with barely a pause, between the costume of the ancient world, and that of feudal Europe; there is just a token nod in the direction of Byzantium and a brief mention of Charlemagne. Racinet seems to have had the widely held 19th-century belief in the nobility of the costume of the classical period, which was seen as 'timeless', and 'artistic' draperies. This point of view leads him to a major over-simplification when he claims, for example, that clothes in ancient Greece were, on the whole, loose-fitting, when we know that they were often highly complex in cut and construction, and — under Persian influence — tailored and fitted.

Why he has so little to say about costume in pre-medieval France is not clear. Admittedly it was a time of great political confusion — France was little more than a collection of Gallo-Roman and Teutonic tribes within constantly shifting frontiers — but there was enough in the way of surviving artefacts (funerary monuments, illuminated manuscripts, jewellery, and a few textiles) to enable some of Racinet's fellow costume historians to cover the period adequately. One is forced to the conclusion that he believed that it was truly the Dark Ages in the sense that the costume was neither graceful nor artistic. Like many other historians of his time, Racinet was more attracted to the bright colours and attenuated Gothic lines of the costume of the 14th and 15th centuries as revealed in the charming illuminated MSS which he reproduces (though he is a bit vague on dates . . .) Most of all he revels in the elegance and ornament of costume from the 16th century onwards, ending with the startling extravagancies of dress during the *Directoire*.

Of course his prejudices show. Some are well-founded (though perhaps over-emphasized) such as the importance of French fashions in the history of dress. Others are somewhat more eccentric, as in his notion that Puritanism was a dominant strain in 18th century English society and dress (one suspects a dig at the English, uneasy friends and colonial rivals for much of the 19th century). Some of his comments are perhaps wishful thinking, the result of a fairly prudish age: as when he claims that women in the later 16th century wore pants under their farthingales; such garments were, however, the sign of a courtesan (see Bertelli's Venetian courtesan in *Noblewomen and Courtesans*) and were not adopted until the early 19th century when clinging, transparent neo-classical gowns made this kind of underwear essential.

Like many late 19th century costume historians, Racinet may have held the view that the dress of his own time was ugly and unappealing, particularly for men. Thus he concludes the story of men's dress in the early 19th century, with the '*admission définitive du pantalon dans la tenue des hommes élégants*'; with trousers, men's fashion has virtually come to a full stop.

Again, like many of his contemporaries jaded with the incessant changes that are the essence of high fashion, Racinet turns to the more static regional costumes of contemporary Europe with their bright colours and traditional decoration. Even in an increasingly industrialized Europe, such costumes continued to be worn in peasant societies and – particularly in central Europe – they were given a boost by a sense of burgeoning nationalism.

Outside Europe clothing is linked much more to the rites of human passage, of birth, marriage and death, of seasonal toil on the land, of religion and of festivals; it is often bound up with intricate tribal and caste systems. Inevitably costume historians like Racinet tend to discuss their subject within a European structure of society (anthropology was very much in its infancy) unaware of the extent to which dress outside Europe has evolved in response to very different political, religious, social and cultural movements. To be fair, in many cases Racinet does try to place clothing in this area within some kind of social context, but he lacks the detailed knowledge of civilizations very different to his own and is forced to rely over-heavily on the kind of information provided by travellers' tales. The areas that interest him most are those which were, either in the past (India) or the present (China, North Africa), part of France's colonial history; in addition there was a great vogue in the arts for 'japonaiserie' that must have inspired his selection of a considerable number of plates of Japanese costume.

Given the enormous subject matter undertaken by Racinet, it is a truism to say that the reader will find over-simplifications and errors both of omission and emphasis (occasionally compounded by the process of selection, compression and translation in an abridged edition). We may sometimes be mildly irritated by his prejudices, amused at his attitudes (like many 19th-century costume historians there is the occasional tendency to pronounce in a moralistic way on the sartorial foibles of mankind), but we are always entertained. Above all, we are *informed*: for Racinet's monumental work is the result of an impressive amount of research, much of which for reasons of space (accompanying texts, glossary, cut and construction tables, bibliography etc) has had to be omitted. It is hoped, however, that this selection from *Le Costume Historique* will introduce a new generation of readers to what is still one of the great classics in the history of dress.

---

**Publisher's Note**

Racinet's Le Costume Historique was originally published in magazine, or partwork, form over a period of several years. Later, in 1888, it was organized into a work consisting of six, large-format volumes of around 2,000 pages. It is this edition of Racinet's master work that has been translated, re-organized, edited and re-designed to produce this book.

The six-volume edition often betrays its origins as a periodical; sometimes plates are included on furniture and ornaments (Racinet's other main work was on this subject), presumably to help meet deadlines in the face of what must have been staggeringly difficult logistical problems. Probably for similar reasons, the huge amount of text is sometimes ordered illogically.

We have solved this problem by removing most of the material on furniture and ornaments, and by re-ordering entries to construct a chronology; however, Racinet's main organization of four sections has been kept.

Necessarily, too, the text has been edited and pared down from the original. But the meat of Racinet's text – the caption material for the illustrations – has been kept, and his voice and his opinions have been left intact, even when contentious. For Racinet was writing more than 100 years ago, in a very different age from our own: an age of colonialism and continuing exploration; of prejudices and poor communications; of different political and social structures.

So we have corrected Racinet's obvious, gross errors, but ignored his minor oddities. To do otherwise would silence the authentic voice of the 1880s; and also undervalue the magnificent achievement of a remarkable man.

# SECTION ONE

## THE ANCIENT WORLD

THIS, THE OPENING SECTION of the book, traces the development of costume from the beginning of civilization to the end of the ancient world, which Racinet defines as being around 400 AD, at the time of the decline and fall of the Roman Empire.

This period obviously caused problems for Racinet, and, as a result, both the organisation of the section and some of the detailed information in it betray his uncertainty about his material; sometimes, also, his certainty about information that we now know to be false. His examples of prehistoric costume, for example — of megalithic, paleolithic and Cro-Magnon — are included with the illustrations of costumes from Barbarian Europe on page 38; his sources for these illustrations are not known, though they may have been influenced by the prehistoric cave paintings discovered in 19th-century Europe. Similarly, on page 20, Racinet refers to the Amazons, female warriors renowned in myth and legend, as if they actually existed.

But this confusion is hardly surprising. In Racinet's time, archaeology was far from the academic study of today, able to call on all the resources of modern science and forensic analysis. It was a new enthusiasm, a plaything of men of means, whose idea of the scientific approach tended to be to dig a trench through a site in search of treasure.

So Racinet had only a few sources on which to rely. The first of these was monumental sculpture, which itself was not always reliable. He complains, for example, that on Roman statuary, ladies are often represented as Greek goddesses. Sometimes, the nature of his material leads Racinet into fascinating diversions from his theme: the scenes depicted on Trajan's Column, a prime source for his pages on Rome, lead to a lengthy discussion of sacrificial rituals.

In the case of Egypt, however, Racinet is on firmer ground. Egypt has been of special interest for French academics for many years; since, in fact, Napoleon had brought the Rosetta Stone — eventually the key to the decipherment of hieroglyphics — back to France following his Egyptian expedition. As a result, Racinet was able to draw on a mass of sculptures and tomb paintings. This explains the length and level of detail of his Egyptian pages.

Otherwise, Racinet relies on his artists' interpretations, or those of artists of previous generations, of descriptions of costume given by classical writers, poets and historians. His pages on the costumes of the High Priests and Levites of Israel, for example, utilise 16th-, 17th-, 18th- and 19th-century interpretations of descriptions in the Book of Exodus. These are likely to be fairly accurate, but the same is not necessarily true when the illustrations are derived from the work of classical writers. But we must remember that Racinet did not have the benefit of the 100 years of classical scholarship that has changed our understanding of ancient history since his time.

# EGYPT

GODS, GODDESSES AND PHARAOHS

THE MOST AUTHENTIC INFORMATION AVAILABLE on the subject of ancient Egyptian costume comes from the study of the sculptures and paintings of the period. These images were not influenced by the arbitrary imagination of the artist, but followed convention and custom, as can be deduced by their uniformity of style. Many of the images are of gods and goddesses and of rulers dressed as gods. But in the convention of the times these were represented in human form, and, as a result, they give us a portrait of the people who worshipped their deities through the successive generations.

**1.1** Pharaoh Ptolemy Philadel-phus, wearing a tall mitre bearing the royal cobra and a loincloth, called a *schenti*.

As well as a wide necklace and bracelets, Ptolemy has an apron that appears to be made of leather and points outward at the front. This was tied on to the body by cords and could either be held up a cage of canes or by metal bands.

**1.2** This Cleopatra, one of the six Egyptian queens of that name, has plaited hair bound by a ribbbon bearing the royal cobra. The two feathers of the headdress denote the highest rank, while the sun, globe and ram's horns are symbols of fertility. In her right hand is an *ankh*, a symbol of life.

**1.3** A more warlike Ptolemy Phila-delphus. His headdress consists of a war helmet and a mitre decorated with ostrich feathers.

**1.4** Osiris, the god of death, the underworld and the afterlife.

**1.5** Mut, wife of Amun and mother-figure of the Egyptian pantheon.

**2.6** The goddess Anoukis in her conventional colours, carrying her usual papyrus sceptre.

**2.7** An unnamed goddess, whose headdress is a tall mitre with a pair of ram's horns protruding at the front and back.

**2.8** Queen Nephertari, wife of Rameses II. This fragment shows an Egyptian women in her best finery, with a transparent dress and an eye enlarged with kohl.

**2.9** The war standard of Rameses III. The two raised arms symbolize victory.

**2.10** The great god Horus, who symbolizes the eternal nature of divinity.

**2.11** Movi, the Egyptian equi-lent of Hermes, is symbolized by the ibis, a sacred bird whose feather tops his headdress.

**2.12** Amun-Ra, the supreme god, with his characteristic headdress containing two long, straight feathers. The sceptre with a grey-hound's head is a symbol of life.

**2.13** Mandoulis, a sun god whose cult was based in Nubia. He wears a striped headdress and a tall, red mitre, with a yellow disc.

**2.14** Khnum, the "maker of gods and men", who fashioned nature and mankind in the small bowl in his right hand.

**3** The interior courtyard of a rich Egyptian's house.

## HEADDRESSES AND HAIRSTYLES

ANCIENT EGYPTIAN STYLES OF DRESS WERE INFLUENCED to a great degree by the hot climate and the burning sun. Women often wore only a girdle and a *klaft* to cover the head. The *klaft* was generally made from a thick, striped material and was fixed at the temples. It fell in folds over the shoulders, sometimes covering the ears and sometimes revealing them. Some women, though, wore headdresses that had been specially designed to show off the shape of their heads – examples can be seen in the second strip.

———— • ————

Egyptian women oiled their bodies in order to keep their skin supple in the intense heat, and also used quantities of cosmetics. They coloured their eyelids green or black to make their eyes appear larger and painted their cheeks white and red. The veins on their foreheads were traced in blue, while carmine was put on their lips and their fingers were dyed an orange-red colour with henna.

The most usual colour of clothes was white in all its shades, while headdresses were made of striped or embroidered material. Cotton, linen and wool were all used. Necks and ankles were normally bare, but adorned with richly worked necklaces and bracelets, made from gold, coral, pearl, agate, onyx and chalcedony.

The main figure in **2** is that of a woman playing a mandola – an ancient stringed instrument – taken from the Necropolis at Thebes. She is wearing a collar formed from six strings of beads, and has two bracelets on each forearm. Her dress, which reaches to the floor, is made of linen, and is so thin that it may well have been made in Asia rather than Egypt.

The main figure to her right is that of Rameses II, King of the 19th Dynasty. His crown is decorated with a cobra, a sign exclusive to the Egyptian kings.

The headdresses in **1** hide the hair, but those in **2** generally reveal it. The Egyptians took great trouble over their hair, often plaiting it intricately and adding artificial hair or wearing it in ringlets. The rich wore wigs of natural hair, while the poor made do with wool.

Rameses and the lady to the left of the mandola player both have thickly plaited hair, its volume probably increased by the use of hairpieces.

Sometimes the additional hair was attached to the headdress – as is probably the case with the figure to the right of Rameses, where the headdress is similar to a small skull cap. On other occasions, the additional hair is attached to the natural hair, as in the figure at bottom centre, where the headdress is a pointed hood, completely independent of the plaited hair.

Immediately above this figure is a different hairstyle that may show either ringlets or very fine plaits; in the bottom left-hand corner the hair is long and smooth, showing that Egyptians who wore their hair short had it cut severely.

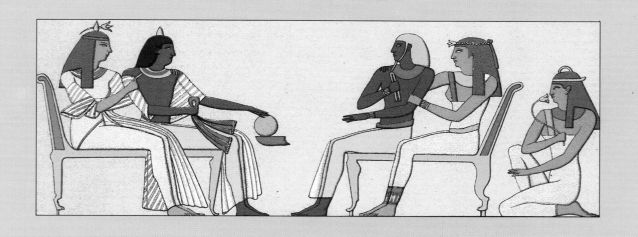

## EGYPTIANS AT WAR

THE WARRIOR KINGS OF EGYPT led their armies into battle personally, riding on chariots and brandishing bows, arrows and battle-axes. A tame lion, dressed for battle, normally ran in front of or behind the king's chariot.

————— • —————

**1** Rameses II, wearing a helmet decorated with the royal cobra and encrusted with precious metals. Wide ribbons flow out behind it.

His body is covered with a leather-lined bronze cuirass and a metal gauntlet protects his forearm from the sting of the bowstring. His six-ringed collar supports an enamelled pectoral.

A typical war chariot has two wheels and is open at the back. In this picture, however, the sides are open. The chariot is probably made of bronze, as is Rameses' bow and arrows, while the arrowheads are iron.

Normally the warrior had a charioteer on his left, but here he has the reins attached to his own body. The horses wear a fringed headdress running half-way down the neck and a tasseled coat, tied at the chest. This coat was often woven in colours in the Baylonian style and sometimes embroidered.

The other figures in **1** show various different headdresses and hairstyle: some have loose hair; others have plaited hair with metal or leather coverings.

**2** The absence of cavalry in the paintings and bas-reliefs of Egypt suggests that there was not a cavalry force as such. The mainstay of the army was the infantry, protected by chariots posted at the front, back and sides of the marching body.

Here the chariot carries an ensign. Each corps had one, placed high on a pole so it was visible to all around. The emblem was usually religious and the god was represented either in human form or by the appropriate animal emblem such as a sparrow or a lion. In this picture the royal standard is a vulture. To the left of the chariot a priest is burning incense.

The soldiers accompanying the chariot are heavily armed. Their shields have small peepholes, so that the soldiers can see out without showing their faces.

Their white tunics are tied at the waist and their heads are bare. Their toes, however, are protected by pointed shoes called *tabteds*, made from plaited palm leaves tied with cords.

**3** Victorious warrior kings slaughtering their defeated foes. In 3.13 a hugely over-proportioned Rameses III kills captives of a number of different races; their hands are tied behind them.

Rameses is wearing a bronze helmet and his cuirass is decorated with the wings of a victorious sparrowhawk. The cords of his quiver go around his body and are hooked at the front. He is armed with a bow and a battle axe and wears a metal gauntlet as a wristguard.

3.20 Rameses II killing an Ethiopian with his battle-axe. Here he is simply wearing a *klaft* and the striped *calasiris* that was the national military costume. Only the cobra stands out on his forehead as the sign of a ruler.

3.14 & 15 Bronze battle-axes, fixed to the handle with leather strips.

3.16 A bludgeon of acacia wood.

3.17 & 18 Canes, about 3ft long, carrying hieroglyphics and having a small thumb hook at the end. They are thought to have been a badge of office.

3.19 An Asian prisoner and 3.12 a Negro captive wearing a chief's feather, a wide baldric and large earrings.

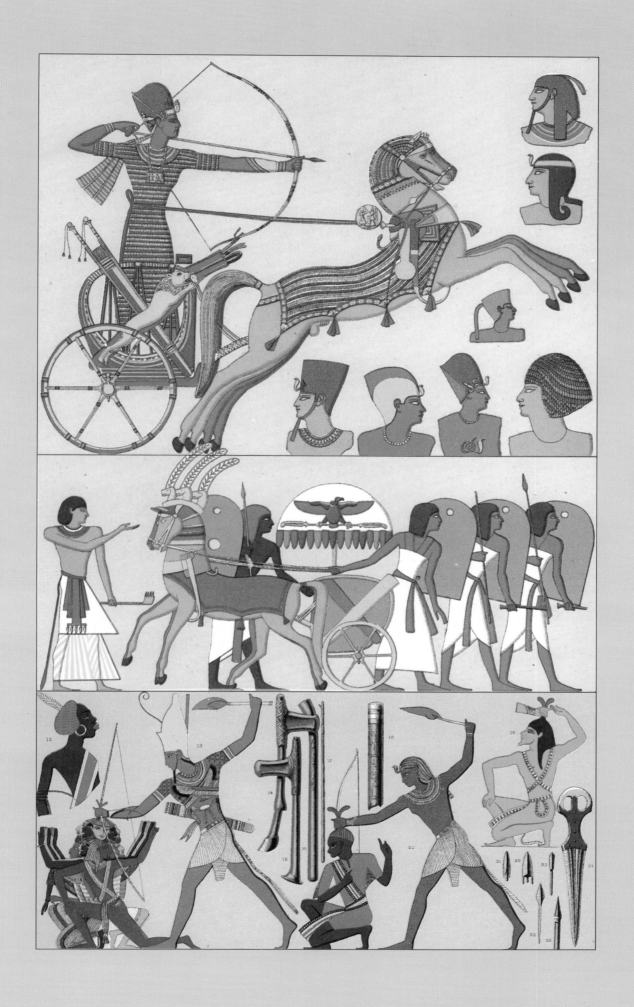

# ASSYRIA

### ASSYRIANS – PERSIANS – MEDES

ASSYRIAN SCULPTURE DIFFERS FROM THAT OF EGYPT, in that the subjects treated do not come from all the various classes of society. The standard images are scenes of war, hunting and religious ceremonies in which the principal figure is the king. The monuments from which these illustrations are taken were built by the Persians, who took on the customs of their defeated foes; the Persians had conquered the Medes, who had themselves overrun the Assyrians.

According to Plutarch only kings of Persia could wear an upright tiara, encircled by a diadem. Others had to wear the tiaras at an angle. The royal tiara was a truncated cone, topped by an upright point. The ordinary conical bonnet worn by Persians was made of wool and had a point that either leant backwards or forwards.

The royal stole was dyed crimson, edged with gold and decorated with precious stones. The long Medo-Persian robe, called a *candys*, was made of linen or cotton and was worn only by the king, his principal officers and his eunuchs. A belt was an essential part of Persian costume: the king's was made of gold. Footwear was not so stylish, though. The Greeks reproached the Persians for their "miserable" looking sandals, which did not complement the rest of their fine costume.

1 A hunting scene with a king accompanied by two pages, one of whom carries his feathered arrows and the other his lance. All three wear laced boots and a double belt, and the king wears a golden diadem with long ribbons hanging from it. Apart from this, his costume only differs from that of his servants in its richness.

2 On the left are two foreigners bearing gifts: their clothes different from those of the Assyrians and the edging on their garments is not made from tassels. Their boots, with toes that curl up, resemble those still worn in Persia today.

The central figure is a king, wearing a tiara and diadem and carrying the royal sceptre shaped at the top into an apple.

To the king's right is a eunuch with the king's weapons and his sceptre, which has a wrist strap at the bottom and a radiating disc at the top.

The winged figure accompanying the eunuch is a god. He carries a square basket in one hand and a pine cone – a symbol of nature – in the other.

3 A chariot pulled by three horses and driven by a charioteer. The horses' heads are decorated with fan-shaped plumes.

The king is wearing his usual upright tiara and diadem and carries a curved bow and some arrows. Behind him are two eunuchs bearing sceptres. They both carry quivers; one also carries the king's sceptre and the other a parasol to shade the king from the sun.

4 The king followed by two eunuchs. The king is leaning on his bow and raising a dish, preparing to make a sacrifice. A eunuch is waving a fly swatter to keep insects away from the dish, and next to him a priest assists.

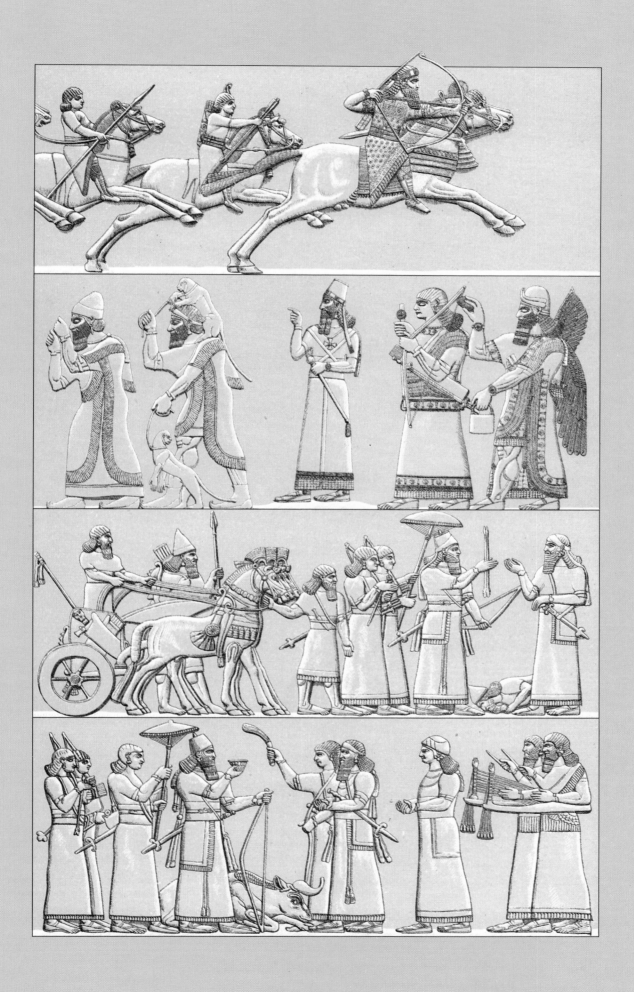

# ISRAEL

## PRIESTS AND LEVITES

THE IMAGES OF THE HIGH PRIESTS and Levites opposite (8, 9, 10, 18, 20 and 21) date from the end of the 16th century to the middle of the 19th century, and are interpretations of descriptions in the Book of Exodus. We know very little of what effect the turmoil and upheavals of those times might have had on Hebrew sacred costume: the influences of Egypt, Babylon, Assyria and Greece must all have had their effect.

We do know, however, that Moses chose those who would serve in the sanctuary exclusively from the tribe of Levi, after their exemplary conduct in the affair of the golden calf. They were divided into two classes: the priests and the Levites.

The high priest, or the "anointed priest" (so called because his head was anointed with holy oil), was in charge of the general administration of the sanctuary and the forms of worship. Some of his garments were common to all priests: leggings, a tunic, a belt and a high bonnet.

In addition, the high priest wore a violet tunic that had bells hanging from it to alert people to his presence in the sanctuary, an *ephod* (13 & 14), which was a type of corset of Egyptian origin, fixed at the shoulders and made from linen and decorated with gold brocade, and a pectoral (14). Moses called this "an ornament of justice": it was square, embellished with precious stones and worn on the chest.

According to Exodus, Aaron, the first high priest, wore an ephod decorated with twelve precious stones representing the twelve tribes of Israel.

1, 2, 11 & 12 show the influence of Egyptian headdresses on those worn by the Hebrew High Priest. 1 and 2 show the symbolic *fleur de lys* that had replaced the cobra as a ruler's decoration at the time of the exile from Egypt.

8 A man wearing a tunic such as

Aaron would have worn beneath his *ephod*. In Hebrew this tunic was called a *mehil*.

The neck of this garment was hemmed and woven so that the edges did not tear. It had a fringe made of small bells, so the wearer could be heard in the tabernacle. Examples of this decoration are common on pictures of royal clothes through the ages and have been found in Egyptian tombs.

3, 4, 5, 6, & 7 A variety of small bells. Sometimes these were enamelled and sometimes they were made of metal, so different sounds could be made when they were struck together.

13, 14, 16 & 17 The *calecon*, the basic article of Levite costume. It was shorter than that worn by the Egyptians, so Moses decreed that a long tunic should be worn on top of it.

19 A fitted undergarment with tight sleeves, which in this case stops at the knees. It was worn by the priests under their ceremonial costume.

15, 16 & 17 Examples of belts worn by the Levites. They were often made of snake skin (15 & 16), following Egyptian custom.

Moses did not specify whether these should be coloured like those worn by the high priests or whether they should be all white. The belts were wrapped around the body several times and the ends hung down.

# PERSIA & PHRYGIA

## AMAZONS – PARTHIANS – PERSIANS – PHOENICIANS

THE ROMAN POETS DID NOT REALLY DIFFERENTIATE between the Parthians, the Persians and the Medes, and the name "Phrygian", synonymous with "Trojan", sufficed for the group as a whole. Indeed Strabon echoed Xenophon in saying "the Medes and the Persians have many similar customs." This confusion, and the limited number of relics available for study, makes it difficult to specify to which group certain articles of costume should be attributed.

The basic elements of costume were a simple tunic, gathered into one or two belts and worn with or without sleeves; a long robe with long sleeves; and a coat of various lengths, with or without sleeves and open at the front.

1, 23, & 24 Amazons. These three female warriors show the range of Amazonian costume. They did not always follow the stereotype of leather casques, bared right breasts and double-headed axes.

5 & 6 Parthians, wearing feminine headdresses that imitate the style of the Medes and the Persians. The tiara curves backwards in Phrygian fashion.

7 A Phrygian or, more precisely, an Armenian, wearing a long tunic with sleeves beneath a short, sleeveless tunic.

8 Paris, wearing two belts, one of which is hidden by his clothes. His tunic is blue and his *chlaeane* light blue.

10 & 19 Persians, wearing in one case a bonnet and in the other a mitre or tiara; both wear a baggy tunic that is pulled back at the sides by a belt and has wide sleeves, revealing very narrow sleeves underneath.

11 & 25 Mitres in the true Phoenician style. The extra pieces, called *redimicula*, are tied under the chin.

17 The King of Persia at the time of the Lower Empire, wearing a pearl-studded crown which radiates outwards and is fixed at the front with a diadem.

18 This beautiful headdress in Phrygian style, tied on with a decorative band, is typical of Phoenician costume.

20 Parthamaspare, King of the Parthians, wearing the two tunics that Strabon attributes to the Persians (they can be recognised by the two sets of sleeves). The coat is fringed on three sides and appears to be rectangular in shape.

22 A captive Armenian, wearing a long tunic with sleeves.

26 A young man, taken from a Palmyrenien bas-relief, wearing a short tunic, gathered in with a narrow belt and a light coat with short, narrow sleeves that is probably the Persian *candys*. His trousers are narrow and reach down almost to his ankles.

Other illustrations include: 2 – a fly-swatter; 3 – a fragment showing a woman's costume; 4 & 13 – thrones; 9 – an Armenian crown with bow and arrows; 12 – Tigrane, King of the Armenians; 14 – the typical Parthian crown and weapons, the bow and arrows in a quiver; 15 – a Persian shoe; and 21 – a Phrygian shepherd: Attis the beautiful, beloved of Cybele.

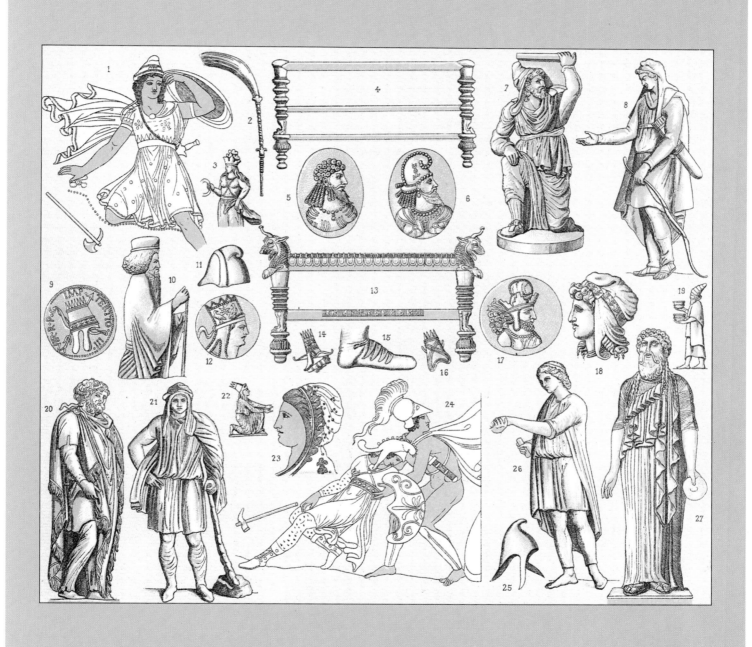

# GREECE

## THE LAND OF HOMER

THE GREEKS WORE CLOTHES THAT DID NOT OPEN at the front, unlike ours today. Nor did they cling to the body except where they were fastened by a belt, or where the softness of the material fell against the contours. The basic garment in Greek costume was the tunic, or chiton, which could be made of either linen or wool.

One of the most interesting outer clothes is the *palla*, because it falls somewhere between an over-garment and a chiton. It is fixed at the shoulders, leaving the arms bare, and is not attached at the sides but held at the waist with a belt and fastened at the hips. The women in 1, 4, 6 and 14 are wearing variants of the *palla* called *pallulae*, which stop at the waist.

But one thing is certain whether the *palla* is worn by musicians, actors or gods, it is a distinctly feminine garment.

2, 7 & 11 The *talaris* tunic. The sleeves could be long or short and were usually wide so that they hung gracefully from the arms. The garment was made of linen and fastened with a belt. Both men and women wore the *talaris* in Greece, but the Romans thought it an unworthy garment for a man and never adopted it.

6 A type of cloak that probably belongs to the same family as the *pharos*.

7 & 11 The small *chloene*. This is an outer garment and is often mentioned by Homer. It is very simple, being made from a square of warm material; a piece of metal was attached to each corner so that the robe hung in beautiful folds.

8 A himation, which is a smaller version of a chlamys; the long chlamys reached to the ground and became the Roman *paludamentum*.

This garment seems to consist of a rectangular piece of material with two additional drapes that end in points. It is attached to both the arm and the shoulder by hooks that join the ends together, and the folds are held by a hem.

These pleats are characteristic of the himation. The tunic worn beneath it is made from a remarkable crêpe or goffer material.

9 The Doric *podere* tunic. This garment is embroidered with stars; the actual material is transparent. The woman wearing this costume has a necklace of pearls and bracelets and anklets entwined like serpents. The light shawl, also embroidered with stars, is called a *pharos*. This was a fine, brightly coloured garment that was generally fastened with a pin. Homer says that it was worn by women and children.

12 A long tunic, gathered in with a belt, whose absence of sleeves suggests that it is of Doric origin. It is left open at the sides above the waist. 15 shows a chiton of a similar but simpler style, without openings at the sides.

Other illustrations include: 16, 17 & 18 – men and women relaxing at a feast; 19 – a vase with a stopper and a label; 20 – a purse; 21 & 22 – glass bowls for fruit; 23 – a bread basket.

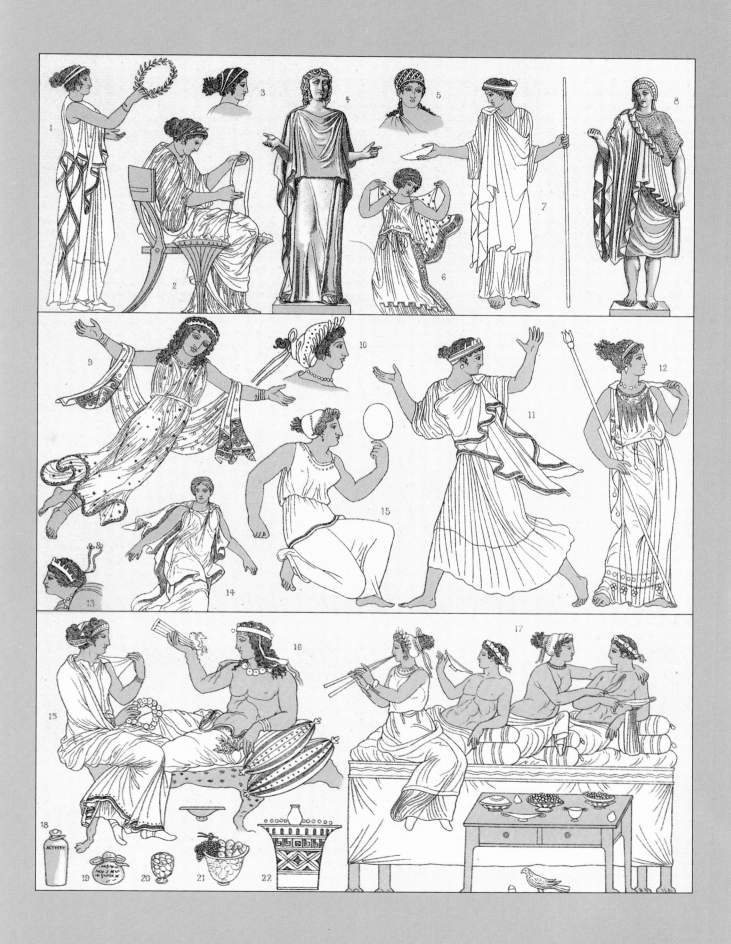

**1.1 & 6** Greeks wearing the chlamys, the standard garment of the young people of Athens. This was made from a rectangle of material, but falls in triangular points.

The chlamys could be worn in a variety of ways. In 1 it is held by a brooch at the right shoulder so that the left arm is covered while the right arm remains free. In 6 it is fixed on the chest, almost at the throat, and thrown back over the shoulders.

Both men are wearing hats from Thessaly at the back of their necks, indicating that that they are travellers. One wears felt shoes that go half way up his leg, while the man in 6 is a messenger, carrying a *caduceus* and wearing leggings rather than shoes.

**1.2** A woman wrapped in a light pallium.

**1.3** A man wearing a *podere* underneath a pallium.

**1.4** A woman wearing two exterior belts, the *strophion* and the *zona*.

**1.5** The *catastictos* or *zodiote*. This was a robe of many colours, "spotted like the coat of the panther".

**1.7** A pallium, the famous overgarment that Homer assigned to gods and heroes and named the *pharos*. In his poems the *pharos* is sometimes described as brilliant white and sometimes as brightly coloured.

It was made from a rectangular piece of woollen material, attached at the throat or on the shoulder by a brooch. In this example, though, the *pharos* is not fixed by a brooch, but thrown over the left shoulder to hang down the back, rather like a Roman toga.

**2** A Greek woman's toilette was an important of her daily routine. Women would cover their entire bodies each day with perfumes and ointments, pomades and oils.

**2.1 & 2** Women washing. Fresh water was mixed with scented waters and "ambrosial liquids".

First the women would wash the dye and powder of the previous evening from their hair. This could be of various colours: ebony; sky-blue; honey-coloured; dusted with golden powder; or even red. Whatever colour the hair, the eyebrows were always painted black.

Here the clean hair is is ready to be curled with hot irons. The woman in **2.2** is holding a mirror, or possibly a clay compound used like a soap.

**2.3, 4 & 5** Women at various stages of dressing. The fine material of their costume barely covers their bodies.

At one time such transparent items of clothing were worn as supplementary articles: the veil that the servant in 10 is offering to her mistress, for example. Under the rule of Pericles in Athens, however, moral standards were relaxed and transparent materials were used as tunics.

**3** The first step in dressing was to wind a band of material beneath the breasts (far right). Next came a tunic of transparent material. There were several types: long, without a belt or sleeves, in the Ionian style (left centre); or short, with a belt (right centre).

Over the tunic was pulled a second short, sleeveless tunic. Again, there are several types, as shown on the left of **3** and in **4**. The tunic shown third from the right in **3**, trimmed with animals and flowers, is called a *zodiote*.

The *palla* was a type of overtunic attached at the shoulders with brooches and gathered at them to fall in double pleats over the breasts. The process can be seen in **4**.

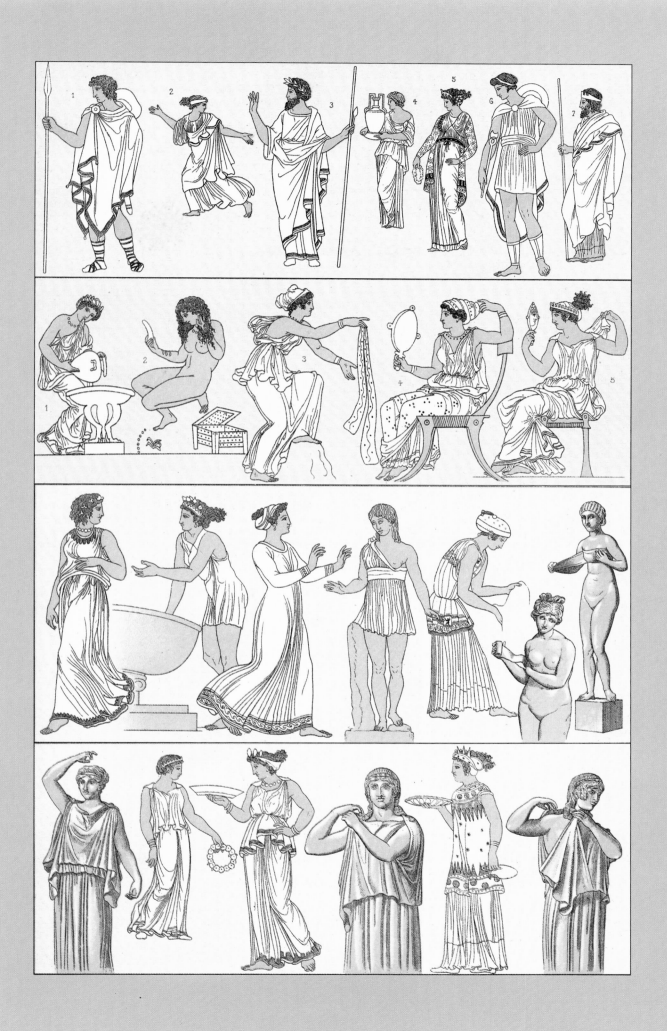

# THE HEROIC AND HISTORIC AGES

THE DIFFERENT AGES OF GREEK MILITARY COSTUME can be distinguished by the dimensions, if not the type, of the weapons carried by the Greek soldier. Large shields from Argos, javelins and short swords are of the age called "heroic". With the "historic" age came a reduction in the size and weight of shields and an increase in the length of javelins and swords to twice the size that they had been previously. '.

18 An officer, whose armour is made from pieces of bronze held together by leather-covered ropes and lengthened by a double *lambrequin*, also made of leather. The under-garment is a short-sleeved woollen tunic.

He is wearing a low, rounded helmet with the visor and leather chin straps drawn up and a red plume like a fan. His baldric is made of leather and his sword has an ivory handle (26). His shield is round and convex, made from two pieces of wood with an ornamental bronze plaque. Inside it are red tassels (48).

This picture is taken from a vase-painting that shows the combatant's arm reaching through one handle to hold on to another, thus enabling him to manoeuvre the shield with more dexterity.

20 A heavily armed infantryman, an *hoplite*, wearing a bronze helmet with a strong, wide chin strap of the same metal, an ornamental crest and a plume of horse hair.

5, 10, 29 & 55 Helmets of the *heroic* style with rounded casques, no visor and tall crests. The exception is 29, where the crest has been removed as a mark of defeat.

1 & 16 confirm the theory that the Greeks carried a cloak on their left arm if they did not have a shield.

21 & 22 Illustrations from a vase showing soldiers marching.

50 A *peltast*, a light infantryman. The *pelta*, a name first given to a small shield by the Amazons, was made of wood or of wicker-work covered with leather. 49 shows in detail the double clasp of his belt and 34 shows his casque with its high plume; see also 52, 57 and 59.

23 A cavalryman, who would have ridden without stirrups, probably with just a piece of cloth on the horse's back. He has three protective discs of bronze on his cuirass, and leather leggings. He is carrying a sword (detail in 35) and spurs are attached to his sandals.

39 A *phalangite* – so called because he fought as part of the phalanx formation – wearing the helmet of Minerva. This was a leather head-dress with three tails of leather covering the back of the neck (38). His one-piece cuirass is made of bronze and fastened at the waist by a bronze belt (28).

46 A victorious soldier. Pinned to the top of his lance are the cuirass and belt of his vanquished enemy.

41 An archer wearing a leather hat with a neck-covering that falls a long way down his back (43) and leather leggings (44).

19 The goddess Pallas Athena, armed with a golden lance and an aegis.

17 Diana the Huntress.

40 A hand clad in a *coestus*. This consisted of straps of leather twisted around the hand, sometimes as far as the elbow, whose purpose was to help the boxer in hand-to-hand combat.

25 & 37 Mummies of a civilian man and woman. Mummification would have taken place in Egypt.

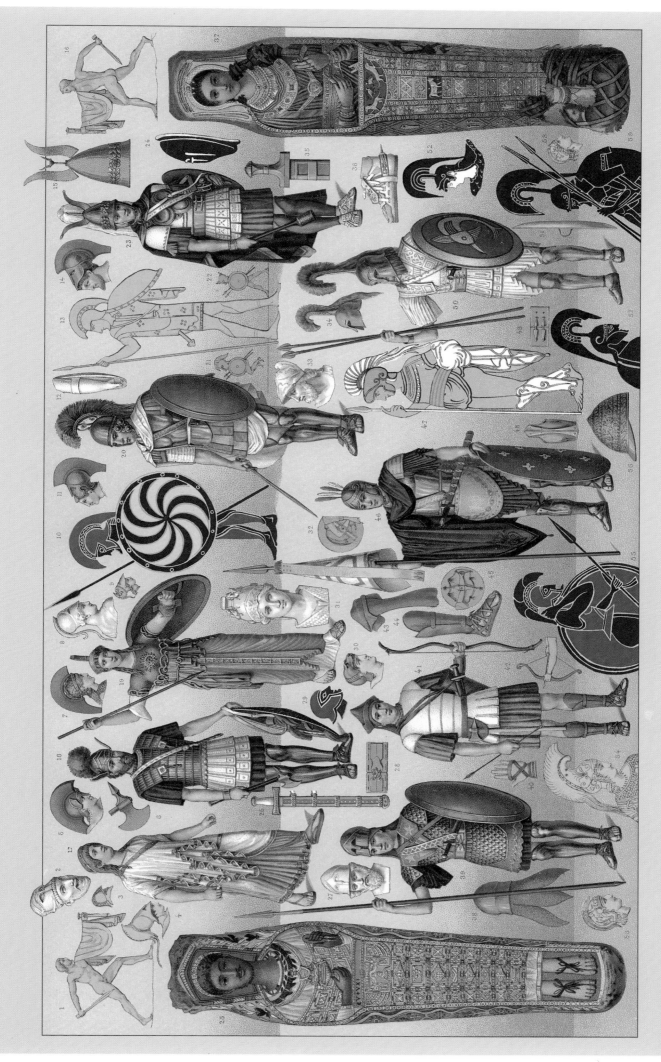

# THE ETRUSCANS

AN UNKNOWN CIVILIZATION

ANCIENT HISTORIANS, SUCH AS HERODOTUS, believed that the Etruscans were of Asiatic origin, and the Etruscans themselves claimed in their annals that they came from Lydia. Nothing is certain, however, apart from the fact that they occupied a part of Tuscany in North West Italy.

The Etruscans left tombs, paintings, sculptures, furniture, vases, jewellery and many other artefacts that make up our main source of information about them.

Striking analogies can be drawn between the Etruscans and the Lydians, particularly in the case of the tombs. But although the genius of the Hellenic influence is quite apparent in these works of art, archaeologists claim to be able to discern numerous qualities which would appear to reflect the Etruscans' Asiatic origin.

1 & 5 Amazons retiring from battle. One is wearing a feathered helmet while the other has a helmet with a double crest. Their tunics are pleated in scalloped folds.

2 & 3 Achilles with his chariot of war, driven Automedon, his charioteer, and accompanied by Patroclus. This picture is taken from a description in *The Iliad*.

4 A Persian wearing the winged helmet of Hades, which made the wearer invisible, and carrying a Scythian bow.

6 Iris, messenger of the gods, carrying her emblem, the *caduceus*.

7, 9, 11 & 12 Helen and her young girls pursued by Menelaus. The costumes are completely Greek, while the vigorous depiction of movement is the essence of Etruscan style.

8 A musician playing the double flute. The Etruscans introduced this instrument to Italy at the same time as the bronze trumpet.

10 Mercury, messenger of the gods, with a beard, a belted tunic and small boots.

13 The master of a gymnasium.

14 A warrior, wearing a pointed helmet similar to those worn in Thrace. The shape of this defensive armour recalls the Mongolian or Circassian helmet. It seems to have been covered with a felt bonnet, a practice common when the warrior was not in battle. The subject here wears laced boots known as *Tyrrhenian* boots.

15 A chariot pulled by a team of four. It is driven by a Phrygian and its wide, studded wheels with eight spokes are exactly like those on the Assyrian chariots in the sculptures at Nineveh.

16 & 18 Examples of men's hairstyles.

17 A helmet with a long, swaying crest.

19 A typical peasant, dresed in a tunic and cloak. His low-crowned, broad-brimmed hat is called a *petasus*, and his leggings are straps of leather wound around his calves. He is carrying a staff with a forked end, the mark of the labourer.

20 An Etruscan warrior wearing a Boeotian helmet with a raised crest.

21 A helmet or bonnet.

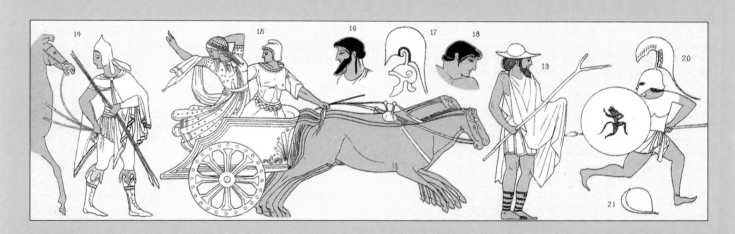

# GRECO-ROMAN

AN EXCHANGE OF IDEAS

THE GRECO-ROMAN PERIOD IN COSTUME marks the transition between the costume of "heroic" Greece and the establishment of the Roman Empire. Rome came to dominate Italy around 275 BC, but was still a republic until Augustus first donned the imperial purple in 27BC. Since Rome was founded – according to Vergil – by Aeneas, who fled from the Greeks sack of Troy, the new republic adopted many facets of Greek culture. The Greek gods and goddesses were worshipped under Latin names, and costume – and changes in costume – passed from one culture to the other.

1 A chariot with a charioteer in Phrygian costume in a portrayal of the abduction of Helen from the "heroic" period of Greek history. The scene is watched by a seated Muse.

2 Sculptures of the deities known to Romans as Juno, Vulcan, Venus, Mars and Diana; but to the Greeks as Hera, Hephaestus, Aphrodite, Ares and Artemis.

3.6 Juno, wearing Ionian costume and holding a sceptre in her left hand, sits on a throne.

3.7, 9, 10 & 11 The *klismos* or *clismos*, a chair with a low seat and a high back with a concave backrest, from which the Greek philosophers would give their lessons. The Romans also used it as a teacher's chair, but called it a *cathedra strata*.

3.8 A group of women talking, attended by a slave. The slave, who holds a fan of feathers, wears her hair short as a sign of servitude. Her dress is worn without a belt and has narrow sleeves that are tight at the wrist. The purity of line indicates its Ionian origin.

The principal lady in the group is wearing a large veil that covers almost all of her features: the costume of a Greek virgin.

4.14 An unusual headdress that resembles a *pileus*, the ordinary headdress of sailors, fishermen and artisans. It is worn without ties and set back slightly so that the hair is showing. Unusually, a veil is attached to it.

Felt bonnets were worn exclusively by men. Their shapes varied from nation to nation but always preserved the same general character of a bonnet without a brim.

Phrygian and Greek bonnets were shaped like eggs, as were those worn by free Romans.

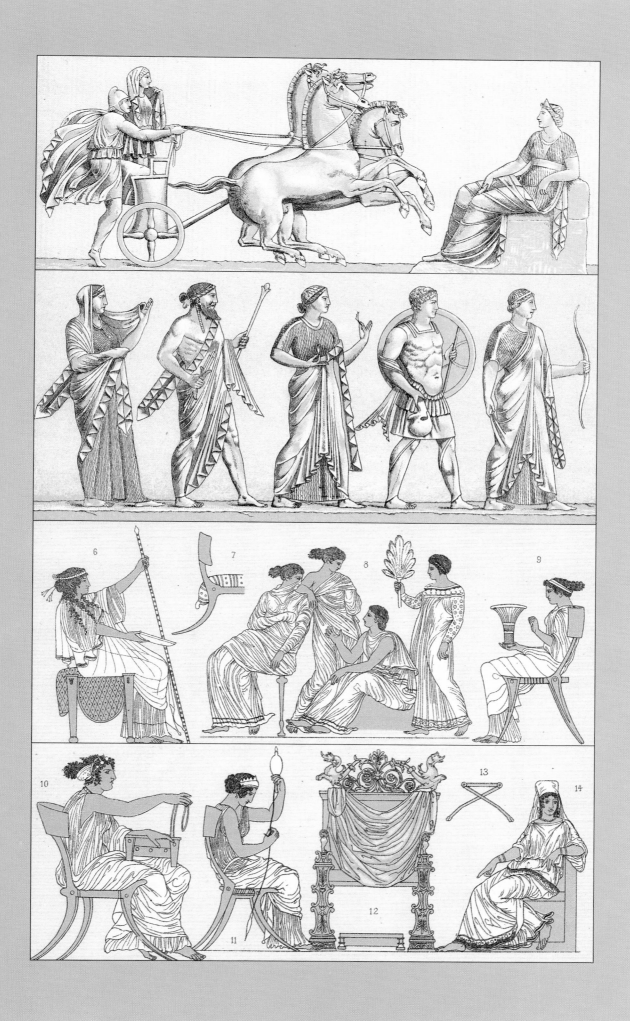

# ROME

## THE PRIVILEGE OF THE TOGA

THE TOGA WAS THE PRINCIPAL OUTER GARMENT worn by the Roman citizen. It was a civilian costume; in the army a military cloak was substituted – either the *sagum* or the larger *paludamentum*. A Roman citizen who wore a toga was called a *togatus* and in the days of the Empire this was a status symbol; the working classes were only allowed to wear togas on feast days. A foreigner was never permitted to wear one, and nor were slaves, though an enfranchised slave could. A Roman who lost his right to the freedom of the city also lost his right to wear the toga.

Togas were made in various different colours. The emperor wore a purple toga, while the toga of a well-to-do citizen was made of white wool of a very high quality. The artisans and the poor wore togas made of dark-coloured wool. The toga *candida* was dyed especially white and worn by those seeking election, hence the term "candidate".

The early toga was not the amply-pleated, sweeping garment that is illustrated in the examples opposite, but a much simpler affair. Unfortunately we do not know how it developed into the grand toga of Imperial Rome.

**1.3** An emperor.

**1.5** A senator wearing his toga draped over his shoulders.

**1.6** Alexander the Great.

**1.10** A senator.

**1.11** Nero, of whom Suetonius said that he never wore the same garment twice. Here Nero is wearing a very feminine costume. His tunic, a *collobium*, has half-sleeves and hardly reaches to his knees. As a contrast to this civilian, effeminate costume he is wearing a military chief's cloak.

**1.13** An orator wearing his toga draped over his head, but leaving his face visible.

Despite the number of works of art depicting Roman women, not a great deal is known about their costume. This is because in much of Roman statuary women are shown as Greek goddesses.

The principle female outer-garment was the *palla*. This was sometimes draped over the head (**1.8**) and was short enough to reveal the *instita*, the decorative hem of the robe called a *stola*. The latter was worn over a chemise and gathered into two belts, one below the breast and the other round the hips, to create a hanging fold (**1.4**).

**1.7** A seated woman wearing a *palla* that covers her arms.

**1.9** The muse Calliope wearing a *palla* in a complicated arrangement similar to that of a toga.

**2** Most of these examples of headdresses are taken from Roman works of art. A few, however, are Greek in origin. Numbering clockwise from the top left, they are:

1 – a wig; 2 – stone carving of Faustina, wife of Antoninus; 3 – Plotina, wife of Trajan; 4 – Julia, daughter of Titus; 5 – a woman, after Caylus; 6 – Zonobia, Queen of Palmyra; 7 – Livia, wife of Augustus; 8 & 9 – the same Greek head shown from different angles; 10 – a stone carving of a Greek woman wearing a veil; 11 – Faustina, wife of Marcus Aurelius.

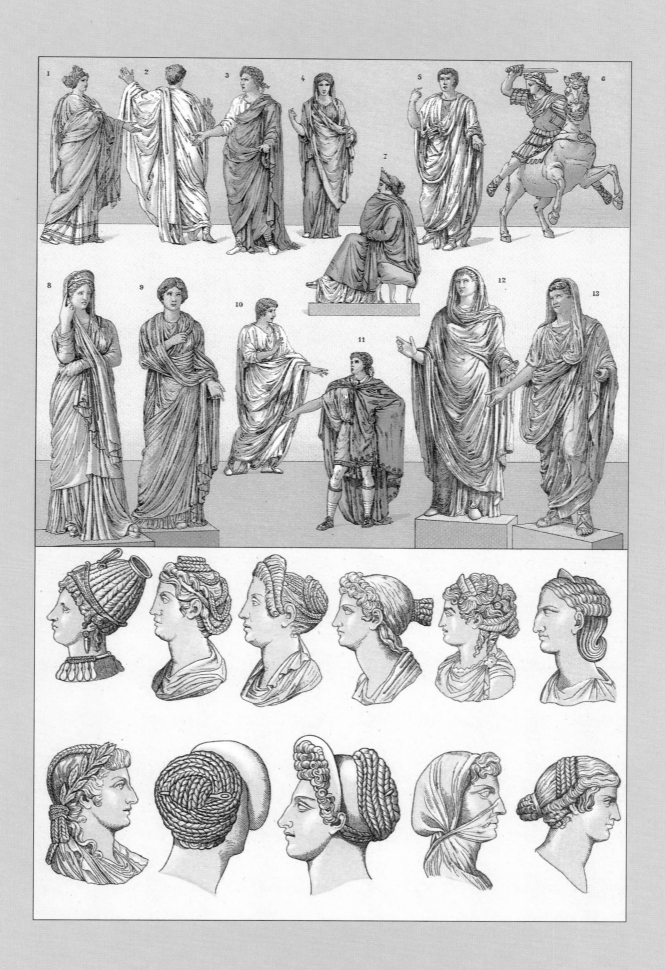

## SACRIFICIAL RITUALS

SACRIFICES PLAYED A MAJOR PART in the religious and civil life of Rome. They had a dual purpose: to placate the gods and goddesses at whose whim all lived; and to foretell the future by means of augury. Far-reaching decisions were taken on the basis of the health of an animal's entrails.

As a result, the ritual was often performed, or at the least supervised, by the highest in the land. These stylized scenes from Roman life are taken from Trajan's Column.

**1** A sacrifice dedicated to Mars, in which three animals are to be slaughtered: a pig, a cow and a bull.

The animals would be led three times round the place of sacrifice to purify them, then their throats would be cut. Here the procession takes place round a camp and the Emperor Trajan plays the role of *martialis* and priest by pouring wine on the altar fire.

The man leading the bull and carrying an axe is called the *popa*. The man following him is the *cultrarius* – he delivers the final blow to the victims with a sacred knife. Both these men are wearing a sacrificial robe called a *limus*. This was secured at the waist by a belt and hemmed with a band of purple.

**2** The sacrifice of a bull and some fruits. A pineapple is among them, and as this was normally dedicated to Cybele it is probable that the sacrifice is to her. Again Emperor Trajan supervises the ritual.

**2** (centre) Trajan appears once more, wearing a different costume.

**2** (right) *Victimarii*, the servants of the priest conducting the sacrifice, hold the animal down so that the *popa* can deliver his blow with the back of his axe. All the participants are wearing ceremonial laurel crowns.

**3** A fragment showing a sacrifice to Neptune. A *popa*, armed with a mallet, holds a bull at the top right; this was the animal traditionally sacrificed to appease Neptune.

**3** (centre) A sacrifice in which incense is being burnt at an altar as a votive offering to the gods. Incense was a feature of all sacrifices, but in this case no animals are involved. The ritual is performed by a woman, with the assistance of a small girl.

The two pillars with heads of Hermes in the background suggest that this was probably a sacrifice to Mercury.

**3** (right) A sacrifice to either Cybele or Bacchus. It appears that the priests are attempting to foretell the future by examination of the entrails being burnt on the altar.

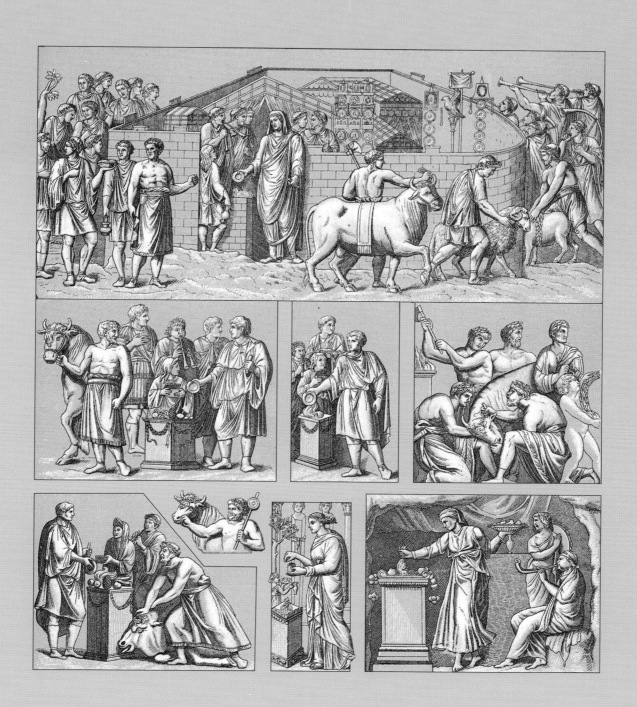

# THE MIGHT OF ROME

THE TRUE MIGHT OF ROME lay in the strength of its legions. For around 400 years these tough, well-disciplined troops dominated the known world, with only occasional setbacks. In the cities, gladiators – equally tough and professional – entertained the mob with blood-curdling spectacles.

1 The Roman military salute: the unsheathed sword is vertical.

8 A centurion carrying a vine stock, his badge of rank. His scabbard is covered with nail heads and his helmet has a silver crest with a plume of dark feathers.

9 & 22 An infantryman *"impeditus"*, that is, "loaded", on the march. His cooking utensils and clothes are slung from a pack on his back, and counter-balanced by the weight of the helmet on his chest. He is wearing traditional soldier's sandals, called *caligulae*.

10 A tribune from the Rhine Army. There were normally six tribunes in a legion, each commanding a cohort. He is wearing a *phaleroe*. Of Greek origin, this was made of round plaques of gold, silver or other metal, upon which were engraved the heads of a gods, emperors, or military leaders.

11,12, 17 & 32 Gladiators. Those in 11, 12 & 17 are wearing helmets that completely cover their heads, with just holes for eyes. They each wear a *campestra* – a type of skirt folded round the hips.

21 A cavalry officer wearing a dalmatic. His sword is longer than that of the infantryman so that he can reach the enemy from horseback. His shield, a *parma*, is made of painted wood decorated with bronze. This was also used by troops who carried light weapons.

23 Caesar, wearing the purple of an *imperator*, or "chief general" of the republic.
His *parazonium* (26), has a leather scabbard, which is decorated with bronze. His *cinctorium* is also made of pieces of bronze (detail in 27) and his tunic, fashioned from leather, has elaborately decorated shoulder pieces and short, fringed sleeves (detail in 19).

24 The *triare*, the basic infantry soldier. At this time his equipment is still almost entirely like that of a Greek warrior.
He is wearing a bronze helmet with chin straps, a crest and a hanging plume. His surcoat recalls the Greek cuirass made from animal skin or linen. His undergarment, called a *subarmale*, is made of wool and has wide short sleeves, and his pectoral is made of bronze.
His sword, called a *gladius*, has an ivory handle and scabbard (25). The Romans, unlike the Greeks, always carried their swords on the right side. His shoulder belt is made of painted leather, and the greaves, called *cnemides*, are iron. In his right hand he is holding a *pilum*.

30 An ensign-carrier. Each cohort had its own ensign, as did the subdivisions, called *maniples*.

33 A footsoldier from the Eastern provinces of the Empire. Instead of a metal *lorica*, he is wearing a dalmatic made from numerous pieces of leather, arranged in double layers and studded.

34 A cavalry standard-bearer, called a *vexillarius*. The *vexillium* was a standard or flag (detail in 29) peculiar to the cavalry. It consisted of a piece of square cloth attached to a horizontal bar and surmounted by two bronze eagles. The *parma* is made of painted wood and has an iron boss.

# BARBARIAN EUROPE

## ENEMIES OF THE ROMANS

THE ILLUSTRATIONS OPPOSITE ARE by no means taken from the same period of history. They are representative of the warriors that that fought the Roman Empire: Celts and Gauls, Germans, Teutons, Slavs, Scythians, Finns and Tartars. There are also Asiatics – the Goths, Visigoths, Huns and Vandals who banded together at the time of the great invasion of the Barbarians from the North during the fourth and fifth centuries. Their repeated attacks brought about the fall of the old Western Empire, 500 years after the battle of Actium and 1,200 hundred years after Romulus. Yet Rome did not even exist at the time when some of the stone-age peoples pictured here first roamed European soil.

1 A megalithic warrior, carrying an axe whose stone head has been pierced to take a wooden handle.

2 Also megalithic, a man wearing a rough woollen hood, shirt and trousers, a fur vest and a necklace of boar's teeth.

3 A man from the "barrow" people, named for their burial mounds.

5, 7 & 8 Cro-Magnon men from the palaeolithic age.
  5 This Cro-Magnon carries a flint-stone knife, with a bag containing flints. His shoes are made of skin and are lined with hair (10).
  The man in 7 carries a wooden spear and has wooden club attached to his belt. His tunic is made of bear's skin.
  The man in 8 appears to be a chief. He is holding a spear with a barbed edge, a lance with a wooden shaft, a dagger made of ivory from a mammoth (11) and a leader's baton made from a stag's antlers (9).

22 A Bronze Age soldier, with a helmet of thick leather, covered with feathers that hang down and cover most of the raised part. His cuirass is made of hemp and the tall, elliptically shaped shield is made of painted wood and reinforced with strips of bronze.

25 A warrior with a long cuirass that crosses over at the front. The helmet is made of leather with bronze studs and he is carrying a long sword with an iron blade and a bone handle. His forearms are protected by armbands (27).

26 A chieftain with a gold helmet plated with a crest and a horse-hair plume (sideways view, 28). His military cloak and tunic are made of red wool.

30, 35 & 37 Bronze Age warriors. The warrior in 30 carries a short bronze sword and a bronze-headed lance. His cuirass is made of strong leather. (Details – 43, 44 & 36). The warrior in 35 shows a bronze helmet with wings of feathers. His shoulder belt supports a bronze sword and is decorated with bronze. (Details – 31, 39 & 41). In 37 the warrior's fringed cloak is attached by a bronze fibula. (Details – 31, 39 & 41).

33 A Bronze Age chieftain. The top of his bronze helmet is pointed and decorated with a feather from a white heron. His cloak, breeches and tunic are made of white wool. His cuirass is very long and made of strong leather with bronze studs, while the belt has a bronze clasp from which his sword, knife and daggers are hung.

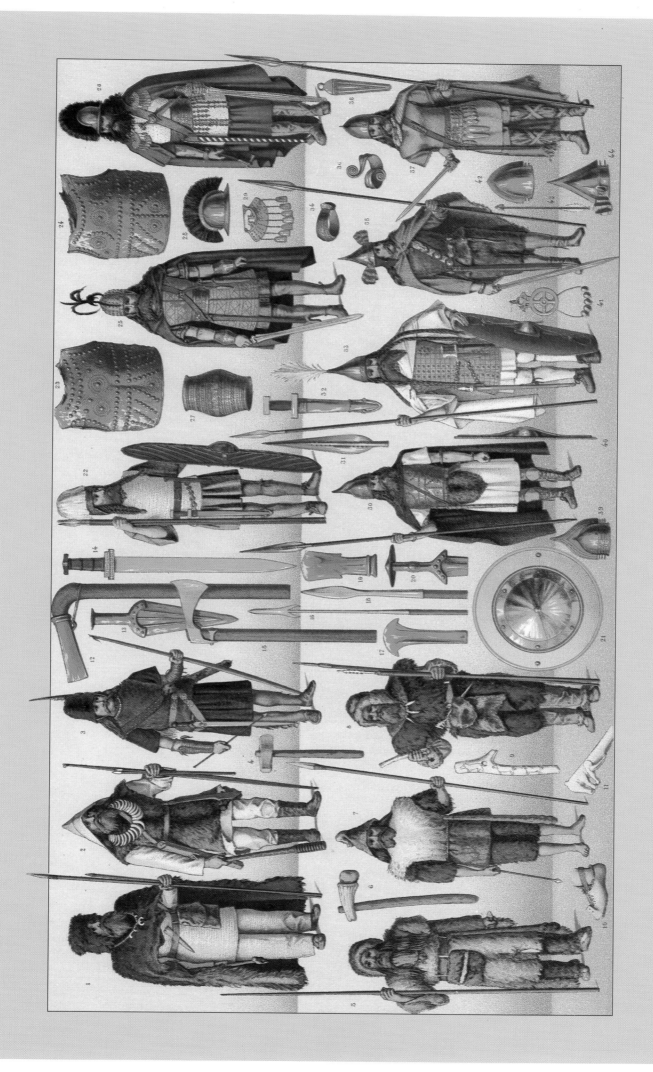

# BRITONS & GAULS

## INEFFECTIVE FINERY

THE GAULS AND THE CELTS – THE ANCIENT BRITISH – filled the entire ancient world with the sound of their weapons, until once victorious they proved unable to develop an organized sense of nationality. As a result, they lapsed into a state of military decadence two or three centuries before the birth of Christ.

Their military leaders carried splendid weapons and had magnificent horses and chariots. Over a tunic embroidered with flowerets of gold, a chief would wear a gilded cuirass or a shiny coat of iron mail – a Gallic invention. This was beautiful but ineffective, and in 58BC the Gauls were conquered by Julius Caesar.

1 The chief *Sutticos de Rouen*, with his hair tied in a pony-tail.

2 A chief in everyday dress: his hair is loose and he is wearing a collar of coloured beads.

3 A warrior, with hair tied up.

4, 5, 6, & 8 Gallic women. Like the Romans they used cosmetics: their hair was often powdered with white ash; they washed their faces in beer-foam; and darkened their eyebrows with liquid taken from the garfish. They wore long robes, often with aprons, and like Gallic men had a passion for jewellery. The barefoot woman in 4 has loose hair and a tunic with long, wide sleeves. The woman in 5, also barefoot, wears a tunic hemmed with a red band that is cut to look like a fringe.

The next women, 6, wears shoes, but her head is covered with her cloak in the style of a Roman pallium. This could be a sign of age, widowhood or captivity. The style of headdress in 8 was common in Gaul, and became so among female slaves in Rome.

7 A peasant, wearing a tunic with two vertical stripes and a belt.

10 A warrior leaning against a menhir. The helmet, cuirass and shield are decorated with studs and points; his shoes, called *Gal-*

*lica*, have thick soles and are tied at the instep.

11 An armed peasant wearing a Phrygian hood. His outer garment is the famous *caracalla*, described by Strabon as the "Gallic *palla*".

9, 12, 13 & 14 Peasants wearing different types of *bardocunulle* – a hooded cloak. This was the origin of the monk's cowl.

16 A warrior wearing a helmet called a *berru*, so named because it was found in 1872 at Berru in France.

21 An infantryman carrying the ensign of the golden boar, a Gallic symbol of excellence. His tunic is striped with bright colours and his cloak is military, of a type called a *sagum* by the Romans.

22 & 23 Gallic horsemen were famous for their bravery. Here the ensign of the golden boar is also used as a weapon.

33 A warrior ready for combat, wearing an iron helmet (39) with chin straps, horns and a crest.

34 A soldier carrying the *carnyx*, the horn of war.

35 A Gallic chief with a bronze helmet decorated with two large wings from a bird of prey.

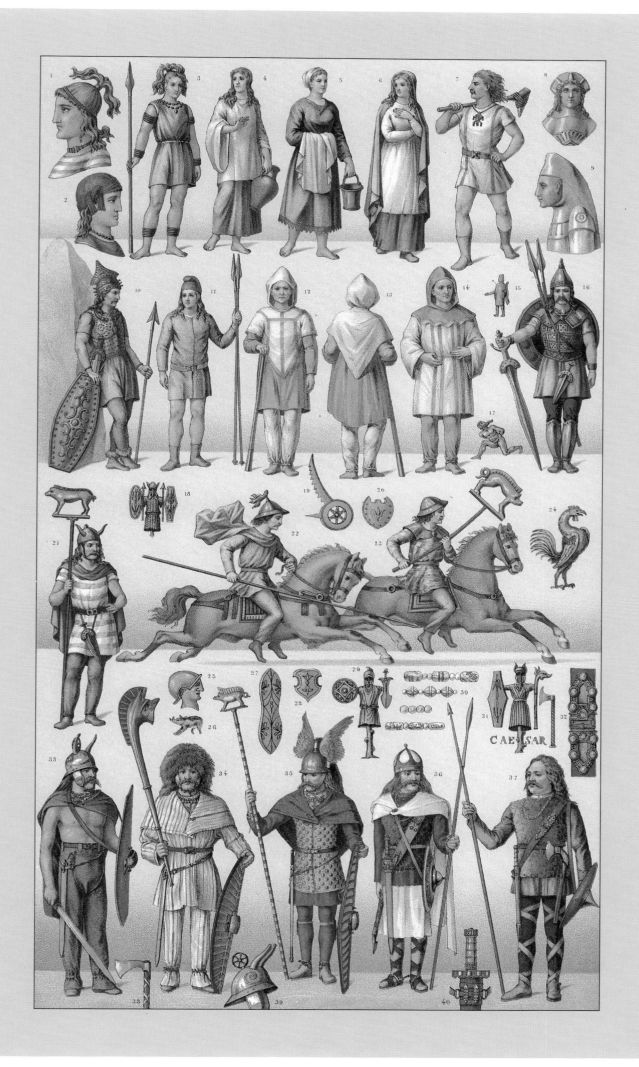

# SECTION TWO

# 19th CENTURY ANTIQUE CIVILIZATIONS

RACINET'S TITLE FOR THIS SECTION is somewhat clumsy, but it is hard to think of a better one. He uses it to take in all those areas of the world in which costumes did not, in the 1880s, conform to Racinet's idea of the mainstream of European style and fashion.

This concept creates a number of curious anomalies. Racinet appears to have started by using the phrase "antique civilizations" to cover those societies that, to his eyes, were actually uncivilized, even though he is rarely condescending: thus his treatment of the natives of Oceania (a term used confusingly, to include parts of the Far East as well as Australia and the Pacific Islands), the American Indians and Africans. Racinet obviously shared the 19th-century fascination with the costumes and customs of societies that in many cases had been known for less than 100 years and that were still being discovered and investigated in his time. He shared, too, an interest in Rousseau's concept of the "Noble Savage" – an appreciation of the basic, natural virtues of humanity, uncluttered by the paraphernalia of an increasingly mercenary and industrial society.

Suddenly, though, Racinet has to change tack, as he turns from the simplicity of nomadic tribesmen to the complexity and subtle sophistication of societies older than, and very different to, his own: China, Japan and India. Here he becomes surprisingly critical – at least in the case of China, becoming particularly indignant about the opium-smoking habits of the Chinese Imperial Court: whether or not they existed, he seems to ignore the notorious involvement of the European powers in the opium trade with China. But much of Racinet's information and comment in these areas – and, indeed, in this whole section – comes from travellers' tales and reports. The section continues with yet another category of "antique civilizations": those of the Middle East and Turkey. These societies are different again. Turkey, for example, is covered here. At the time, Turkey was still the focus of the Ottoman Empire, which was clinging on to its sphere of influence – once its possessions – in Europe, and had a well-developed and old-established bureaucracy. Yet since the style of dress is far different from that of the main European tradition, Turkey is discussed here. Racinet still has the time to write with disapproving relish, though, of Persian dancing girls and coffee-making rituals.

The sources for the illustrations in this section appear to be both contemporary prints and engravings, and, in an early use of the medium, photography. Source photographs are referred to several times in the text, mainly in comments about the way in which an illustrator has made a change from the original.

⚓

# OCEANIA

MALAYS – PAPUANS – ABORIGINES

THE ANTHROPOLOGIST RIENZI claimed to have identified four distinct races among the archipelagoes and islands of the Pacific Ocean. Later, though, it became accepted that there are only three principal races: the Malays, who used to inhabit the coasts until invaders chased them inland; the Papuans, fishermen who live principally along the shores; and the nomadic Australian Aborigines.

1, 15 & 17 Papuans. The warrior in 1 wears only a loincloth, with an amulet in the form of a human figure round his neck. His hair is decorated with a wooden comb and a plume of feathers, and a sabre called a *peda* is worn round his neck.

15 shows a simple woollen tunic with a fringed hem. The shoulder belt is decorated with feathers and the hemispherical leaf hat is adorned with shells.

The grass-skirted warrior in 17 has first dyed his hair red in lime water, then whitened it with powder made from pulverised coral. The effect is crowned with a diadem of cassowary feathers and a headband of small shells. The warrior's comb is adorned with a plume of feathers from a bird of paradise.

3 & 18 Members of the Kanaque tribe from New Caledonia, dressed for a feast day. Styles were varied and individual, but most tied their hair up with brightly coloured material topped with a plume of feathers. Some wore beards, while others shaved with sharpened oyster shells; but nearly all pierced their ears. The warrior (18) wears a mask designed to frighten his enemies.

8 & 10 Aborigines, who did not know the bow and arrow, but relied on wooden spears and boomerangs (13 & 14).

9 An Arossien, from San Cristobal in the Solomon Islands. A warrior tribe, equipped with bows and arrows, spears and bludgeons (5), the Arossiens often pierced their noses and hung ornaments, such as parrot feathers, from them. Here the hair is tied up with a bamboo comb and decorated with fringes that hang down on either side of the parting. The bracelets and belt are made from white, red and black beads of shell, and are used as currency.

11 A native of the Admiralty Islands. Here the warrior's face is painted white and his hair is decorated with hibiscus and feathers. He has a collar of small shells and as a chest-ornament wears a white ring of shell with fine scales attached. The arm bone of an enemy hangs round his neck. His bracelets are made from large shells, and he wears a finely worked loincloth.

12 A Vitien warrior, whose hair has been reddened either with lime water or the bark from a tree soaked in coconut oil, then curled back around the head and decorated with a comb of parrot feathers. He wears a collar of shells, pigs' teeth and rats' or bats' jaws.

19 A New Hebridean warrior, with a wooden helmet whose visor has a human face painted on it. This mask opens at the level of the mouth and ends in the form of a beard. His chest is covered with a decoration of plaited bulrushes, from which hang three pendants made from teeth. His spear is heavily spiked with barbs made from human bones.

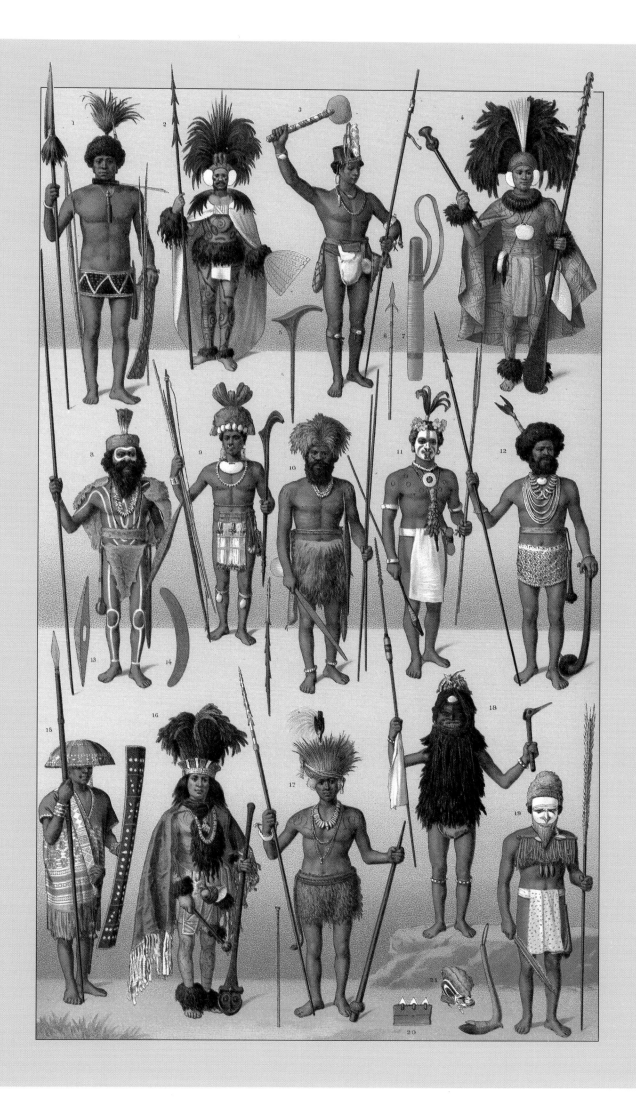

## JAVA – BORNEO – SINGAPORE – PHILIPPINES

AMONGST THE TRIBES OF OCEANIA it was often the custom for mothers to flatten their childrens' noses artificially, and to encourage the use of varnish to darken their teeth. Tribesmen would make themselves more attractive – and more frightening to their enemies – by covering their bodies with tattoos.

———— • ————

**1 & 9** A Javanese woman and man. The woman wears a light turban and long and full trousers that are gathered in around the waist by a narrow thong. Two chains hang from a gold collar studded with gems.

The man (9) is similarly dressed, but with a cut-off conical bonnet and a garland of flowers.

**2 & 19** Natives of Borneo in battle dress. The upper body (2) is protected by a breast-plate of fish skin. The loin cloth under the breastplate ends in a small apron at the front. The helmet, like a thick forage cap, is of woven cane. The war jewellery consists of a collar and bracelets made from tiger claws.

The second native (19) shows several variations in dress. The front of his helmet represents a human face, while its top is made of the skull of a rhinoceros bird decorated with argus feathers. His sword hilt is decorated with the hair of those he has defeated and on the ground is a basket, used to carry severed heads.

**5 & 7** Karens from Borneo. The man's clothing is for everyday wear and the woman is in full ceremonial dress.

**12** A warrior of the king's guard from the Islands of Hawaii.

**15** A Binua, from Singapore, wearing full battle dress. The lance is entirely wooden and the blowpipe, the national weapon, is much shorter and more inaccurate than later versions, such as those tipped with iron points (19 & 24).

The Binua's clothing and jewellery are made entirely from natural materials: a leopard skin hangs over one shoulder, and his hat is crowned with feathers.

**16** A Malay from Borneo. He has a Muslim's shaven head, and a hat in the shape of an inverted basin that serves as a parasol. Malays usually carry two daggers: one at the front and one slung over the shoulder.

**18** A woman from the Timor Islands. Her upper body is covered in a tissue of silk, threaded with gold and she wears a silk cap and a dyed cotton skirt that is Javanese in style. Unless in the presence of strangers, a skirt would be her only garment.

**23 & 24** Dayas in hunting and battle dress. The bun hairstyle (23) shows Polynesian influence and the breastplate (24) is made of vegetable fibres.

**25** A child's fly swatter.

**30** A Philippino Indian fisherman. This armour looks like chain mail, but is, in fact, made of vegetable fibres.

**38 & 39** Daya women. The sleeveless jacket (38) is made entirely of cotton. The small wooden box attached by cords serves both as a pocket and and a bag. The second woman (39) wears only a loincloth, which goes down to the knee. Her hat is made of woven straw and her bracelet of brass wire.

## MALAYSIA – INDONESIA

THE PEOPLES OF MALAYSIA, where a poorly turned out man invites scorn, are the best dressed in Oceania: even in the poorest, most distant islands the Malaysians never go about naked. Clothes are generally made from local products, but blue materials and cotton are also imported from the two Americas.

The principal item of the male costume is the *sarong*. This is made from a piece of material called a *pagne*, six or eight feet long by three feet wide, which is wrapped round the hips and sometimes secured with a belt. Women use *pagnes*, too, though in their case they are knotted at the throat and hang down to the ankles. Women's hair is usually tied up at the back of the head and fastened with a pin made of horn, buffalo or brass.

———— • ————

All the illustrations in **1** & **2** are of natives of Gorontalo, a town on the Bay of Tomini in Celebes.

**1.1** Alfour de Tondano, ruler of Gorontalo, in ceremonial dress that copies the ancient national costume. He wears an elegant loincloth of richly coloured silk. A white headscarf covers the hair, which is held up at the front by a silken headband containing the feather of a bird of paradise.

**1.2** Contemporary ceremonial dress. The scarf crossing shoulders and chest is held in place by a belt; this device was used in the company of Christian women as a symbol of faith. The costume is made of cotton and the scarf of silk.

**1.3** & **4** Sailors, both with cotton costumes and silk sashes. One headscarf (3) is of cotton; the other is of silk.

**1.5** & **6**, and **2.1** Catholic women, wearing chemises, handkerchiefs round their necks and aprons. Showing both European and Oriental influences, these are devotional garments.

**1.5** & **6** show the same woman from two different angles. She wears an enormous wooden hair comb, which rises above her head in the shape of a cross. This is topped with artificial flowers from which are hung small chains of brass encrusted with shells.

**2.1** This woman wears a gilded belt and carries a fan of gilded leaves; her necklace is made of glass beads.

**2.2** One commentator says that "the chiefs wore either a Christian costume, which tended to give them rather a starched appearance, or a Muslim costume that suited them a great deal better."

Here the chief has adopted a Muslim style of dress, but the shoulder sashes, crossed over the chest, may indicate that the man is a Christian and perhaps the husband of the woman next to him.

**2.4** A warrior dressed in a chequered Malay sarong, a short open jacket and a headscarf wrapped round the head like a turban. All these garments are made of cotton. In his left hand he carries a *kampilan*, a type of sabre whose blade is wider at the tip than at the hilt. The tall narrow shield is called a *salawako*.

**2.5** A member of the Gorontalo militia in his uniform.

**3** The majority of Oceanic tribes do not cut their hair short and wear nothing on their heads. The characteristic style is shown on the left: the hair has been allowed to grow long, and is fastened at the back with a bamboo clasp; the forehead and nose are decorated with markings. Short-haired styles, with and without a headdress, are shown to the right.

# AFRICA

SENEGAMBIA – THE GUINEA COAST – WEST AFRICA – ABYSSINIA –
SOUTHERN AFRICA

THERE ARE MANY DIFFERENCES between the African tribes, differences that manifest themselves in varying styles of costume. The widest variations in costume, however, are those between the inhabitants of Senegambia and the Guinea Coast, on the West of Africa, the Abyssinians, to the East, and the Southern Africans.

1, 6, 8 & 14 M'Pongue women, from Gabon, wearing either a piece of cloth wrapped round their hips or draped, short pantaloons and belts. Their chests are bare, but decorated with strings of carefully chosen beads. They attach a *moondah*, or ornament, to these necklaces, the most popular motif being a tiger's claw.

3 A chief of the Yoloff tribe from Senegambia, wearing a blue robe of cotton – the standard material in this part of Africa. The material would almost certainly have come from India.

7 An Abyssinian, wearing a cotton military cloak that is held in place with a black panther skin. This is decorated with a large piece of red leather in the shape of a cross and partly edged with silver. He wears cotton leggings and a wide piece of cotton is wrapped round his body.

9 A chief of the nomadic Peul tribe, from Senegambia. The Peuls are famous for their jewellery: bits of glass, gold coins, red beads and large collars.

10 A Galla chief. These fierce tribesmen cover themselves only with a loincloth of leather or animal hide. Their hair, thickly buttered, is either worn loose or in plaits. The ivory bracelets are a count of enemies defeated.

11 A Berta from the Upper Nile. Famous warriors, the Bertas use iron-headed javelins, curved daggers (12) and short knives (13). The hood is made from the skin of a black monkey and topped with an ostrich feather.

15 A Basotho, from Southern Africa, wearing a short panther skin cloak fixed on the chest with a strap that is covered with a large bronze collar. His loincloth and greaves are made from antelope skin, and his headdress is of ostrich feathers – the mark of a brave warrior.

20 A warrior from the Guinea coast. His cylindrical headdress is made from plaited rushes, red wool and shells.

21 A Bakalais witch doctor from Gabon. From childhood, future witch doctors must wear a special loincloth, fixed around the hips by a belt of white beads and decorated with a type of red chenille, and strings of large coloured beads round the neck and chest.

22 A Zulu chief from Natal. The strips of animal skin round his arms and legs show him to be a hunter and warrior, while the leopard skin on his chest marks him as a chief. His otter-skin headdress is decorated with large vulture feathers and his cloak is made of buffalo skin.

23 A Pahouin warrior from Gabon. Famous hunters, they can also work iron, making assegais (24) and axes (25). This warrior is wearing a loincloth made from the skin of a black monkey and carrying a bag decorated with a fringe made from a cocoa plant.

## TIMBUCTOO – CROSSROADS OF AFRICA

BECAUSE OF ITS SITUATION, Timbuctoo has become the principal station for caravans crossing Africa. The majority of the native inhabitants of Timbuctoo are Negroes, but alongside them live Arabs and Moors who stay in North Africa for business reasons. As a result, the local costumes are similar to those worn on the Mediterranean coast of the African Continent.

———— • ————

**1**. The *gandoura*, left, with wide sleeves, coral jewellery and a hood decorated with bows of silk or cotton. Unusually for this part of Africa, women are not compelled to wear veils. Far right is a *tarboosh*, an undervest and a jacket embroidered with silk.

The central figures in **1** are Chillouks, from the Upper Nile. They wear few clothes, but pay considerable attention to their headdresses. Men cover their hair with clay, gum and cattle dung in in order to sculpt it into shapes such as helmets or fans.

The right-hand figure of the pair is a king, wearing a regal headdress that consists of a fur fixed with large pins. His companion wears a panther skin and necklaces of shells and ivory.

**2** A Chir, left, from the Upper Nile, with plaited hair partly covered by a cotton cap. His loincloth is made of fig leaves and his necklace and bracelets from ivory. In one hand he carries a pipe with an earthenware bowl and a long wooden stem, and in his other hand a javelin.

To his right are two Niams-Niams tribesmen (the name means "big eaters"), tattooed with patterns of lines, zigzags and squares. Their loincloths are made of animal skins and belted at the waist. The straw hood, left, worn exclusively by men, has a a flat top decorated with feathers. They carry javelins,

barbed lances and, right, the *troumbache* – a sabre with many curved blades.

To their right are two Bazy (sometimes Bary) from the White Nile region. The Bazy men do not wear clothes, but smear their bodies with yellow ochre. Their headdress is very similar to that of the Niams-Niams and the Chillouks: a pile of curled and plaited hair, decorated with rodents' teeth, left. The woman, right, wears a beautiful loincloth covered with shells and pieces of glass.

**3** A Hottentot, wearing a cloak of dyed skin and trousers with a bead necklace and a circular metal pendant. Remarkably, the Hottentot tailors cut clothes with only a knife and a needle made from a bird's bone.

To his right is a rich woman with a double-sided cloak: the outside is dyed and the inside is the skin of a panther. Her belt is made of glass beads and her necklace is a double string of beads.

Next is a Hottentot warrior wearing a panther skin tunic and a headdress of long feathers held with a headband. His ear is pierced with a bone and he carries an assagai.

Sarah Bartmann, right, wearing the national costume, became famous in Paris at the exhibition of 1815 under the name of the "Hottentot Venus".

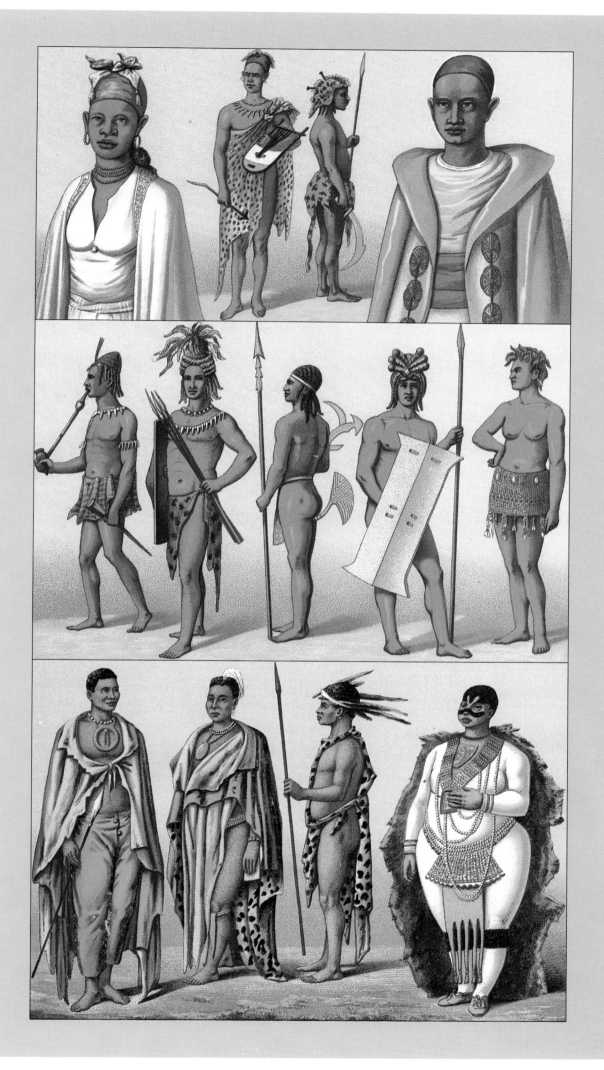

## SOUTHERN AFRICA – SUDAN

THE XHOSAS, FROM SOUTHERN AFRICA, are a handsome people who take great care of their appearance. The equatorial climate means that they do not require much clothing and tattoos are the basis of the costume for both men and women. These tattoos have a heraldic function, with special designs denoting individual tribes. Men and women both oil their bodies heavily, the height of luxury for a woman being not just to rub perfumed oil into her skin, but to make her body shine with the oil. Before applying oil, men smear their faces and bodies with a red dye to which the women add sugar from a sweet-smelling plant.

This care of the body extends as far as removing the hair from all parts of the body except the armpits: both men and women shave off their eyebrows.

Various hairstyles are adopted, by men and women. Some cut their hair to leave only a large clump, which is woven into pieces of wood to form a latticed cone. Others shave the crown, plaiting the sides with fine strips, or keep tufts at the sides and weave them through pieces of brass.

Many women allow their hair to grow naturally long and curly: they use it as a sort of pin cushion in which to keep a knife or a pipe. Sometimes they plait their hair round strips of bark. This arrangement may take many days of work, but when finished it can last for six months or more.

The principal garment worn by the natives is a piece of animal skin with the fur worn against the skin. For a man, this is usually a simple loincloth; for a woman, it is more circular in shape, sometimes covering the entire body. The hunters carry assegais and shields made of animal skin. Around their necks are knives with handles of ivory or boxwood and round-ended blades. For long marches or hunting they wear leather sandals, held on with leather strips that pass over the instep and through the big toe.

1.1 A Bechuana warrior.

1.2 A Basotho hunter. The feathered instrument is meant to deceive game; it is stuck in the ground to attract inquisitive animals, and can be quickly retrieved to spear them.

1.3 A Xhosa from Grahamstown.

1.4 A Bechuana.ı.

1.5 A Matabele.

2.1 & 2 Zulus.

2.3 A Bechuana tribeswoman in ceremonial costume.

2.4 A Matabele tribeswoman.

2.5 A Xhosa woman.

3 Senegalese tribesmen and women, from the lands by the *River Senegal* in Western Sudan. There are a large number of different tribes in Senegal, all with different styles of costume.

One style, left, is a long tunic worn with talismans around the neck. Next to him is a man wearing a *pagne*, made of dried leaves. With the man to his right, he is wearing leopard-skin shoulder straps with ammunition pouches attached at the waist.

The woman to their right wears a yellow turban with a blue and white striped border: headgear of mixed colours is a characteristic of Senegalese costume. Her chemise, worn underneath a carefully draped *ferdah*, another native garment, has comfortable wide sleeves.

The man on the far right is wearing the ample sleeves of his tunic rolled up over his shoulders.

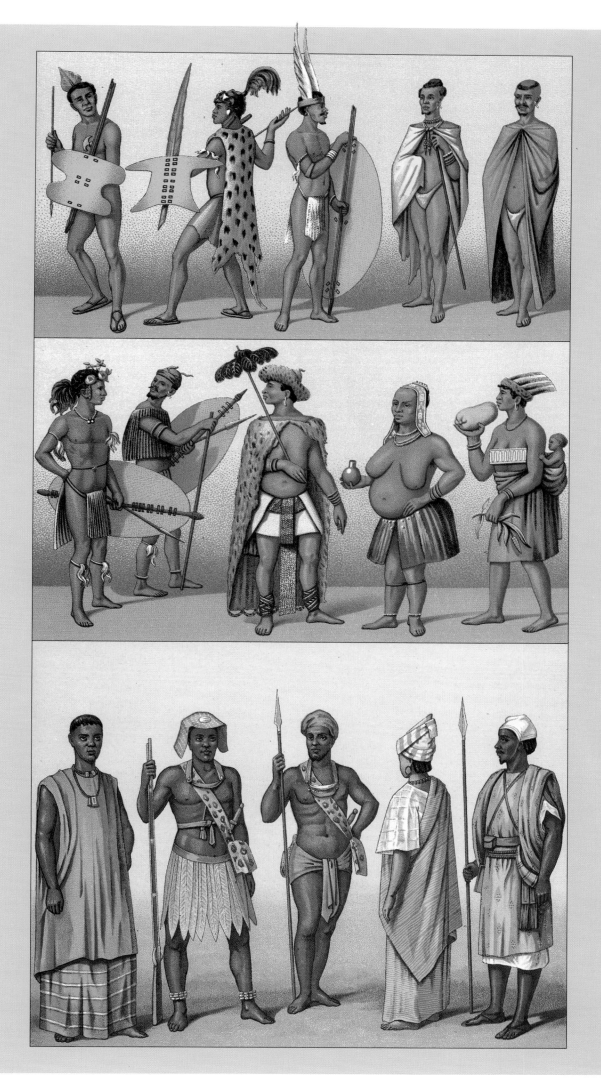

## BERBERS: KABYLES AND KROUMIRS

THE BERBERS ARE OFTEN CONSIDERED to be the most ancient of the Africans, and are divided into many groups. However, according to Jules Duval, the most important of the Berber tribes is that of the Kabyles, who live in the Atlas Mountains and in Algeria and Tunisia.

Brave and industrious warriors and tradesmen, the Kabyles value their nationality more than their lives. They have been Muslims since they were invaded in the seventh century. However, Kabyle women are allowed to go out without covering their faces, to join in at feasts and even dance with the men. This freedom allows them to play an important role in society.

———————— • ————————

The Kabyle national costume is extremely simple, consisting of a a cap, a woollen shirt called a *derbal*, which can be worn with or without a belt, and a leather apron. The outer-garment is a hooded cloak called a *burnous*. The girls' curly hair is never cut whereas the boys' heads are shaved.

**1.1** A water-carrier. From the age of 12, girls are obliged to fetch water twice a day in vessels such as this. It weighs around 60lb and the barefoot girl rests it on her back, with the base tucked inside her belt.

**1.2** A woman carrying milk and her child. The baby is carried on the back in a belt that serves as a hammock. She wears a cushion-like headdress in order to help support the weight.

**1.3** A man wearing the simple costume of a worker in the fields. It consists of a short *derbal*, a long leather apron, hanging from the neck and a straw hat with a tall crown and a wide brim as protection from the sun.
**1.4 & 5.** A simple yet feminine costume, shown front and back.

**2.2** A Kabyle woman wearing the glorious *thibeximin* on her forehead. This is a round plaque, decorated with pendants, which denotes that she is the mother of a boy. She is also wearing large, dangling coral earrings and a double brooch that fastens her cloak.

**2.1 & 2** The Kroumirs, with the Kabyles, the Mzabites and the Ouchetettas, inhabit Numidia. They live in shacks and not in tents like the Arabs, but, as with the Kabyles, the family lives in one room.

The Kroumir costume is similar to that of the Kabyles. It consists of a large shirt made of wool or cotton under one or two *burnouses*, depending on the season. Arms, legs and neck are never covered, and when they are not barefoot their shoes consist of pieces of leather with the corners folded back over the heel and toes and tied on with cords crossing over the instep of the foot.

The Kroumir women's costume does not really differ significantly from that of the Kabyle. The woman in **2.1** is a Moor, and is not wearing the double brooch or the *palla*, but her costume is essentially similar to that of her neighbours.

**3.2 & 4** Every day a Kabyle woman has to make couscous and fetch water. Here we also see her equipped with a vase and a long hooked stick to help in the collection of olives. Another woman (**3.4**) is gathering figs, a major source of food for the Kabyles.

**3.3** The daughter of the Grand Kabyle, wearing a traditional ancient cap, which was once black and is rarely seen today. Her face was probably tattooed in childhood, and such patterns are often seen between the eyes and on the nostril. Frequently the tattoo is in the shape of a cross, perhaps as a reference to the Kabyles' former Christianity.

## ARABS – ALGERIANS – MOORS

"MAY GOD ORDAIN THAT YOUR WIFE gives you five sons!" is a common Arab saying. The number five is significant because it recalls the five fingers of the right hand, which has the power to ward off all the evil eye. As a result, the number five is thought to brings happiness, and is often drawn on the doors of houses, or shown on a child's fez. The rich embroider the design on their clothes in gold or silver, and sometimes symbolize it by the use of five coins.

———— • ————

This inequality of the sexes is made apparent from the earliest days of childhood by the importance given to everything that concerns the boy: the first hair-cut at two years old when he is also allowed to wear the *burnous*, and circumcision at the age of seven. All these ceremonies are performed with great solemnity.

Girls, by contrast, are prepared by their mothers from babyhood for manual work, as a mark of their inferior status.

**1** An Arab tent. The Arab women hide their treasure at the foot of the main pole: normally, a goat skin containing earrings, necklaces, coral beads and jewels.

**2 & 3** A range of Algerian, Arab and Moorish costumes.

The Algerian shirt is short with baggy sleeves which fasten at the wrist. The everyday costume of the people is a *haik*, a pair of small leggings and, according to circumstances, a turban or a red woollen cap.

Often this is worn with a short jacket, with or without sleeves. Baggy culottes are worn with large folds that go down to the bottom of the leg; watches and purses are hung from belts. Slippers are worn on the feet, but the calves are usually bare: only old people wear stockings and even then only in cold weather.

The Moors of Tunisia wear a fez, or a red hood with a tassel of blue silk, with a small white calico bonnet beneath it. Next comes a waistcoat: with buttons – a *farmela* – or without – a *sadria*; then an embroidered jacket, trousers, attached to an undershirt with laces, and stockings. Shoes, called *sebbat*, are worn outdoors, and slippers indoors.

Scribes wear a kaftan: a large coat that reaches down as far as the heels. A *zouka* is a type of kaftan that stops at the knees, and another variation is a *gefara*, a type of small *burnous*.

**2** The central figure is a Moorish girl wearing a *sarmah*, a bonnet with a truncated crown. Designed to show only two curls of hair, this is decorated with ribbons, silk tassels and gold chains. The rich would also add pearls and diamonds. It is covered with a piece of gauze which hangs down the back.

The photograph from which this was taken showed five divisions on the palm leaf at the front: another instance of the symbolism of this number.

**3** An Arab on a donkey, carrying a voluminous parcel, with Arab men and a boy who are dressed in a style typical of that seen in the fruit and herb markets of Tunisia.

# THE SEVEN RACES OF ALGERIA

THE NATIVE POPULATION OF ALGERIA is composed of seven races: first and foremost are the Arabs and Berbers, including the Kabyles; then come the Moors, the Turks, the Kouloughlis, the Jews and the Negroes. However, the style of their clothes, as regards colour and design, follows certain recognizable idioms throughout the Algerian population.

———— • ————

**1.** Kabyle women in ceremonial dress. The hairstyle of the central figure indicates that she is married, but the lack of a round jewel called a *thibeximin* on her forehead means that she has either not had a son, or has had a girl since having a son, and so been forced to remove it. Her robe has fringed edges, and is covered with enamelled jewels and brightly coloured, patterned drapes. These are arranged to fall in fine soft folds, fastened at the hips and shoulders and thrown back over the head like a veil. The flat headdress is characteristic of the mountain-dwelling tribes who carry things on their heads.

The toilette is scrupulous on ceremonial occasions. Hair is dyed as dark as possible with a mixture of oak apple, antimony of sulphate and copper pyrites. The substance is mixed with olive oil, then heated until it forms a paste.

The hair is covered with this paste for three days and then combed through. The eyebrows are also dyed in this way. Every woman carries somewhere in the folds of her costume a little case of worked reed with a fine tube of silver or iron. This contains kohl for use on the eyes. Rouge, used on the cheeks, is made by chewing walnut shells.

**2.1** A Negro from Oran, wearing a *haik* underneath his *tarboosh*, with gold earrings and a *burnous.*

**2.3** A Berber tribesman, wearing a silk turban with an embroidered border without the *haik*. The grey *burnous* is lined with blue.

**2.2** and **3.2 & 4** Kouloughlis women. The headdress of the woman in **2** is almost as high as that of a man who is wearing two or three *tarbooshes*, one on top of

the other. A band of cotton is wrapped around the headdress many times, securing the muslin *haik* that falls over the shoulders and frames the face, allowing the hair to hang loose on one side.

Over her dress she is wearing a garment of striped cotton. It has a hole for the head to pass through, rather like a chasuble. The young woman in **3.4**, with her forearm heavily tattooed with square patterns, is also wearing this garment, but in this case it is made entirely of muslin. **3.2** A woman wearing indoor clothes. Her robe has very large sleeves, and her corsage consists of a waistcoat with long epaulettes tied with a yellow silk belt.

**2.4 & 5** and **3.1 & 2** A young Moorish boy and three Moorish women. The young boy is wearing a red fez from Tunisia. His waistcoat is made of embroidered silk and his shirt is cotton.

The woman next to him is wearing a bonnet fastened by a golden throat strap. A flat turban of striped silk is wound around the bonnet and beneath it is a piece of material tied under the chin and completely covering the neck.

To her right is a Moor from Andalusia, wearing a simple waistcoat of orange silk, attached at the breast by a button. Her hair is loose while her head is covered with a casually tied piece of blue cotton material.

The cone-shaped bonnet worn by the girl in the blue dress to her right is set far back on the head, hardly covering her loose hair. Her dress is decorated with golden embroidery on silk on the chest and has short sleeves. Underneath she is wearing a blouse of fine cotton with loose three-quarter length sleeves.

## ALGERIA – TUNISIA

ETHNOGRAPHICALLY, ALGERIA AND TUNISIA cannot be separated, as both are peopled by the same categories of races: the Berbers, the Arabs, the Moors, joined by the Jews and the Negroes from the centre of Africa. The women of this mixed population with their various costumes appear here as they would in the desert or the mountains, or when they bustle about in the narrow streets of the North African towns.

1.1 An Arab woman wearing a *gandoura*, gathered in at the hips with a belt of camel skin. Her *burnous* is thrown back over her shoulder and a scrap of material is tied round her head.

1.2 An Arab woman from southern Algeria. Her *haik* is made of fine material and covers her head and shoulders, with a bonnet and turban over it. She is also wearing a white woollen robe and a cloak, attached in the manner of the Greek *palla* with brooches on the shoulders.

1.3 & 5 Kabyle women, wearing *haiks* – one coloured and one brown – over woollen chemises. When they walk they have to lift the *haiks* a few inches and tuck them into their belts. One women (3) is wearing a traditional bonnet called a *ichaoun*; the other is bareheaded except for a red ribbon from which hang two large rings of white metal.

1.4 An Arab woman wearing a turban made of camel skin, secured by strips of wool and covered with the classic *burnous*. Beneath the *burnous* is a *gandoura*.

2.1 A young Kabyle mountain dweller, wearing a *beskir*, a light piece of material that frames the face with a *ichaoun* around it that floats a muslin veil. Her large tunic is gathered up into her belt.

2.2 An Arab woman with a flat headdress to facilitate carrying things on the head and a necklace made of sequins.

2.3 A well-to-do Arab woman dressed for the town with a long veil over her head. The bottom half of her face is covered by a *beskir*, a piece of material knotted at the back of the head and reaching down as far as the knees. Her *haik* is made of light material and her stockings are silk.

2.4 A Jewish woman from Constantine. Her corsage is heavily embroidered and her robe is open to show a tunic with wide sleeves. Her apron is also embroidered.

3.1 A Moor from Algeria, wearing indoor costume. Outdoors these women were so hidden by their clothes that all that could be distinguished was their overall stoutness, considered highly desirable. Often, women were so large that they could hardly walk.

3.2 An Algerian woman wearing a large veil fastened at the bottom, as is typical in the region. Attached to her necklace is an amulet: a common practice among all classes, as a protection against the evil eye.

3.3 A most interesting costume, consisting of a garment attached at the sides by a double brooch. This seems to have more in common with the Greek *palla* than anything usually worn by a Kabyle woman.

The flat headgear, however, makes it clear that this is a Kabyle costume, and the theory is supported by the fact that the woman is also wearing a *haik* without a veil.

3.4 A Tunisian peasant.

## ARAB SOCIETY

IN ARAB SOCIETY, THE PEOPLE beneath what we may call the aristocracy belong to one of four basic groups. These consist of the land owners, the farmers, the domestic servants and the labourers.

——— • ———

**1.1** A Moorish woman dressed for the town.

**1.2, 3, 4 & 5** Moors who live in the country, the last being a beggar.

**2.1** A regular soldier from Tunisia, occupying himself by knitting. He is wearing European trousers and two fezes. Both in Tunisia and Algeria, the custom is to collect fezes, and wear more than one at the same time. Here, one is made of red felt and the other of white. The Tunisians are experts at the manufacture of fezes, and export millions of them to other Muslim countries.

**2.2** A man is of mixed origin, known as a *Berrani*. In the province of Oran, the Arabian *Berranis* were normally herdsmen, while in Tunisia they were porters and labourers.

This *Berrani* appears to be a hunter. He has all the necessary equipment: rifle, cartridges, knife and water-bottle.

**2.3** A woman carrying wood.

**2.4** A Tunisian woman, carrying her child when going to fetch water.

**2.5** This costume is similar to those of the Kabyles. The over garment is like a Greek *palla* and is fastened by a *fibula*. However, the difference between this and the Greek garment can be seen here where the back of the robe covers the head and is fixed by the *haik*. The robe is also hitched up into the belt to make walking easier.

**3.1** A Jewish woman from Algeria.

**3.4** A servant.

**3.2 & 3** Professional dancers. In Arabian society dancing is confined to two types of people: slaves and women who dance professionally. Professional dancers are themselves divided into two classes: those who dance in rich houses and those who dance in the streets.

The first category are generally employed as the major source of entertainment for the harems. The lyrics of their songs are decent and respectable and their dances are composed of gracious and graceful movements. Their feet do not leave the floor. Some dance while others sing, accompanied by a tambour or a small mandolin. The songs are melancholy and the same tune is repeated 12 to 15 times until sheer exhaustion obliges the dancers to stop.

Public dancers are found only in the Algerian towns. Here the dancers are accompanied by a musician who is playing playing a two-stringed instrument called a *rabab* and by an old woman marking time with a *daraboukkeh*. The dancers have castanets attached to both hands which they shake vigorously at first, gradually softening their sound.

The dancers wear baggy striped pantaloons and transparent tunics. They move the lower part of the body from their hips and their arms, and their dance ends with a gradual slowing down until they rest immobile.

**3.5** A peasant from Algeria playing the tambour. Music is a feature of Arab life and accompanies most events, funerals as well as feasts. The tambour is perhaps the most popular instrument: the musician uses an eagle's feather or a piece of shell to pluck the strings, never his fingers.

# ESKIMOS

### HUNTERS OF THE ICE FLOES

A N ESKIMO'S DIET CONSISTS PRINCIPALLY of fish and sea-mammals. A solitary fisherman, the Eskimo needs both experience and bravery in the pursuit of prey such as sharks and narwhal, both of which can put up a deadly fight. The Eskimo fishes with great skill, and his cunningly designed equipment reflects his objectives: to capture and carry.

1 A sledge and huskies

2 A snow shoe

3 to 12 A range of hunting equipment and weapons, generally made of wood, with iron tips set in walrus bone.

13 A lady's boot, made from tanned seal skin. The upper part of is made of cloth.

14 An Eskimo woman carrying her child in her hood.

15 An iron knife whose blade and handle are at right angles to each other.

16 A sealskin bag. These were used as shoes for dogs.

17 A stone lamp set in a wooden base.

18 A woman's costume, made of sealskin lined with fur and embroidered with red woollen braid and white and green leather. The leggings are detachable.

19 & 20 Sealskin hunting pouches, decorated with leather.

21 A stool made of embroidered sealskin decorated with bearskin.

22 A woman's tunic – a short blouse made of sealskin and lined with wool. It is embroidered with wool and silk, and the sleeves and neck are trimmed with fur.

23 A man's costume made of sealskin with wool braid. The gloves are made of bear's paws –

complete with the ferocious claws.

24 An iron household implement with a wooden handle.

25 A *Kayak*, the canoe used by solitary fishermen. It is made by stretching black-painted sealskin over a bone shell.

26 A hook made of walrus bone, used for dragging dead seals over the ice.

27 A sealskin muzzle, placed over a dog's snout.

28 A tobacco box of walrus bone with an iron clasp.

29 A fisherman with a spear. The spearhead is made of walrus bone tipped with iron.

30 A walrus-bone knife.

31 A harpoon, both ends of which are made of walrus bone. The wooden shaft comes off when the prey tries to escape by diving.

32 A wooden paddle with spatula-shaped ends of walrus bone.

33 & 34 Spears.

35 A sealskin boot with cloth uppers.

36 A portrait of Juliana-Judith-Margarita Okabak, a 22-year-old Eskimo woman.

37 Inside a winter home.

38 A mother and child.

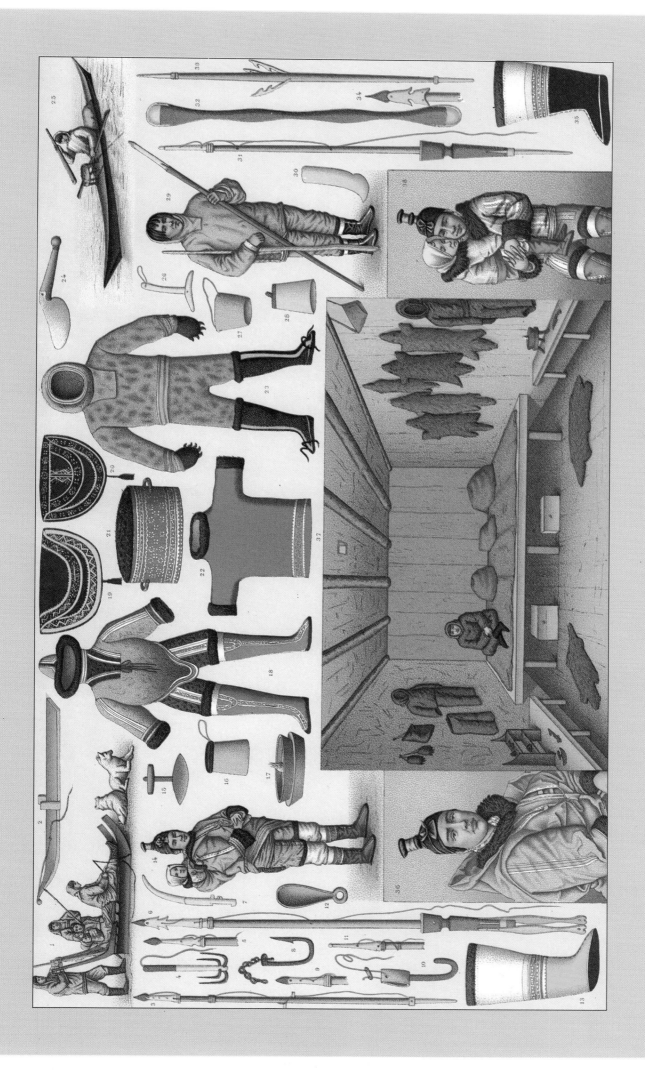

# AMERICAN INDIANS

### NORTH AMERICA – YUTES – SIOUX – JOWA

THE NATIVE INDIANS OF NORTH AMERICA were once one of the largest groups of hunting peoples known to history. Hunting was the source of their entire livelihood, until the coming of the Europeans and the introduction of guns, glassware and *eau de vie*. These things developed into necessities for the Indians, who paid a high price for their trade with the devastation of their lands. Expert horsemen, their costume was ideally suited to the needs of the rider, the hunter and the warrior.

———— • ————

**1.1, 2 & 3** Yute chiefs, from the Great Salt Lake area of Colorado. Yute chiefs do not wear headdresses because their characteristic slight elongation of the skull is considered a mark of beauty. To achieve it, the skulls are flattened during childhood.

One of the most traditional items of Indian costume is the tunic. Finely decorated with fringes and hems, this can be of any length, and is now worn as a ceremonial garment.

Since they live in the saddle, the Yutes wear short hunting vests with long trousers made from hide or wool. A characteristic touch is a piece of wool or leather divided in two and tucked into the belt, as in **1.1**, or drawn back each side over the thighs and buttoned into place, as in **1.3**. This is intended to protect a horseman's legs without hindering movement.

The hunting vests, worn over an under-vest, have long, flared sleeves that are fringed at the wrist. In **1.1** the vest is decorated with a baldric made of embroidered moose hide. In **1.2** it is decorated with a breastplate of feathers and dyed strips of leather.

Yutes covered their hair with grease and either wore it loose (**1.2**) or plaited back from the front with the pieces at the side.

**1.4 & 2** Sioux chiefs. Also great horsemen and hunters, the Sioux have a costume similar to that of the Yutes, with the difference that headdresses are worn. Feathers for these are generally taken from wild cocks and pheasants, but chiefs take them from from eagles and birds of prey. Each headdress is designed by the wearer to fit his own self-image, and its style often determines the name: "Big Chief Bustard", for example, or "White Crow".

**1.4** is a chief's son. Decorations are sewn on to his woollen leggings and his shoes are made of cotton. In the other illustrations moccasins are worn. These are made from the treated hide of a moose or stag.

**2.1** Chief Sioux Yanctons, with a necklace of animal hair and bears' teeth. The extravagant headdress of the Ponka chief (**2.2**) is made of feathers mixed with strips of dyed red leather. These cover the head and spread outwards to cascade down the back.

The Minisoufaux chief (**2.3**) is wearing a cotton cape trimmed with a long leather fringe and his hair is lengthened at the front with two red fox tails. The Sioux Sisistas chief (**2.4**) wears an under-shirt whose whiteness and cut is typical of the region.

**3.1, 2, 3 & 5.** Jowa chiefs from Kansas. The fur bonnet is (**3.1**) decorated with a feather and a piece of metal, three more of which can be seen on his cravat. A metal disc is also attached to the glass necklace in **3.2**. Here the blouse is made of appliquéd cotton, and the riding trousers are part wool and part leather. Embroidered leather gaiters and a woollen cloak can be seen next to him, in **3.3**.

## NORTH AMERICA – FOXES – SACS – KAW – KILLIMOUS

FOR MANY YEARS, THE EUROPEANS who colonized North America thought of the native Indians as one homogenous people. In fact there were made up of a large number of different tribes.

Today, the Indians can be divided into two main groups: those that are still nomadic, such as the Sioux and the Yutes; and those – generally the weaker tribes such as the Californian Indians and the Cherokees – who live on reservations.

Costume changed with the changes in life-style. The tanned skin of a bison, still with its mane, was once used as a bed or a blanket. Now however, with the exception of their moccasins and gaiters, many Indians have stopped wearing skins and traded them for woollen clothes, finding these more practical and more becoming.

1.1 & 5 Indians from the Fox tribe in Kansas. The chief of the Foxes (1.1) is wearing a fur bonnet with a woollen star on it and a plume made of fur and cotton. His necklace is made from the skin and teeth of a bear. The Fox brave (1.5) is wearing a similar necklace and has a feather at the back of his head, probably from a wild cock or a pheasant.

1.2. An Indian from New Mexico, with red and white face-paint and a mirror hanging from his necklace. He wears a large woollen blanket as a cloak, and his trousers are fringed and decorated with red horizontal lines and blue crosses.

1.3. A chief from the Sacs tribe from Kansas, wearing a cotton turban topped with a feather plume. The lining of his cloak is appliquéd, and his woollen trousers are gathered in just below the knees with garters.

1.4. A chief of the Kaw tribe from Kansas, with a huge scarlet cloak and a piece of yellow woollen cloth decorated with white patterns on his chest.

The Indians in Oregon and Northern California are mainly of the Killimous tribe. They are known for their hunting skills and their dexterity with horses. The braves would prefer to wear skins, as their chiefs do, but normally have to be content with a black loincloth.

2.1. A North Californian Indian woman, with a tunic of cotton and a skirt of wool; the crib is made of wood.

2.2. Again from North California, this woman wears a woollen cloak and her child is is dressed in cotton.

2.3. An Indian from the same region, wearing a wicker-work headdress, a large necklace made from coloured glass and stones, a cotton skirt fringed with shell and an apron which is also decorated with glass and stone beads.

2.4 & 5. Oregon Indians. The man's headband and trousers are made of cotton, and he carries a quiver made from skin. The woman is also wearing a cotton headband and has a necklace of red beads. Her apron is of the same style as that in 2.3.

3.1 An Oregon Indian, with a wicker-work headdress and a necklace carved from shells.

3.2. An Oregon Indian. Her long hair is tied with cotton ribbons while her clothes are made of wool. She has the characteristic wicker-work headdress and carries a crib.

3.3. A winter costume, made from different types of animal skin.

## SOUTH AMERICA – GUARANIS – CARAIBES – BOTOCUDOS

ANTHROPOLOGISTS DIVIDE THE NATIVES of the great plain that stretches from the eastern slopes of the Peruvian Andes to the Atlantic Ocean into three families: the Guaranis, the Caraibes and the Botocudos. The latter, like the American Indians of the North, are still primitive hunters. They go about naked and lead a nomadic life, very often not even building shelters. Typically, their legs are thin. This, however, is seen as a mark of beauty, since it is achieved by tying their children's legs together to stunt their growth.

———— • ————

**1** The Botocudos wear bizarre ornaments in their ears and bottom lip, though it would be unusual to find ornaments quite as large as some of those illustrated; both sexes have their ears and bottom lip pierced at the age of seven or eight. The *botoque*, or lip ornament, is slightly smaller for men than for women.

Botocudos go naked except for a girdle of leaves; an example can be seen in the illustration of the man with spears and large earrings, and details are shown above and right.

The other natives in **1** are Camacans: a branch of the Tapuyas who are direct ancestors of the Botocudos. The Camacan chief's crown made of feathers is one of the most beautiful articles of costume to be seen on the banks of the Amazon. The red and green parrot feathers are sewn into a type of woollen hood. Camacan women are skilled at spinning cotton, and make their only garment from it: a short apron, as worn by the woman in the bottom left-hand corner.

**2** The basic population of Chile is composed of native Indians and Spanish Creoles. The Chilean men are in general excellent horsemen, robust and adroit, used to taming wild horses. Their bridles are made of simple strips of leather and their saddles are merely a piece of skin or material. Riding without stir-rups, they spur their mounts on over the steepest ground.

The entire Chilean population wear the short cloak or *poncho*, the national costume. This is worn by both men and women, and by those who adhere to local custom as well as by those who follow European fashion.

The costume in 2.2 comes from Santiago, the capital of Chile, while the costumes in 2.1, 4 & 5 are more rustic and tend to be worn by the native Indians.

The *poncho* is a dalmatic without sleeves, reminiscent of the Roman tunic. It is a quadrangular piece of material, 10ft long by 6ft wide, with an opening for the head. The *poncho* covers the head and the top part of the body, but does not descend lower than the knees and often stops higher than that.

The most highly valued *Ponchos* are those from Arauca. These are made from the finest wool and chamois from the Andes. A *poncho* of this type takes nearly two years to make and is very expensive. The Chileans favourite colour for *ponchos* is turquoise-blue, but they may be also dyed yellow, green or red; they are often decorated with bands, sometimes patterned with delicate designs and figures.

The woman's *poncho* is a smaller version of the man's; women turn the basic *poncho* into an elegant garment, sewing and decorating it with exquisite care.

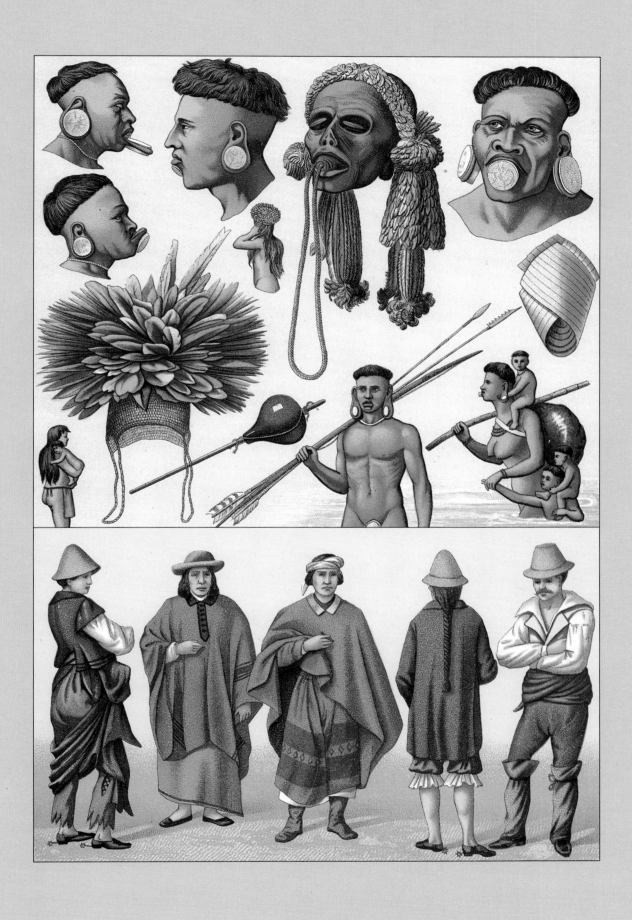

# MEXICO

MEXICAN INDIANS – CREOLES – SPANISH

THE POPULATION OF MEXICO is composed of three types of people: the indiginous native Indians; the descendants of the Spanish conquerors of Mexico; and a mixed race, the result of intermarriage between the Spanish and the Indians. The latter group occupy an unfortunate position, being mainly employed as servants to the rich, workers in the capital's diverse industries and door-to-door salesmen and itinerant pedlars.

———— • ————

1.1 A rich Mexican, a descendant of the conquering Spaniards. He is wearing a felt hat, a short jacket of woollen cloth with double epaulettes, cotton *calzoneros* (leggings worn beneath trousers) and a *sarapé* of striped silk. He is not wearing stockings.

In the Spanish tradition, gallants still carry guitars for serenading ladies, but it is rare to see a guitar attached with a silk strap.

1.2 A rich Mexican with *calzoneros* and trousers made of hide, open down the sides. His short jacket reveals a waistcoat of red silk and he wears a sombrero.

1.3 A Spanish Indian woman wearing a double collar across which a narrow strip of silk runs horizontally, with a skirt and short tunic.

1.4 A feast-day costume. The hat is decorated with a ribbon to match the handkerchief worn on the head, and a small embroidered apron is attached to a silk belt. The jacket is left open to reveal a naked stomach.

1.5 A creole woman wearing town clothes: a mantilla and a silk skirt. Mantillas were sometimes made of white and black silk and embroidered with brightly coloured patterns, but those worn by the average women were made of blue- and white-checked wool. She is wearing satin slippers, but does not have stockings.

16 A cobbler, wearing a type of leather scapular that serves as a protective apron. He has *calzoneros* and leather trousers.

1.7 A rich Mexican, with a *sarapé* embroidered with gold.

2.8 An inhabitant of Pobla, wearing riding costume with a very large gold-trimmed *sarapé* of an unusual cut. He has long trousers and *calzoneros* that cover his feet.

2.9 A creole woman, with her hair in a Spanish-style hairnet topped with a diadem. A mantilla is draped over her shoulders and her open woollen jacket.

2.10 A water-carrier, dressed in leather.

2.11 A Mexican Indian chief in his warrior's costume. With small variations, all the Indians of Mexico wear this costume. The headdress is a diadem, decorated with feathers from a bird of prey and the tunic is made of bison skin, prepared and treated by the tribeswomen. The fringes on the tunic are attached to small metal blades that clash together at the slightest movement.

2.12 A Mexican Indian wearing a *sarapé*.

2.13 A parrot-hawker.

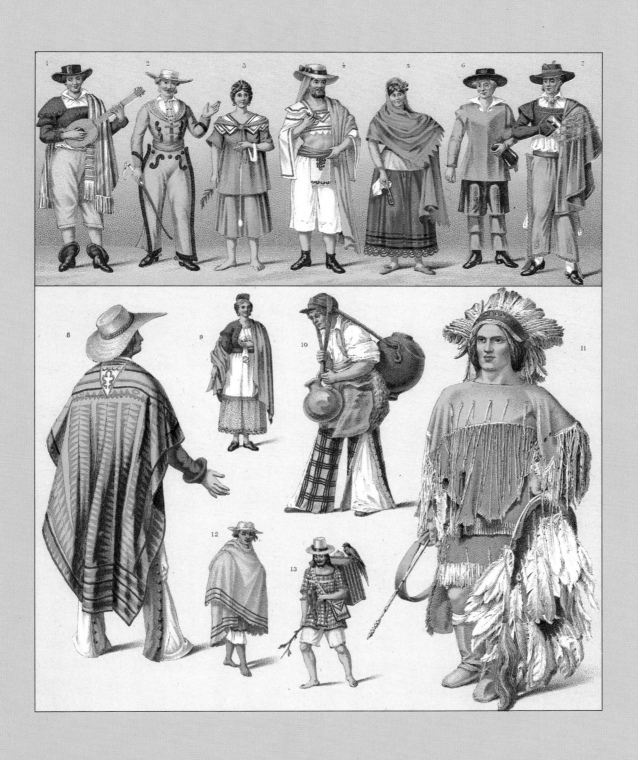

# CHINA

## THE IMPERIAL COURT

THE NATIVE CHINESE POPULATION was overrun by the invading Manchu race in the 17th century. However, the traditional customs of the Chinese won the day over the practices of their conquerors, with the result that the Manchu people adopted many Chinese religious and civil customs. One area in which Chinese and Manchu tastes remained different was women's dress.

The essential items of a Chinese lady's wardrobe are: first, a large under-garment stretching from the waist down to the top of the ankles. This is held up at the top by a belt of cloth and edged at the bottom with ribbons.

Next, a *han-chaol*. This is a blouse made in the shape of a short tunic, longest at the front, where it is gathered in, and going no further down the back than the waist. A lining of silken net is normally worn beneath this blouse to prevent it from clinging to the skin.

The principal items of clothing are: the *haol* – a long dress split at the sides with long narrow sleeves, fixed at the waist with a belt; and the *ma-coual* – an outer-garment with short, wide sleeves.

**1.1** A princess of the Imperial family wearing indoor clothes and a black velvet diadem decorated with artificial flowers. Her hair has been divided into strands and tied with ribbons, and on the back of her head she has a crown of blue feathers and dropped pearls. Her bracelets are gold and her neckerchief is made of red silk.

Instead of a *ma-coual*, she is wearing a short, sleeveless jacket over her robe. The jacket is lemon yellow, this being the distinctive colour of the Imperial family. The five-clawed dragon is also in Imperial colours and it, too, is a prerogative of the royal family.

**1.2** A *niutze*, a young servant girl, wearing her hair arranged in strands, and decorated with arti-ficial flowers and a golden hairpin. Her bracelets are made of pearls and her neckerchief of green silk. The ladies of the Imperial house would have had about 120 servants in their personal service: 100 eunuchs, 10 women and 10 young girls.

**1.3** In China, civil and military service is rewarded by the right to wear certain items of costume, examples of which shown here are the yellow cape and the peacock feather in the hat. The mandarin is also wearing an embroidered chest-piece and a long robe decorated with three- and four-clawed dragons.

On the table next to him is a water-pipe for smoking opium.

**2.1** The Empress Hoang-heou, wearing ceremonial costume, including a bonnet of embroidered satin.

**2.2** A young servant girl, or *niutze*. She is handing her mistress a jade sceptre – an emblem of the highest rank.

**2.3** A mandarin in ceremonial costume, wearing a collar of coral, an embroidered pectoral, silk boots and the imperial yellow cape.

**2.4** The Emperor Thien-Tseu, whose name means "son of heaven", in ceremonial costume. His clothes, his jewels, his jade sceptre – particularly his throne – all exude an appropriate air of grandeur and dignity.

## MANCHU WOMEN

THE MAIN ITEMS OF CHINESE COSTUME are very simply cut, and the material used for them is varied according to the seasons. The cloth that rich people prefer in summer is a type of linen known as *ko-pou*. This is an extremely light fabric. In spring and autumn a heavier material called *siao-kien* is favoured. This material is not dyed and comes from silkworms in their natural state. In winter *touan-tse* is used – a type of satin much stronger than that found in Europe.

When children, Chinese girls wear their hair loose. On becoming young adults, they put their hair in a plait, either leaving it hanging or tying it up on top of the head. Once married, though, women always keep their plait coiled up, usually held in place by two ivory needles.

Beyond these basic rules there are many refinements in hairstyling and many regional differences. In Shanghai, for example, women wear a diadem of velvet and black silk as in **1.**1, 2, 3 & 5 and **2.**2 & 3. In **1.**3 can be seen the cushion of cardboard backed with black silk and placed on the nape of the neck, over which the married lady's plaits are rolled.

Chinese girls wear make-up from the age of about seven or eight. They paint their faces white and their lips pink. "Her face is as white as flour, her mouth is a cherry", in the words of a Chinese song. Eyebrows are blackened, and a small red dot is painted in the middle of the bottom lip and on the chin. The height of fashion is to paint a small stripe of crimson between the eyes and to colour the temples green, black or blue. Elegant Chinese women wear nail-covers, often finely engraved.

Manchu women retain a different appearance to that of their Chinese counterparts, both in their hairstyles and in their clothing. Young Manchu girls plait their hair in the usual way, but married women have a style that is unique – they part their hair down the middle of their heads and knot it over each ear, as in **1.**4 & 5.

Manchu women also wear shor-ter dresses than Chinese women, and their single plaits fall down over a jacket or a waistcoat that is decorated with elaborate embroidery. The clothes are generally brightly coloured and have wide, embroidered borders.

Women commonly carry smoking materials in a pouch hanging from their belts: a strange contrast to the delicate fans and other accessories. Well-to-do women also carry sachets of perfume.

Another peculiarity of Chinese society is their appreciation of tiny feet; at one time children's feet were mutilated in infancy as a matter of routine.

Nowadays, the practice is less common than it might appear, as a result of the influence of the Manchu emperors. Its incidence varies according to class and above all to area. In many provinces, a Chinese woman of good family still believes herself to be dishonoured if her parents have not had the operation performed, since normal sized feet – apart from being thought unattractive – signify that a girl has been born to work and not as an idle member of high society.

A Manchu marrying a Chinese girl, though, would not wish her to have deformed feet. Thus both Manchu and Chinese women of the imperial court, as well as the wives of numerous officials who reside in the capital, have kept their natural feet.

Nevertheless, all women of high rank, whether Manchu or Chinese, wear a boot specifically designed to make the foot look smaller.

**1** A detail from a superbly embroidered piece of Chinese cloth.

**2.1** An empress, wearing a crown with long pendants. She is holding a sceptre surmounted by a mythical beast called a *fong*. Her *haol*, or under-garment, is made of satin lamé, and is covered by a *ma-coual* of red silk, decorated with embroidery depicting a five-clawed dragon entwined with a phoenix. It ends in a striped border lined with gold brocade. Her earrings and bracelets are made of jade.

The raised throne on which the empress is sitting is draped with a green cover rather than padded, following the Chinese custom. She carries a gold scale and a *Yu* stone, both of which are used to authenticate imperial decrees.

Her status means that she can never be seen by the public, but only by the emperor and her personal attendants. In many ways, therefore, her regal position is more or less akin to slavery.

**2.2 & 3** An imperial wife of second rank and her servant. The *Li-Ki*, the fourth of a series of books that define the protocols of the imperial court, gives the emperor the right to have to 300 concubines, all of whom wear a standard costume.

The emperor's wives are classified as follows: first, three wives have the title of *fou-gin* and are considered to be true wives of the second rank. They are referred to as "queens" and their status places them above the other women of the palace, but they are never allowed to aspire to the status of the empress, the premier wife. Their costume is decorated with feathers of five colours.

Next, nine wives have the name of *pin* and are princesses of the second rank – they wear yellow dresses. Then, 37 wives bear the title of *chi-fou*, women of the third rank, who dress in white. Finally, 80 are called *yu-tsi*, imperial concubines, who dress in black.

The various clothes – uniforms, almost – are made in palace workshops, according to patterns fixed by the imperial tailors at the start of the Manchu dynasty.

Here, the princess – in a yellow dress with gold embroidery, worn under a strikingly colourful outer-garment – obviously belongs to the *pin* class of imperial wife. Her hair is lifted back in a typically Chinese fashion, and is covered with a delightful cap decorated with pearls and artificial flowers. A large hairpin holds the hairstyle in place.

Her servant's hairstyle is more original: the hair and small cap have been arranged in a phoenix style to represent the shape of the bird. She is dressed in a short sleeveless jacket, worn over a *ma-coual* of blue cotton; her *haol* allows us a glimpse of green sleeves. She is holding a needle used for picking up opium. This is heated over a lamp and placed in the bowl of the opium-pipe.

There were vast numbers of servants in the imperial residences, employed to perform all manner of tasks. Some did hard manual labour, while others were involved in knitting and small domestic chores.

The rich spent most of their lives inside the imperial chambers in total indolence, smoking opium. This helped to maintain the semi-somnambulant monotony of their existence.

Reclining on their *kans*, that is, pieces of furniture that served as bed, sofa and chair, they did not even need to trouble to extend their hands in order to smoke the opium pipe; servants were always there to assist them in this dubious practice, seizing the moment when their masters and mistresses dozed off to lift the stem to their own lips.

## MANCHU – CHINESE – MANDARINS

CHINESE SHOES are of three types. Some fit feet that have been allowed to retain their natural shape; others are designed for feet that have been made artificially smaller. The third type are designed to give a naturally framed foot the appearance of having been reduced in size. The latter is called a "theatre boot" and is both high and short, raised up under the heel and very hollow at the front. The sole is designed in such a way that one can only move forward by walking on tip-toe.

Manchu women are more relaxed about their costume than their Chinese counterparts, who are used to a closeted life, shut away in their homes. The servant in 1.1, who wears her hair separated in waves and covered with a felt hat, appears to be Manchu. Her clothes are made of cotton and her sleeves edged with velvet.

The parasol that she and the button-seller (1.2) are holding is typically Chinese. These parasols are made from fish skin, whose smell, unfortunately, tends to persist.

1.4 A Chinese lady from *Tong-King*. Her clothes are quite different from those just described, the only common factor being the loose outer garment without folds draped to show any contours of the body. In a country as large as China, though, such variations are to be expected.

1.5 & 6 Two mandarin women. The first is clothed entirely in silk. The second has a shaven head, except for a cord of plaited hair – this style is a result of the influence of the Manchu invaders.

Mandarins are the public officials of civil and military rule, graded according to the importance of their work and decorated with the insignia of their grade. The official dress consists of a robe embroidered with dragons or serpents. It is fastened with a belt and partly covered by a shorter, more austere robe, over which a cape is worn.

The decorations awarded by the emperor for military or civil service are: first, the yellow robe and the peacock feather – given only to the highest dignitaries; and next, the *lan-lin* feather. Soldiers who distinguish themselves are allowed to wear a fox's tail.

2.1 A mandarin dressed in everyday summer clothes. As custom dictates, he is holding a fan in one hand and a handkerchief in the other.

2.2 An official wearing the ceremonial costume of the most senior judges and ministers of state, with a coral collar and peacock feather. His hands are hidden as etiquette demands.

2.3 A woman of importance in ceremonial dress. She is a Manchu – her feet have not been made smaller. Her choice of jewellery indicates her status, since it copies her husband's insignia. The four-clawed dragon worn by senior officials can also be seen in the embroidery of her dress.

2.4 A Chinese lady in indoor clothes. There is no ornamentation, but she has made her hair more attractive with an artificial flower, possibly wrought from silver.

3 A Chinese peasant pushing ladies in a barrow, wearing the plain clothes of the poor. In a society where the ideal of the rich was not to move, the thought of walking or any type of activity was anathema.

# JAPAN

MILITARY COSTUME

THE ANCIENT JAPANESE MILITARY COSTUME appears at first sight to bear a strong resemblance to that of Europe – the principal elements of European armour all appear to be present. However, on closer scrutiny, this similarity can be seen to be no more than superficial. With the possible exception of chain mail, the construction of this armour has little in common with its European equivalent. Japanese weapons are light and are made of leather or lacquered papier-maché. Where armour plating is used, the metal in question is in fact light steel.

———— • ————

The sequence of pictures opposite shows an archer preparing for battle. First he washes ritually, shaving the front and crown of his head and leaving the characteristic spiky tuft at the very top.

1 He dons a silk loincloth.

2 Next is an under robe of light wool, or even silk, which takes the place of the shirt. This is held in place by a knotted belt.

3 He ties up the short, wide trousers in the same manner.

4 He secures his black felt cap with the aid of a silk ribbon.

5 He protects his hands with leather gauntlets, tied on tightly at the wrist with ribbons.

6 He puts on a half-robe or lined jacket with wide sleeves. The sleeves are separate from the jacket below the armpits.

7 He now puts on a second, longer pair of trousers.

8 Silk coverings are worn over the lower legs. This helps to secure the greaves to them.

9 When the greaves are in place, the archer lifts up his trousers and inner robe until they are thigh-high and fastens them with cords. Then he lets the material fall back down, so that the trousers, which previously looked like a skirt, now look like culottes.

10 He fastens the leather greaves with cords.

11 He puts on shoes made of leather with the hair on the out-side.

12 He puts on the first part of the *braconniére*, that is, the part of European armour that covers the hips, stomach and the thighs.

13 The archer attaches armour to his right hand the same way he fastened his leg-armour: by means of a lining of stitched material.

14 He raises the sleeves of his robe arm to the shoulder and ties them with the cords.

15 He adds on the mobile plates that cover his shoulder and arm.

16 For maximum protection he ties the sections of the *braconniére* together using string cords.

17 & 18 The archer from both front and back, wearing all the defensive elements of his armour.

19 & 20 The armour does not prevent movement, since the arch-er is able to sit on the ground.

21 & 22 The fully armed soldier, ready for combat, carrying a 6ft longbow.

## AINOS – MILITARY COSTUME

STRANGELY ENOUGH, THE JAPANESE were not the first occupants of Japan, as the Ainos, a race quite unlike the Japanese in appearance, are thought to have preceded them. The costume of the Ainos is little different from that of the lower Japanese casts. The men wear narrow trousers and a loose outer-garment secured with a belt. The women may wear several dresses, one over another. All of these garments are of a rather crude design.

The Japanese were once men of conquest, with a feudal system of government in which the military were held in high esteem. Despite the fact that they were quick to appreciate the superiority of fire-arms over traditional weaponry, the paraphernalia of the cumbersome military equipment of feudalism could not be thrown out overnight. Hence the old helmets, mail coats and two-handed swords that could until recently be seen alongside the European equipment sported by infantry soldiers.

1 A sword with an iron blade and a handle of lacquered wood.

2 & 3 Ainos, from the Island of Yeso.

4 Prince Daimio in traditional court dress. The greater the number of sleeves, the more worthy of respect the wearer.

5, 19 & 20 A steel sword, its sheath and its cover.

6 & 25 *Betos* – members of a near-criminal class found in the cities.

7, 8, 9 & 10 A mounted general with details from his armour.

11 12, & 24 Examples of iron mail. These are fine pieces of workmanship, with individual links carefully crafted.

13 An officer armed with a bow.

14 *Yakounine* armed with two swords.

15 & 29 Sheaths for lance-heads. The first is gilded. The second is partly lacquered, partly silk.

16, 17 & 18 An officer carrying a standard, with details of his armour.

21 A nobleman carrying a standard and an iron fan, the insignia of a commander. Beside him is a "weapon of honour", carried in front of a senior officer on going in to battle. It is a type of halberd, with a shaft decorated with a pretty mother-of-pearl design.

22 An archer of the lowest rank.

26 A helmet of burnished iron with horns of yellow brass.

27 Detail of the covering for a sword – a lattice work of silk, studded with precious stones.

28 A nobleman in full regalia.

33 A footsoldier from Yedo, with the emblem of his troop. This is made up of mallets whose handles are set in a disk bearing the troop's area name. The leather strips hanging down are for decoration. The outline of a mallet is painted on each mallet-head, with three dots beside it.

31 & 32 Martial arts clothing. The two separate heads belong to a man and a woman whose costume would be identical.

33, 34 & 35 Greaves made from mail and burnished iron with silk and leather added.

# THE MIDDLE CLASSES

THE JAPANESE DIFFER GREATLY from the Chinese. China is a largely egalitarian society, in which everyone except the *tankaderes*, or boat-girls, can aspire to senior office. In Japan the population is divided into castes. One is born into one of these castes and can never leave it. There are nine of them: princes, noblemen, priests and military officers make up the first four, whose members have the right to carry two two swords. The well-educated classes, such as doctors, have the right to carry one sword. Merchants, regardless of their importance, craftsmen, peasants, servants and sailors, who make up the lower classes, are never allowed to carry arms. Beggars and Christians are considered to be lower even than the lowest of these castes.

Men generally wear trousers, which are tight at the calf, and one or more shirts. These are generally made of white cotton, but for the nobility the white cotton is mixed with blue-grey silk. The workmen have insignia on their shirts, indicating the type of work that they do, or the organization to which they belong.

Married women have plucked eyebrows and blackened teeth; they do not wear make-up, neither do they wear brightly coloured clothes. Instead of a shirt they have a tunic of red silk crêpe. All Japanese clothing, whether worn by men or women, is attached with silken cords.

1 Middle class Japanese. The men wear a short shirt, underpants and stockings – all made of cotton – and leggings held up with a belt. A robe or half-robe covers the first layer of clothes and is itself covered by second robe or jacket. The shoes are thin-soled slippers, both warm and water-proof. There is no specific right or left shoe and the slippers are sometimes mounted on wooden bases.

The way the women wear their hair varies from district to district, but large hair pins are nearly always in evidence.

2.1 A *yakounine* (*yakou* means "work" and *nine* means "man") in cavalry dress. *Yakounine* were police officers of the middle order of society.

2.2 & 3 A senior officer of the taikoun in city clothes. A young girl is handing him walking sandals that are mounted on wood (indoor only flat shoes are worn).

2.4 A lady in city clothes – the sombre colour of her garments suggests that she is married.

2.5 A *yakounine* wearing a short over-garment over his robe, fastened by a belt.

3.1 A Japanese in civil costume. These clothes are quilted and are therefore worn in winter. He has a light box covered with knotted cords in his right hand, while his left hand seems to be making a gesture that may indicate his profession: a doctor, or perhaps an acupuncturist.

3.2 A townsman in a summer outfit, holding a large straw hat and the fan on which he would write a list of the things to do that day.

3.3 A pilgrim wearing white clothes that symbolize sorrow and carrying a beggar's bell. Those who make a pilgrimage to the "high mountain" to purify themselves do so by using money given by the public.

3.4 A member of the privileged classes. This costume is worn by students at the college for interpreters at Yedo university. These are given the rank of officers, and have the right to carry a pair of swords.

## WOMEN'S COSTUME

IN JAPAN, AS IN CHINA, a well brought-up girl is skilled at both reading and writing. Japanese women are elegant in their bearing and supremely well-mannered. Despite their complete lack of legal rights, Japanese women enjoy a considerable amount of freedom in practice.

———— • ————

In public, Japanese women generally go bare-headed, but hold a parasol made of silk stretched over a delicate bamboo framework. Like the fan, the parasol is considered *de rigeur* as part of any respectable lady's costume at a social event.

The over-garment, or *kimono*, worn by women is of the same cut as that worn by their menfolk, and is common to all social classes. However, the rich have robes made of linen, whilst those of the poor are of calico. The family coat of arms is often embroidered in silk on the sleeves and the back of the flowing outer garment.

1.1 This shows how the robe is hitched up when walking, so that the wearer does not trip up. It is also possible to see where the openings of the wide sleeves begin and end. The bottom of these sleeves are closed because they also serve as pockets – the only pockets found in Japanese clothing. Small items such as a fan and a piece of thin white paper, which serves as a handkerchief (1.5) are stuffed in to the front of the robe or hung from the belt.

When Japanese are entertaining, it is the custom for guests to take home any uneaten food. Once again the sleeve pockets come in useful, since they can carry the most appetizing morsels that would not be entrusted to the safe-keeping of the servants.

The broad belt, or *obi*, is made of silk and wrapped twice around the body. The way the knot of the *obi* is positioned indicates whether or not the wearer is married. Young girls wear their knot behind their backs (1.2). All Japanese women decorate their hair with flowers, ribbons and needles, but they never wear earrings, or, indeed, any other jewellery.

2.1 & 2 Buddhist monks. All such monks belong to a caste between the nobility and the middle-classes. The small rosaries in their hands are miniature versions of the great Budhist rosary, which is fashioned in the shape of a boa-constrictor.

2.3, 4 & 5 Japanese ladies, with dark, silky hair worn short and dark, well-arched eyebrows.

The Japanese are meticulous in matters of personal hygiene. Young girls indulge in an elaborate washing routine, from which custom releases the married women. Once married, women must shave their eyebrows and blacken their teeth, all of which renders coquetry redundant. Hair is worn in a cunning scaffold style, secured with pins that are very often made of expensive tortoise-shell.

Neck, shoulders, stomach and arms are rubbed with milk to keep them white. Eyebrows are darkened with black crayon and lips are coloured.

The lady with a fan in figure 2.3 is wearing a quilted robe. Her wide belt is held in place by a another much narrower belt, fastened with a buckle. She does not wear shoes – when inside their houses the Japanese stand and sit on mats of woven rice straw.

2.4 A lady playing a three-stringed instrument called a *sam-sim*.

**1.1, 6, & 7** Women's hairstyles. The first three examples depict the traditional woman's hairstyle, a creation that may take a morning to complete. Because of the length of time involved, working women can only restyle their hair once or twice a week.

Usually, women allow a tuft of hair to grow over their foreheads. The rest of their hair is divided into two "wings" that meet beneath a large bun of false hair held in place by a tortoise-shell comb, knots of material, and needles with heads of coral and glass, the glass beads being filled with coloured liquid.

The three women here are each wearing a *kimono* with a narrow collar, and an *obi* knotted at the back.

**1.2 & 4 and 2.11 & 13** Japanese ladies in winter and summer costume. In winter, working women go out wearing one or two quilted coats and keep their faces warm under a hood wrapped around their heads.

The pockets of their long-sleeved robes act as gloves for their hands. **1.2** shows an example of the wide sleeve of the traditional Japanese robe being used as a pocket. In **1.4** the figure holds a pole on which is hung a paper lantern. **1.11** shows a parasol protecting its owner against the snow.

**1.3** A young servant girl. She has her handkerchief coiled up coquettishly round her head. She is wearing a jacket with a flower pattern on it. This jacket crosses over at the waist and is held in place by a strikingly coloured belt to which are attached some braces of the same colour. She is wearing a striped apron that is laced with flower patterns. It is a piece of ordinary silk which has been given a finish and whose folds have been heavily ironed in horizontal lines.

**1.5** A rich lady in ceremonial dress. This lady's hairstyle is held in place by a halo of giant pins made of yellow and brown tortoiseshell; her lips are painted; she has her hands tucked into the folds of her belt in an elegant posture.

**2.8** A young lady attending to her toilette and examining the hair at the back of her head with the aid of a hand-mirror.

**2.9** A street seller. This huge clutter shows different types of coloured wicker basket, which could be put to a variety of uses. All the seller's wares are heaped up on the side of two cages that obviously contain more items, held in reserve. His dress consists of a hat of bamboo bark, a jerkin and trousers of blue cotton, and a *kimono* held tight around his body by a shredded sash.

**2.10** A lady in town clothes.

**2.12** Young ladies resting.

**2.14** Ladies bathing. This scene shows the three stages of a lady's toilette. The women begin by washing themselves all over, crouching down in a tank. Then they wash the upper body using warm water from various small pitchers. Finally, they wash their faces, kneeling before a tub.

This last operation is a lengthy one, owing to the large quantity of white make-up that Japanese women wear.

**3** A family scene inside a Japanese house, just before going to bed. Thick dressing gowns have been taken out of the trunks in which they are kept during the day and mats have been piled up at the end of the room. A small wooden pillow has been placed on top of the pile: the Japanese rest their heads on this at night.

93

## THE JAPANESE AT HOME

JAPANESE LIFE is at its most convivial within the home. There are no sofas or beds, because the Japanese sleep, sit and kneel on mats, which cover the floors of every house. As a result, there is little or no need for any furniture.

Sitting cross-legged is common in Japan, in ceremonies and rituals as well as in normal domestic life. When a Japanese receives a guest, the host and visitor first kneel, then exchange greetings; they only start to talk after saluting each other by placing their hands flat on the ground and bowing their heads towards each other – the lower the better.

———— • ————

Kneeling is such an important part of Japanese life that even if craftsmen are engaged in awkward tasks, they still attempt as nearly as possible to stay cross-legged.

At meal times, a cloth of woven straw is placed over the mat on the floor, then a large cauldron containing rice is placed in the centre and everyone, seated around in a circle, fills up his or her porcelain mug.

The mats are made of finely woven rice straw and are six feet long by three feet wide. In fact, straw mats are so fundamental to Japanese life that they are used as rough units of measurement.

1.1 A washer-woman at a wash-house.

1.2 Japanese ladies at bed-time. They are sleeping under a simple quilted cover and lying on a mat. Their heads rest on a wooden pillow, topped with a small cushion.

The nightlight behind their heads is designed and decorated in a way that has symbolic significance. The white colour denotes purity, while the pagoda-like construction reflects the positive distinction that the Japanese draw between natural and man-made fire in their conception of the elements that make up their world: man-made fire is worthy of worship.

The Japanese do not use wax in their lanterns, but a type of vegetable fat that is coated on to a paper cylinder wrapped in silk.

The wooden framework behind contains drawers for make-up.

2 A public official and his family. All public officials of whatever rank carry two swords. One is a small personal weapon, and the other is a long sword of office. When sitting, the sword of office is placed across the knees or to one side.

The group to the right shows an orchestra of women. Groups like this are usually made up of one or two guitar-like instruments, a cello-like instrument called a *biwa*, and a *gotto*. The latter is similar to a harp, but is lain down to play.

3.2 A lady kneeling in front of a mirror with a make-up box beside her. Young middle-class ladies accentuate the whiteness of their teeth by putting brilliant-red carmine on their lips. They can be distinguished from married women by their yellow tortoise-shell hair-pins and their broad brightly coloured sashes.

Married women adopt a much more severe appearance: they wear no ornamentation in their hair, and they blacken their teeth. The clothes of both sexes are done up by cords – the Japanese do not use buttons.

# INDIA

## THE RAJPUTS OF TELINGANA

R AJPUTANA WAS A STATE IN NORTH-WEST INDIA, in the southern part of Hindustan called the Deccan, between the Arabian Sea and the Bay of Bengal; the Deccan being part of a British governmental division called the Bombay Presidency. The name derives from the fact that the various separate parts of Hindustan were ruled by the Rajahs of the royal Rajput family.

The Rajputs – whose name means "Children of Kings" – believed that they were descended from the Kchatryas, the ancient Kings of India who were called "the Children of the Sun and Moon". In the 17th century, there were still 100 independent Rajahs, each capable of raising a cavalry force of 25,000 men, and the Rajputs, warriors through and through, were always eager to take up arms at the first sign of trouble.

———————— • ————————

The illustrations here show the last chiefs of the Hindustani Kingdom of Telingana, of which Golconde was the capital. This city was destroyed by the Mongols, and replaced as capital by Hyderabad, four miles away.

1.1 Djihan-Khan, wearing an unusual turban, quite unlike that worn by Muslims in that it comes over the forehead in a point. Made of fine silk, it is held in place by a golden ribbon with pearls and an emerald in the centre.

At its top is a golden jewel, representing the sun, set with large rubies; this fastens a spray of fine feathers that bend down under the weight of two diamonds. A band of pearls and fine stones is attached at the base of the feathers and hangs down on either side of the turban like a necklace.

An under-jerkin covers all the upper body, and is fastened by a belt at the waist. Rich and poor alike wear this type of costume, designed to give protection against the sudden changes of weather

characteristic of the region.

Wide silk trousers taper down beneath the jerkin to a narrow fit at the ankle. Then come velvet slippers, slightly turned up at the toes and leaving the heels exposed.

Over this costume, Djihan-Khan wears a wide robe of an almost transparent muslin, held by a silver-plated belt that is inset with precious stones. Beneath it are two sashes of cashmere with gold bordering – a badge of rank.

1.2 Schah-Soliman, carrying a shield made of rhinoceros hide and decorated with six metal rivets. This Rajput is smelling a flower: a reminder of the interest that Indians of rank showed in perfume.

2.1 & 2 Mogul emperors, wearing identical clothes. A cloth turban ends in a point over the forehead; and a golden band set with pearls and precious stones surmounts it. At the turban's crown a jewel representing the sun supports a spray of feathers – a royal symbol.

# THE CONQUERING MOGULS

THE MOGUL EMPIRE WAS FOUNDED IN 1505, but Aureng-Zeb was the Emperor responsible for its geographical expansion: he had acquired some 64 million subjects before his death in 1707 at the age of 88. The Court of the Grand Mogul – as the Mogul emperors were known – was one of the richest imagineable, drawing as it could on all the riches of Hindustan.

———— • ————

1.1 The Emperor Djehanguir, who ruled from 1605 to his death in 1627, sitting on his throne beneath a parasol. The apparent simplicity of his costume is most elegant: he has a most attractive pearl and diamond turban, and his delicate robe is made from fine cotton from the Dacca region. The golden throne, silk rug and silver railings are all traditional, though one would have expected the Emperor to have been wearing rings on his fingers.

Inset, with a spray of feathers, is another Emperor, Djehander-Schah, who was crowned in 1712, but beheaded a month later.

1.2 & 3 Mogul women, wearing veils of thin muslin, with jewels on their foreheads, ears and hands. Their robes are made of fine cotton from Dacca, and their trousers, of embroidered silk, come from the valley of Kashmir. Their breasts are supported by cases made from a very light, flexible wood, joined together in the middle and strapped on behind.

After washing, Mogul women apply sandalwood powder as a perfume, then highlight their eyes with antimony. They paint their nails a vermilion colour, using the sap of the *maldroni* plant.

2.1 A Mogul woman who has coloured her upper body and face yellow with saffron dye.

2.3 The Mogul Emperor Farouksiar, who died in 1719, and, inset, the Emperor Houmaioun, who died in 1556.

Houmaioun is shown dressed for an audience at court. On such occasions the Emperor would receive his courtiers kneeling on a carpet or cushion, which is placed on a raised platform.

Farouksiar, by contrast, sits on a throne beneath the traditional parasol, with his feet on a foot-stool. The traditional costume on such occasions is the *raz* – a long, muslin robe, worn tight across the chest and wide and flowing at the base.

The illustration of Houmaioun is interesting because it contrasts so strikingly with that of Farouksiar. In the former, the artist has set out to convey an abstract quality: primarily, greatness of spirit. Houmaioun, it was once said, would have been a greater Emperor had he not had so much goodness in his heart.

Always trying to behave honourably to his unworthy brother, who frequently betrayed his trust, Houmaioun was forced to spend most of his adult life fighting to retain his throne; he even spent 13 years in exile. Here, his image is powerful in its simplicity: his greatness does not need the material trappings of power in order to show through.

The illustration of Farouksiar is quite different. He ruled at a time when the Mogul Empire was beginning to crumble. He was the figurehead for a court faction that effectively ruled in his name. As a result, Farouksiar needed to wrap himself in all the symbols of sovereignty in order to have any credibility whatsoever.

## CLASSES AND CASTES

THE PEOPLE OF INDIA ARE DIVIDED by a number of different racial origins and religious beliefs; and within these divisions there are numerous sub-divisions of class and caste – each with their own costumes and traditions. A small selection from this cornucopia is illustrated on the opposite page.

—————— • ——————

**1.1** A Brahmin jewel trader, a follower of Shiva, carrying a sample of his wares in his hand. He has a small silk turban, of which one fold hangs down over his forehead, bearing the insignia of his sect. A large gold medallion lies on his chest.

A billowing tunic falls below the knees, covering wide trousers of Turkish design, and a cashmere shawl is worn as a sash slung over his shoulder.

**1.2** A Rajah of Gingy in the Karnataka, a follower of Vishnu. The folds of his fine silk headdress are wound tightly, leaving the ears exposed, and a small shield of rhinoceros hide and a bow and quiver hang from his shoulders.

**1.3** A Pathan Muslim, wearing a muslin turban wound in the style of his religion. The remainder of his clothing, however, appears more typical of the Hindus.

**1.4** The Rajah of Tanjore in the Karnataka, a member of the *Mahrat* caste and an adherent of Vishnu. His turban is made of embroidered silk and is decorated at the front with a brooch holding an eagle's feather in place. He is wearing diamond earrings, a white muslin robe, a cashmere belt and a plaited shoulder belt.

**2.1** The wife of a craftsman from Amritsar. The majority of working women in the Punjab are employed to clean cashmere shawls, which are sent to the markets of Hindustan.

This washerwoman is wearing a *choli* – a small jacket with short sleeves that only goes down to the bust. Otherwise, her main item of clothing is a straight skirt. Her feet are bare, and her skin is exposed above the waist.

**2.2** The wife of a jewel trader, covered with gemstones. She has a pearl-studded gold ring in her nose, and six or seven necklaces. The sleeves of her *choli* end in jewels, which also glitter on her bust.

**2.3 & 4** Women of the *Mahrat* caste. This is one of the aristocratic castes of India, and these ladies live shut up in enclosed *zananah*. They are wearing pleated skirts with light corsets that do not cover their breasts. One lady – with a parrot on her hand – has bare feet, since she is indoors and walking on carpet. The other carries a piece of betel leaf in her hand.

# DANCERS AND A WEDDING

INDIAN WEDDINGS CAN LAST FOR ANYTHING from two to 30 days. Children of the relatives and friends of the happy couple – who are carried in a litter – lead off the wedding procession, and the adult guests follow on behind the litter. Usually the litter, which is used for all types of procession and celebrations as well as for weddings, consists of a light bed or sofa surmounted by an arched bamboo pole that has been carved with likenesses of real or mythological animals.

In **1**, though, the litter is a *chaupal*, one of the most ancient types. It is decorated with flowers and has lanterns round its base. This *chaupal* is almost identical to the *jalledar*, the type of litter used by Rajahs, except that the latter also has an embroidered awning as protection against the sun.

Servants are carrying the litter, and next to them stand more servants: two bearing pots of flowers on the ends of poles; two carrying small standards that display the households' colours; and others carrying supplies of the indispensable betel leaf. Musicians are playing trumpets, tambourines and oboes.

**2** A *canceni* dancer, with four accompanying musicians.

There are three classes of dancer in India: the *devadases*, who only perform at religious ceremonies; the *nartachis*, who dance at some ceremonies but are not allowed to enter the temple; and the *cancenis*.

The latter are found at all Indian parties and festivals, and in most rich households. They perform erotic dances that tread a fine line between art and indecency.

The dancer's costume is nearly identical to that ascribed to Latchimi, the wife of Vishnu and goddess of beauty. Her black hair, shiny from coconut oil, is swept back over her forehead, to end in a single plait.

The earrings, nose-ring, collars, ankle-bracelets and half-brassiére also recall the goddess. Like most *cancenis*, this dancer is an adherent of Vishnu, as can be seen from the mark on her forehead.

**3.1** The wife of a Gujarati jewel trader, a follower of Vishnu and a member of the *Vaysias*, or merchant, caste. She is carrying a wooden roller that holds bracelets, and is herself a kind of walking advertisement, with bracelets, nose-rings and collars of different sizes.

**3.2, 3 & 4** *Cancenis* dancing girls, adherents of Vishnu. The manageress of a dance troop such as this buys attractive young girls of four or five years old and teaches them how to dance and sing for a number of years before they appear in public at about 10 or 12.

Their clothing is luxuriant, consisting of a pretty pearl-edged skullcap and a huge veil. This is wound several times round the head, and then tumbles down in voluminous folds at front and back, before being covered by a transparent sari. They also wear figure-hugging trousers of embroidered silk and short-sleeved *cholis*.

As they dance, the *cancenis* spin round with their hands in the air, making their veils rise and their folds billow out.

# PEASANT COSTUMES

ON PREVIOUS PAGES WE HAVE SEEN RAJAHS, emperors and middle-class traders and merchants. But India is a huge continent, and many of its people are peasants. The costumes of these less wealthy Indians are shown on the opposite page.

———— • ————

1.6 A group of women from the mountains of Assam. Unlike the uncivilized Garro, these mountain people tend to keep in contact with the people of the plains, and wear similar clothes to them: long embroidered and fringed tunics and tartan-like shawls, worn folded into a square or knotted over the chest.

Both sexes wear very crude jewellery, though the women have adopted the heavy earrings that are a feature of plains costume.

1.7 Women on a pilgrimage, wearing cloth turbans and the white stigmata of their sect on their foreheads. Their necklaces are made of glass and coral, and their *cholis* are made of a white fabric – in the case of the seated lady it has been darkened or torn; this lady also wears a sash and a coat, knotted at the chest.

Woman take all their cooking utensils with them on pilgrimage, and all along the pilgrims' route abandoned pots and pans can be found. This is because caste members believe that the gaze of a non-caste member defiles the pot: if they only suspect that a pot has been glanced at by a stranger, pilgrims will abandon it. Pilgrims actually reduce their ration of rice so as to be able to afford a new pot each day.

1.9 A Manpouri woman, from Eastern Bengal. She is a member of one of the lowest castes, the distinguishing feature being her dark skin.

2 Girls from Kashmir. The Kashmir women are renowned for their cold, mask-like beauty, and are thus the source for most *cancenis* dancers, who are sold in early childhood to dealers from the cities of Northern Hindustan. In slightly more wealthy families, however, the girls are sold not as dancers, but as temple servants.

The Kashmiri costume is notable for its long, full clothes. It consists of a long embroidered bonnet, covered in jewels, and a long satin tunic, under which can be seen a pair of figure-hugging trousers.

3 Mina women. The Mina were once known as *Pal* people – *pal* being the name for a fortified wall of the type built to link their scattered houses. Later, the Mina became dispersed in the Jaipur region, and adopted the Hindu customs of local *djat* growers.

The Mina wear similar jewellery to that found in the Assam mountains. An original item, though, is the nose-ring that clips on to the upper lip after passing through the nostrils.

# SRI LANKA

WEDDAHS – SINGHALESE – MALABRES – MOORS

THE ISLAND OF CEYLON, OR SRI LANKA, is situated at the southern extreme of the Indian peninsula at the entrance to the Bay of Bengal. The native population is divided into four races: the Weddahs, or Beddas, who live in the mountains; the Singhalese, ancient invaders from India who are known as Kandiens in the centre of the island and Singhalese on the coast; the Malabres who also came from India after the Singhalese; and, finally, the Moors. Like the Hindus, the Singhalese still have a caste system, despite the fact that the English tried to abolish it.

1.1 A novice.

1.2 A Kandien priest, wearing a yellow robe – yellow being a sacred colour. This is simply a length of material wrapped around the body, leaving the right shoulder and arm bare. For religious reasons, such robes must be made and dyed in the space of a day.

1.3 A Jew, whose costume is remarkable for its good taste and quality of material. All his clothes, including his turban and even his Indian slippers with gold brocade and turned-up toes, are made of silk.

1.4 & 5 These two children are probably Parsees. The former is dressed in cotton and the latter in beautiful silk with gold brocade.

1.6 A Singhalese woman of the middle caste, from the coastal area. Her *canezou* is made of cotton embroidered at the neck and with a lace collar.

2.1 A sailor from the Maldives, wearing an Arabian bonnet, cotton clothes and a belt of printed material.

2.2 Kandien nobles. Despite the attempted abolition of the caste system by the English, costume often reflects the old caste traditions.
The *comboye*, worn by both men

and women, is the most important article of national costume. It consists of a piece of material wrapped around the hips and fastened with a belt, whose size is an indication of status.
The beret is also a mark of nobility and is forbidden to ordinary people, as are gold and silver jewellery.

2.3, 4, 5, & 7 Middle class Singhalese, with costumes appropriate for the hot climate and their sedentary habits.
The men wear cotton clothes: coloured *comboyes* that reach to the ankles and small open jackets. Their heads are always covered and their hair is worn in a bun.
Women's costume is the same as the men's except that they substitute a *canezou* for the jacket.

2.6 and 3.1, 2, 3, 4 & 5 Hindus. Their skin is often very shiny because it is customary to cover their bodies with oil many times a day to combat perspiration.
Men nearly always have shaved heads, except that in some castes a tuft is left at the back of the head.
Women tie their hair back, unless they are widows in mourning or are being punished for some offence, in which case their heads are shaved. They wear saris, which are draped around the body and pulled over the head at the approach of a man, even when they are indoors.

# THE MIDDLE EAST

TURBANS AND BONNETS

THE PEOPLES OF THE MIDDLE EAST ARE HIGHLY SKILLED in the art of winding a turban. However, although there is a long tradition behind the method used – an Ottoman tradition in fact – the many different styles that appear in the illustrations opposite demonstrate quite clearly that there are no hard and fast rules. A turban's appearance can be changed to match a particular costume, to comply with local fashion, or, indeed, to satisfy a personal whim.

A turban is generally made from a 15ft- or 16ft-long square of material. Two people are required: one holds two corners while the other takes the opposite bottom corner in one hand, so that the top corner that is left falls diagonally.

Both people turn the material inside out simultaneously – as if they were wringing out wet washing. To adjust the turban on the head, the roll of material is taken in the left hand with a small length kept outside the hand. The roll is then placed on the temple close to the left ear and wrapped round behind the head, almost completely covering the right ear.

When it has been wrapped round the head two or three times in one direction, the material is turned the other way and the left ear is covered. The two ends are then fastened over the head.

**1.1, 2.5, 3.1 & 5** Persian head-dresses. The first is a *coula* made of lamb's skin. The traditional Persian headgear, this was generally replaced in the late 19th century by a smaller bonnet of black lamb's skin. The second is a felt bonnet as worn by an Arab nomad, with a pointed top.

The Ilyate girl in **3.1** is engaged to be married. Her bonnet is decorated with golden threads and crowned with peacock feathers, while her hair hangs loose over her shoulders and down her back.

The Dervish (**3.5**) from South Persia is a Muslim monk. Some such monks wear red bonnets, which are embroidered with edifying maxims in coloured silk; others wear a pointed bonnet with a turban. This often bears the words of a saint in black lettering. In this example the bonnet is encircled by a turban made of camel skin.

**3.2 & 4** An Indian Thug from Hindustan, wearing a muslin turban peculiar to this group, and an Indian Dervish monk, wearing a pointed bonnet from Kashmir.

**1.2, 5, 3.4, 4.2, 3, 4 & 5** Head-dresses from Afghanistan. The first is a turban of striped muslin, wrapped around a pointed bonnet and set off by an eagle's feather. Next is a turban made of cretonne, worn over a small bonnet with pieces hanging down over the cheeks.

**3.4** and **4.2** are probably father and son, with white turbans of different styles and sizes. The same is true of the blue turbans in **1.5** and **4.4**, again worn by father and son.

**4.3 & 5** Two cotton turbans, the second with ends that hang down the back and a Persian hairstyle beneath.

**1.3** A muslin turban worn by a Catholic bishop in Senna, a town near Baghdad.

**2.1** A Turkoman wearing a bonnet made of black lamb's skin.

**2.2 & 3** Kurdish warriors.

**1.**1 & 3 Young Ilyates from Vera-mine. The Ilyates are nomads, living in tents and travelling through Persia from the Tiger to the frontiers of China.

**1.**2 A woman from Teheran pre-paring a meal. There is neither table nor cutlery, and all the dishes are put on a table cloth on the floor.

Stretched out on a soft mattress, the woman is about to plunge her hand into a mass of rice with herbs. This is the principal food, and meat is only provided once the guests' initial hunger has been assuaged.

Water, the only drink, is taken from a cup or a wooden spoon dipped into the water-container.

**2.**1, 3, 4 & 6 Outside the house, Persian women wear baggy panta-loons that entirely hide their skirts. Each leg of the pantaloons is attached to the belt independently of the other.

The muslin or cotton veil encircles the head, drapes down the back and is then brought round over the chest by an attachment round the neck called the *hyader*.

The face itself is covered by a length of percale called a *roubend*, which has a narrow eye-slit. The lady in 1 is drawing back her *roubend*; 4 is holding her panta-loons in her hand; and the lady in 6 is attaching her *hyader*.

**2.**2 & 5 Persian women from Trebizonde in indoor costume, with light shawls tied round their hips. Shawls, made from wool or linen, are much favoured in this region.

**3** The servants of a rich Persian. Some of these will be slaves; others will have been hired temporarily from a market. The servants have many different roles, but the most important of them is the pre-paration of tea and coffee, and a type of pipe, called a *kalean*.

Coffee has been drunk in Persia since time immemorial. It is pro-duced in abundance at a low price and drunk at all times of the day. Tea is prepared in a samovar and taken with sugar.

The *kalean* is just as popular. The tobacco used normally comes from Chiraz. It is very mild and made more so by being washed three of four times before it is smoked. Nevertheless, the smoke is cooled by water in the *kalean's* carafe.

It is a servant's responsibility to light the pipe and fit a wooden tube, adapted to take the place of a rubber tube with a crystal end that is specially reserved for the master of the house. The wooden tube is presented to guests – it is extremely rude to refuse it.

Women also smoke the *kalean*, and pass it round on social visits after drinking coffee. The servant in the bottom row, second from the right, is lighting the pipe which she will offer to her mistress or to guests.

**3.**1 This servant is carrying an *affabeh*, used to moisten the fingers and wash the mouth.

**3.**3 A servant serving coffee.

**3.**4 A servant offering refresh-ments.

**3.**5 A servant carrying cold water.

Male servants perform the same functions for the man of the house and his guests.

The costume of the female ser-vants demonstrates that the Per-sian women do not wear body linen. They frequently take warm baths, though, and these can be had relatively cheaply in villages as well as towns.

All these servants have their fingers and toes dyed with henna, and obey strict rules of behaviour. For example, they are never al-lowed to take their turbans off in front of their mistress.

—————— • ——————

**1.1** A young Dervish from Chiraz.

**1.2** A servant girl preparing coffee, surrounded by all the instruments necessary for her task.

She starts by heating the grounds on a sieve. These are then compounded using a cylinder and a flannel. The coffee is boiled in a coffee-pot; two drops of cold water are used to clarify it, and the coffee is then served boiling, without sugar, in little porcelain cups from China that are placed inside silver cups.

**1.3** A Turkoman girl in a costume that shows she is engaged to be married.

**2** Musicians, accompanying the dancing girls in **3**. One plays a large tambour, another a smaller wooden tambour. The musician is playing a small guitar, an instrument widely used in Persia. To his right is a man playing a *zourna*, a type of oboe called a *zamr* in Arabic. This is particularly popular at dinners and celebrations.

On the far right, the musician is playing the *kemangeh*, the instrument most favoured by Persian singers for accompaniment of the voice. The most valued of these instruments are made in Chiraz, where they are decorated with ivory and mother-of-pearl.

**3.1** A Persian woman wrapped in a *hyader* with a *roubend* attached round her neck. This pose may well be a prelude to the dance that is shown to her right. This illustration clearly shows the way in which the *roubend* crosses the chest to hold up the large cotton cloak enveloping the head.

**3.2, 3 & 4** The names "dancer" and "courtesan" are almost synonymous in Persia, and serve only vaguely to distinguish one from another. Only women dance; a Turkish or Persian man would never be seen doing this.

Dancers are of low status. They are required to perform at weddings, feasts and ceremonies. Only a short while ago they used to appear at ambassadors' receptions.

As in all Asiatic nations, the tune for the dance is sung not by the dancer herself, but by another woman or a little boy. The rhythm of the dance is rarely quick; the action consists of the striking of attitudes and of passionate movements executed with a languorous air.

Certain of the dance movements show the particular genius of the Persians. That is, that although they do not have theatres, they take keen pleasure in performing dramatic representations of a piece from one of their favourite poets.

The Dance of the Bee is one such composition – its movements are shown in **3.2, 3 & 4**. The scene is drawn with a staccato rhythm. The dancer pretends to have been bitten by a bee which she follows while taking off her clothes.

Her naked body is often covered with tattoos of flowers, palm trees, animals and even large reptiles that crawl around her legs.

It is customary in the royal house-holds of Persia to announce the rising and setting of the sun with the sound of the tambour.

This is placed on the highest terrace of the palace, and the solemn salute is performed by three musicians (1.1). The tradition probably derives from ancient sun-worship, since the feast of *Nourouz*, that is, the spring equi-nox, is still celebrated in consider-able style – even though the celebrants are Muslims and despite the reproaches of the Turks

1.4 A dignitary presenting the pipe of ceremonies.

1.3, 4 & 5 An important official, who is responsible for the *kalean*. For all rich Persians this was an item of great luxury and expense, but the king's pipe was covered in pearls and diamonds and worth considerable sums of money.

This dignitary is wearing the ancient national costume, with a gold lamé robe that reaches to the ground. This item of clothing can be known by a number of different names, depending on the cut and arrangement of the sleeves that can be buttoned to cover the under-garment.

A *caba*, for example, is wrapped tightly round the loins and buttons down one side. A *bagali* crosses over the chest for a short way and buttons down one side as far as the hips. The *tikmeh* buttons down the front, while the *biruni* is ample, with large sleeves thrown casually over the shoulders. Perhaps the most magnificent garment in Per-sia, though, is the *katebi*. This is

lined and trimmed with superb furs down its entire length, includ-ing the shoulders and the cuffs.

The headdress shown here is a *kulah* – simpler to wear than a turban since it can be taken off in one piece. It is either made of lamb's skin or a black wool called astrakhan, lined with another less fine, grey skin and topped with red wool. A cashmere shawl is wrapped round it, forming a turban that stays attached to the bonnet when it is taken off.

The dignitary also has a *kangiar*, a dagger worn by the rich and the military (lawyers and men of letters carry a writing case instead of the dagger). His beard is excep-tionally long for a Persian, but it is black and thick.

This is fortunate, because a blond beard is considered a disas-ter, and is dyed in a complex way. First it is dyed an orange-red colour with henna, and then dark green with a paste made from leaves of the indigo plant. The paste is then out and the beard exposed to the air for 24 hours, after which time it goes black.

2 These figures show the typical costumes seen in the busy streets.

2.1 & 5 Men preparing *kaleans*.

2.2 A man carrying fresh water to sell to thirsty passers-by.

2.3 A tea-vendor.

2.4 An Indian Dervish carrying the coconut in which he collects alms and the horn that he blows to attract attention.

114

# THE ORIENT

CHRISTIAN MONKS AND NUNS

THE COSTUMES OF THE CHRISTIAN MONKS AND NUNS of the Orient go back to the distant past. Some of them come from institutions that have only left a vague memory of their existence. Authors such as Father Hélyot and Schoonebeck have filled in an important historical gap by trying to record the dress of religious orders that have disappeared, while at the same time noting the regulation costumes of their own period. Their labours remain the best guide on the subject and it is from their drawings and commentaries that the following is taken.

**1.1 An early Knight Templar.** The habit of the knights was white and at first did not have a cross; this was added later. Founded in 1118, the Templars existed to protect travellers and pilgrims.

**1.2 & 8 Carmelites** in their ancient costume.
In 1287 the Carmelites adopted the white cope and started wearing the scapular. At the end of the 13th century their costume consisted of a black robe with a capuchin and a scapular of the same colour was worn over a white cope and hood.

**1.3 & 6 Mingreliens** in indoor habit and winter habit. This order's origin is as ancient as it is obscure. The habit consisted of a tunic of rough material, tucked into leggings or tight trousers, and a type of short jacket, or, depending on the season, a felt garment reminiscent of the ancient chlamys. The headdress was a skullcap with a bonnet worn over the top.

**1.4 An Armenian monk** of the order of Saint Anthony. The habit, which is entirely black, consists of a long robe, fastened by a leather belt, with another shorter, open-fronted robe worn over it.

**1.5 An Acemete or Studite monk** from Syria, wearing a long long robe with narrow sleeves. These monks wear a type of cope that is open at the sides and has a double red cross on the front.

**1.7 A secular canon** of Saint Sepulchre. The order's costume consisted of a tunic, a cloak and short hooded cloak, all in white.

**2.1 & 6 Nuns** of the Bere order. These women wear the same costume as the rest of the population. Their short, sleeveless jerkins are just like those worn by both men and women in Persia. In Autumn the jerkins are lined with fur and in winter they are worn longer and have sleeves. Their leggings and veils are also like secular garments, but the nuns cover their faces with *roubends* when they go out.

**2.2, 5 Nuns** from an ancient, but unknown order.
The habit consists of a robe worn under a a cloak that cannot be opened at the front: it is really a dalmatic. The veil, worn over a band of white wool that frames the face, is suggestive of a wimple.

**2.3 An Armenian nun.** She is wearing a black robe with wide, three-quarter length sleeves, a black cloak, veil and leggings.

**2.4 A Capuchin nun.** This order was not established until the middle of the 17th century. The tunic underneath is made of coarse brown wool and is tied with a cord; over it is a white cloak and a white wimple with a large white veil. The white veil is only worn outdoors, when going to church.

# TURKEY

## THE HEART OF THE OTTOMAN EMPIRE

IN THE 16TH CENTURY, THE OTTOMAN EMPIRE stretched from Morocco to the Arabian Sea in the south, and from The Black Sea to Vienna in the north. Since then its power has declined, but Turkey still rules large areas of continental Europe. Turkey's northern subjects tend to retain their own European identities in terms of dress – though Turkish influences can be detected; but the Turks of the Southern Ottoman Empire, illustrated opposite, cling to their original Asian heritage.

**1.1** A Bektachi Dervish. The religious men of this order wear a large jade star on their chest and a crescent symbol in their right ear.

Their clothing consists of a long-sleeved coat, a jacket, and wide trousers that are heavily pleated at the thigh and are narrower lower down the legs, where they are held in place by staples. The headgear is traditional: it is called a *hadj*, or crown.

**1.2** A *hammal*, carrying the tools of his trade on his back.

**1.3** An *aiwa*. In Turkish houses the kitchen is separated from the living area, so that cooking smells do not permeate the house.

The dishes are carried on a large tray placed on the *aiwa'a* head; his uniform consists of a long striped apron made of cotton and a cotton cloth draped over the shoulders.

**1.4** A middle-class merchant from Istanbul. Unusually, his dress has not been Europeanized.

**1.5** A *sakka* – a water carrier.

**1.6** A helmsman, called a *caikdji*, from one of the elegant barges that are for hire in Istanbul. His shirt is made of silk that has been boiled before being woven.

**2.1** A Jewish lady from Istanbul. Her headgear was *de rigeur*: a bonnet painted with large flowers lies tightly on her forehead, completely hiding her hair beneath a white border.

**2.2** A Turkish lady from Istanbul in town clothes. The outer garment may be made made either of merino wool or of cashmere, according to the season, and is called a *feradjé*; the veil of white muslin is called a *yashmak*.

**2.3** A Turkish lady from Istanbul in indoor clothes. She is wearing an *entari* with a long train and an ample *chalwar* that almost covers her velvet *paboudj*.

**2.4** An Armenian bride. This traditional costume consists of a trailing dress made of thick silk and a diadem of white flowers resting on two veils. The outer veil, a *telpetché*, is made of gold thread.

**3.1** A middle-class man from Manissa wearing a waistcoat over a shirt whose collar is turned up, but no tie.

**3.2** A lady from Manissa wearing a fez of ancient design that rather resembles a mortar.

**3.3** A Muslim peasant from the Angora region. His clothing is simple, but his jewellery is rich.

**3.4** A Muslim peasant from Angora wearing an outer garment of white felt.

**3.5** A Christian craftsman from Angora.

1.1 A Kurd from Yuzgat, lightly dressed since he would have come to Yuzgat in the summer to graze his flock. His cotton *entari* is striped with red, black, white and yellow, and is held at the collar by a button in the shape of a camomile flower.

1.2 A Kurdish woman from Yuzgat. Her headgear is extraordinary, being composed of numerous different items. The fez is entirely wrapped in white cotton, which is itself almost completely covered by several handkerchiefs painted with leaves. The structure is balanced by large earrings: silver circles with small chains hanging from them, attached to coins that jangle noisily on her shoulder.

1.3 A Muslim tradesman from Angora. In this town, the main occupations are sewing, dying wool, leather tanning and carpet-making. Each type of workman has a distinctive style of dress: this man appears to be a weaver – his cloth belt would have been beyond his means unless he had made it himself.

1.4 A Muslim from Bourdour. His fez – a *tepelik* – is almost the size of a napkin. Made of silver, it is exquisitely crafted.

2.1 A Kurdish woman from Sari Kaya. Unlike the Turks, the Kurds are a wandering people. This woman's clothing is consistent with such a lifestyle.

She is wearing a short *mintan* with embroidered sleeves, which covers the top half of her body in such a way that it does not hinder free movement. Again to make movement more easy, her skirt is tucked into her boots.

2.2 A *bashi-bozouk* from Angora. A *bashi-bozouk* is one who is exempt from military service because of his job: this man appears to be a camel driver. His waistcoat is crossed over at the chest and carelessly buttoned up at the top.

2.3 A Greek lady from Bourdour, whose costume is of ancient design. Her headress consists of a very high fez around which two handkerchiefs have been wound.

2.4 A Muslim servant from Angora, wearing pretty earrings consisting of hollow rings with silver filigree.

3.1 A Turk from Hudavinguar province. These people are nomads, grazing their flocks in vast, rich prairies, and their ancient and noble origins make them the object of great respect. They like to wear jewellery and their clothing is full and rich, being picked out with gold embroidery.

3.2 & 3 Two Zeibeks: a corporal and a sergeant. The Zeibeks are a mountain people whose dress and lifestyle are completely different from those of their neighbours.

The difference in rank between the two soldiers is clear from nearly every item of their costume: for example, the corporal's ammunition belt is simply a string of linked pouches; while that of the sergeant has gilded marking on each pouch.

3.4 A Muslim cavalryman from Koniah. This horseman is one of the volunteer auxiliaries who help to escort travellers and pilgrims.

1.1 An inhabitant of Elmaly, an area famous for its orchards. This man is an apple grower, and can therefore wear lighter, more flowing clothing than if he was a farmer.

1.2 A Jewish lady from Brousse, in indoor clothes. She is wearing an unusual headdress that completely covers her hair, which she must not let anyone see. Her *entari* is made of rich silk and carries floral designs.

1.3 A workman from Aidan, a centre for tanning and cotton-making. He wears a type of brimless hat and a long *pushkul* of blue silk hangs over his shoulders, ending in a thin *saryk*. A long *entari* of striped cotton is attached at the sides with a tie.

1.4 A groom. Such men are a common sight in the East, where horses are treated with reverence. The quality of the groom's dress is important, since it is taken as an indication of the wealth of the household for which he works.

This groom is wearing a *tchepken* of fine cloth delicately embroidered with braid, and a *djamadanof* of velvet dotted with gold. His ample breeches grow narrower as they go down the leg before ending in false gaiters, embroidered with silk, that go down almost to the tip of his boots.

1.5 A Jewish doctor of philosophy from Smyrna, whose costume is as sober as his occupation. His headgear is a type of turban similar to that worn by Muslims, though its oval shape would not be to their taste. He is carrying a long walking-stick cut from a cherry tree.

21 & 3 A peasant and his bride from Brousse. Both are in their wedding clothes: the bridegroom looking particularly elegant in richly embroidered material. The *yelek,* for example, is striped with embroidery of wool and silk in blue and black.

The bride is wearing a fez with a flocked *pushkul.* Her jacket is light in colour, and is embroidered with gold palm leaves.

2.2 A Muslim lady from Smyrna. Her robe is open at the front and held in at the bust by hooks. These are supported by a silver belt with large clasps and delicate silver and gold plating.

2.4 A Christian grocer from Aidan. His fez is wrapped in a handkerchief, and a tastefully coloured *chalwar* hangs down over the top of white socks and black shoes.

3.1 A peasant from Belka, with a fez almost entirely covered by a striped silk wrapping: only the tassel is visible. His robe, of strong silk, is held at the waist by a leather belt.

3.2 A lady from Damas in indoor clothes. Her unusual shoes consist of wooden blocks surmounted by embroidered leather straps.

3.3 A Druse lady from Damas, wearing a headdress whose design dates back to very early times. It consists of a silver tube covered with etched or embossed decorations and encrusted with uncut gems. Sometimes this could be several feet high.

3.4 A Lebanese Druse.

3.5 The wife of a craftsman from Belka, dressed for the town. She has a full robe, over which is laid a silk *tcharchaf,* or kerchief, with long cords that end in silver bells.

3.6 A peasant woman from Damas.

———— • ————

1.7 A Muslim man from the Lebanon, wearing a fez with its tassel hidden under a white muslin wrap. His shirt is made of striped silk.

1.8 A Muslim woman from Lebanon, wearing a thick chain around her neck to which is attached a large silver triangle.

1.9 A Bedouin woman from the Lebanon. Her headdress is made of two handkerchiefs: one stretched over her arms and back like a veil; the other wound round her head.

1.10 A Bedouin man, with flowing robes and characteristic turned-up slippers.

1.11 A Bedouin woman, with a thick veil attached to the top of her headdress.

2.1 A Muslim peasant lady from the Trebizonde region. A *tepelik* covers the whole of her fez.

2.2 A peasant woman from Osmandjik, with a dark robe that is open at the front.

2.3 A Kurdish woman from Palou, wearing a *mintan* whose sleeves have serrated ends. Over it is a robe of striped silk with wide, open sleeves.

2.4 A Muslim woman from Mecca. She wears three long veils, one over the top of the other. The first is made of gauze, and its upper part, which overlies the hair, is embroidered with gold thread and covered with sequins. The second veil, also of gauze, has gold and brightly coloured silk embroidery. The third is of muslin bordered with gilded lace.

2.5 A Kurdish woman from the Sivas region.

2.6 A Muslim lady from Van dressed for town. Her face is covered with a *tcharchaf* made of silk and bordered by large fringes.

2.7 A Bedouin woman.

2.8 A Turkish lady from Brousse, wearing a soft fez wound round with brightly coloured handkerchief. A silk skirt, embroidered with gold, covers her *chalwar*.

3.9 A Jewish lady from Aleppo. Her headdress is really a type of mitre, made of silk and striped with different colours. She has a long sleeveless *entari* of striped silk, which goes over the *chalwar* after a *mintan* the same colour as the *entari* has been put on.

3.10 An Armenian lady from Van. Her fez is wrapped round with a handkerchief, making it into a type of crown. Her *entari* and *chalwar*, made from a thick weave of silk, disappear under a type of broad-striped cape made of cashmere.

3.11 A Muslim woman from Trebizonde wearing indoor clothes. She has a pearl necklace from which hangs the *munuri Suleiman* – the Seal of Solomon. This is set round with pearls and turquoises. She has a satin *hyrka*, which is open in a heart shape at the bust.

3.12 A Muslim lady from Trebizonde dressed for the town. She is wearing a thick black veil and an all-enveloping outer robe embroidered with gold.

3.13 A Muslim woman from Senna, in town clothes.

3.14 A Christian woman from Diarbekir. Her headdress consists of a small silver skullcap with a long cylindrical point, over which thick bands of white cotton have been unrolled.

3.15 A Muslim women from Djeaddelé, close to Mecca.

# SECTION THREE

# EUROPE FROM BYZANTIUM TO THE 1800s

THE THIRD SECTION of the book takes up the story of the development of costume where the first section left off. It starts with the Roman Empire of the East, centred on Byzantium, which rose to prominence after the fall of Rome in the middle of the fifth century AD. At first, Byzantine costume was very much derived from that of the Greeks and Romans; later, though, Eastern influences began to make their mark.

Though Byzantium continued Roman traditions in the East, little was known in Racinet's day about the development of costume in Europe after Rome's legions had left. These were the Dark Ages, when Europe was in turmoil as different tribes and factions fought to fill the vacuum created by the Romans' departure. Europe was exposed to a rag-bag of widely different influences from the steady conquests of the Saracens and Moors in the South to the predatory raids of the Vikings and Norsemen in the North. For this reason, Racinet jumps forward 500 years, to pick up the story in 11th-century Europe.

From this point on, the narrative is unbroken: it concludes at the turn of the 19th-century. Racinet dots around Europe, sometimes writing about a specific country; at other times, he takes Europe in general as his theme and discusses a number of countries within this context. Inevitably, though, many of the European examples are taken from his native France. A certain prejudice — or perhaps understandable pride — can be detected in Racinet's remarks: he tends to overstress the importance of France as a fashion-leader for the rest of Europe.

As Racinet draws closer to his own time, he seems to become more and more confident about the details of costume, about the way in which trends developed and spread and the exchange of influences between countries. This is partly because his sources are becoming more and more reliable. At the start of the Middle Ages, Racinet has to rely on his interpretation of church frescoes and stylised illustrations of the period; a few hundred years later he is helped by the trend towards realism instead of allegory in some artists' work: later he has access to detailed engravings; and towards the end of his story he is able to use illustrations from magazines devoted to fashion.

This increase in the quality of his source material also seems to give Racinet the confidence to indulge himself in some delightful asides to give us a clear view of the man himself, complete with his opinions and his prejudices. He takes the cynic's view of the capacity for common sense of fashion-followers, noting that elegant innovations almost invariably become exaggerated until they are no more than vulgar ostentations, and has some set, though by no means denigratory, views about other nationalities — especially the English. He is quick to puncture pomposity and pretension, as in the case of France's *incroyables*, and also has a keen eye for beauty — particularly in the case of Italian peasant girls. At the same time, he is always ready to denounce what he considers immorality or bad manners with elegant understatement, whether it be in 16th-century Venice or in the England of Hogarth.

# BYZANTIUM

## THE EMPIRE OF THE EAST

WITH THE DECLINE OF THE ROMAN EMPIRE came the rise in importance of the Empire of the East, centred on Byzantium. Here tradition was all, and the only flexibility or variation in costume was in the dress of the Greek and Roman clergy and the Byzantine ascetics.

1, 2 & 3 Byzantine saints at the end of the 10th century, each wearing a pallium, a dalmatic and an embroidered tunic with leather shoes. The saint in 3 has a gold-coloured *super-humeral* – a piece of material that covers the shoulders – over his pallium. This traditional Byzantine decoration was worn by princes and lay dignitaries as well as by the higher clergy.

4, 5, 7 & 8 Officers of the Emperor, wearing cloaks decorated by a *clavus* of golden material.

6 A Greek bishop of the ninth century, wearing a *sticharium* – a tunic that is crossed over right and left by two pieces of material called *clavi* that go down to the feet. He is also wearing a primitive form of chasuble – one, that is, without a V-neckline. His pallium has been decorated at the bottom with small pieces of lead to make it hang properly.

9, 10 & 11 Byzantine ascetics from the ninth century. The much-respected Greek ascetics wore the pallium, as a mark of respect for the ancient philosophers. Ascetics and ascetics alone were entitled to wear this cloak, and only priests who were judged to lead truly ascetic lives qualified for the privilege of the pallium.

12 Heldric, Abbot of Saint-Germain d'Auxerre, wearing a chasuble and an embroidered stole over his alb.

13 & 19 A Roman abbot and bishop from the 10th century, the latter being, in fact, the evangelist Saint Mark in bishop's costume. With his pallium he is wearing a chasuble, a dalmatic and an alb.

14 A Roman consul of the Lower-Empire in the fifth century. The development of this grandiose consular costume coincided with the decline of consular authority to a purely honorific status.
The costume consists of a palmata – a toga embroidered with gold and decorated with a purple clavus – and a *subarmalis profundum* or *lorum*. This was a wide band of material that was wrapped around the body. Eventually it became the sacerdotal pallium (see 16, 17, 18 & 19).

16 & 18 Patriarchs from the same period as the bishop in 6, and with a similar costume to him. However, they are also wearing a *epitrachelium* – a stole made of a golden fabric. The priest in 16 wears a *super-humeral* of golden fabric, rather than a pallium.

17 A French bishop from the 11th century, with a conical tiara made from wicker, circled by gold or silver at its base and decorated at its point by a spherical jewel. He is wearing an alb, a dalmatic, a chasuble and a pallium, and a maniple is hanging from his left arm.

20 Nicephore Botaniate, Emperor of the East, crowned in 1078.

21 A patrician wearing a purple toga embroidered with gold over a dark tunic.

## THE INFLUENCE OF ASIA

THE ALMOST ORIENTAL LUXURY that characterizes the Eastern Empire dates from the period when Byzantium became Constantinople. The emperors, resplendent in gold and jewels, held sway over courtiers whose rank was marked by the grandeur of their costume. Fringes of gold and silver, brocade, golden materials, silk damasks – indeed, all the materials that had been only seen in Asia until that time – were combined with Greco-Roman costume.

———— • ————

The Caesarean crown of laurel, for example, the highest mark of imperial dignity, was transformed into a diadem of diamonds, from which later were to hang strings of pearls.

The Despots, who replaced the Caesars in the East, are always shown wearing a diadem covered with precious stones (6 & 8), or with an equally ornate crown (1, 2, 3, 4, 9, 10 & 11). Empresses also wore a diadem (7), or a crown glittering with jewels (5).

Elements of the imperial costume, such as the palla and the stole, are characterized by the thickness and stiffness of the embroidered cloth from which they were made. This makes them more like forerunners of religious garments than Roman costumes. An outer tunic of fine material covered an under-tunic, and a purple chlamys was worn over both. This was attached at the right shoulder by a golden clasp encrusted with precious stones. From the fourth century until the fall of the Eastern Empire, the sovereign could be distinguished by his *clavus*, a square piece of golden material worn over the chlamys (3).

The emperor's clothes were always coloured in shades of purple. First the Theodosian code, and then the Justinian code, made it an offence for anyone other than the emperor and members of his family to wear any shade of purple, hyacinth or violet.

The Emperor Nicephore (1) is wearing a silk tunic with a stole studded with precious stones. Instead of a chlamys, he is wearing a palla, also made of silk and as richly decorated as the stole. This palla, wrapped around the shoulders and hips, is the original of the bishop's pallium.

The empresses rivalled their husbands in terms of luxury and magnificence. Here they have the same distinctive costume as the emperors: sometimes with a chlamys decorated with beads and fastened with splendid clasps; and sometimes with a type of beaded, ornamented tunic.

The Empress Maria in 5, for example, wears a tunic with wide, ornate sleeves, like those of the Emperor, whose stole is studded with precious stones.

2 An emperor from the early days of Byzantium wearing ceremonial costume.

1, 3 & 5 Nicephore Botaniate, (Emperor from 1078–1081) and Maria, his wife, in ceremonial costumes.

4 Nicephore Botaniate in ceremonial costume.

6 & 7 The Emperor Heraclius, 610–641, and the Empress Eudoxia.

8 Justinian II, twice Emperor – 685–695 and 705–711.

9 Emperor Philippus Bardane, 711–713.

10 Emperor Leon IV, 775–780.

11 Emperor Constantine V, 780–797.

# EUROPE

## THE MIDDLE AGES

THESE FRAGMENTS ARE TAKEN FROM A FRESCO that decorates the vaults of the Abbey of Saint-Savin at Poitou. They depict various Old Testament scenes, in particular the events leading up to the martyrdom of Saint Savin and Saint Cyprien. The costumes are from an age when French fashions were still derived from the Frankish costumes described by Eginhard. Clothes – particularly those worn by men – did not change much for about six centuries, up until around 1100, when they became long rather than short.

———— • ————

During the course of the 11th century, several different types of cap were worn, as shown opposite. Hair was cropped at the front, and left thick at the back and sides, in a style that came to be known as *provencale*. Beards also came into fashion.

At this time, clothes did not vary much in shape or style, but were worn in very different ways. Tunics were common, being worn by virtually everyone, but their fabric and length depended on the class of the wearer: beautiful silk tunics from the east for the wealthy; and short, coarse-cloth tunics with close-fitting leggings for the poor.

**1.1 to 4** Various types of Phrygian cap, with the characteristic scrolled top and curve to a point at the nape of the neck.

**1.1, 3, 4 & 7** A square of material similar to a Roman pallium was worn over the shoulders. It was attached at the right shoulder by means of two ends of the square, which were passed through a brooch.

**1.5** A tunic called a *bliaut* was worn over the chemise. This was a type of knee-length smock, with tight sleeves and an opening for the head.

**1.7** Saint Savin, wearing a wide

*bliaut*, belted at the waist so that the material falls in folds.

**1.8** Footwear often consisted of simple shoes fastened with laces criss-crossing the calf.

**2.2, 4, 5 & 6** Long tunics with luxurious folds were worn by those considered worthy of respect, such as old men and ecclesiastics. In the case of the latter they would have been made of coloured silk, and embroidered with gold thread.

**2.2** A hooded cope was often worn in place of a pallium, and was considered a travel garment. Later, copes similar to this were worn by the clergy.

**2.6** An old man wearing a different type of shoe, made of stiff material and covering the whole foot; some shoes were open at the heel. Heavier wooden outer shoes were worn over these thin ones for walking outside, in rough conditions.

**3.1** 11th-century battle-dress: chain mail and a round helmet.

**3.2** A soldier wearing a tunic with wide, short breeches that covers his hose and is tied at the knees.

**3.3** A horseman ready to ride into battle.

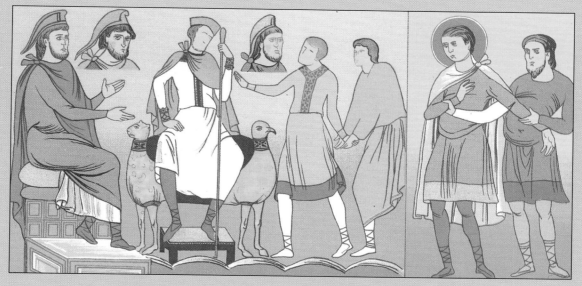

## THE MIDDLE AGES – THE CHURCH

FORMAL RULES GOVERNING ECCLESIASTICAL COSTUME were first laid down during the Meringovian era, and detailed the shape, cut and material of such garments as albs, amicts, chasubles and dalmatics. Bishops' costume was also subject to strict rules, but tended to be much more elaborate, as it included items such as mitres, croziers and rings.

———— • ————

1.2 to 5 Each of these priests is wearing an alb, one of the earliest parts of liturgical costume. Although its name is derived from the Latin *alba*, meaning "white", the alb was often made in different colours, and also of other materials than simple linen. Details such as the embroidered square of cloth at the bottom of the alb show the lasting influence of the extravagant Carolingian age.

Each priest, including the one in 6, is also wearing an amict – that is, a long piece of fine linen wound round the neck like a collar. Before the service, the amict is used to cover the priest's head, and it is lowered at the moment he approaches the altar.

1.1 A priest wearing a dalmatic, named after the robe worn in classical times in Rome. Typically, it would have long sleeves and a tasselled sash.

1.2 The alb was belted in the middle with a piece of cord. Bishops, though – see **2** – would have worn a silk girdle richly embroidered with gold or silver thread.

1.3 to 5 The chasuble, or cloak, is worn over the alb, and cut at the sides to allow free use of the arms: each one shown here has a slightly different cut.

1.4 This priest's chasuble has an embroidered border called an *orfray*, with an added lateral strip to form the shape of a cross.

1.5 Only bishops and mitred abbots were permitted to wear a dalmatic under an alb.

1.6 A priest wearing a type of dalmatic that is split down both sides.

2. Various types of mitre, and other elements of costume that distinguished a bishop from lesser clergy.

Originally a small, round bonnet, the mitre increased in height during the 12th century, with the help of a stiffening of board or fustian. Later, during the 15th century, mitres became more and more ornate. They were manufactured from golden or white silk and studded with diamonds.

The two bishops are each holding a crozier, as a symbol both of their power and as their function as the earthly shepherds of their flocks. To emphasize this twin symbolism, some croziers carried the motto "Guide, Rule, Punish".

Some croziers had figures carved in the centre of the scrolled end; some were shaped out of a pair of entwined serpents. The word *homo* was often carved into the curved scroll to remind the bishop of his mortality.

The bishop on the right has a *sudarium* floating like a pennant from his crozier. This fashion became less popular among male clergy, but continued among abbesses.

Other marks of episcopal rank were *super-humerals*, broad collars made of richly jewelled brocade with a strip of material hanging down over the chest, and gloves. These are said to have had their origin in Church customs, though some cynics have it that their prime purpose was to prevent the left hand from knowing what the right hand was doing.

## THE MIDDLE AGES – ARMOUR

ONE OF THE MOST IMPORTANT INVENTIONS of the early Middle Ages was that of the mail coat. This protected a soldier as well as sheet metal – if not better, since it provided so many more angles from which to deflect a sword cut – but, just as important, allowed the wearer a much greater freedom of movement. Mail developed from the 10th to the 14th centuries, increasing in complexity of design and efficiency.

———— • ————

1.1 A Norman knight of the 10th century, wearing a protective coat made of a strong material – sometimes leather – on to which have been sewn iron rings. The basic coat consists of a tunic with short sleeves that ends in a pair of leggings.

The iron rings are simply laid side by side, and held in place by strong braid and stitches (see detail above). They are not inter-linked, as is the case with chain mail. Nevertheless, this type of mail was such an effective defence against blows that knights sometimes dispensed with the leather doublet that was usually worn beneath it to prevent bruising.

The helmet is made of iron and bronze, and has a fixed nose-piece.

1.2 A different type of mail (see detail above) consisting of strips of beaten iron and nails rivetted on to a leather coat. This dates from the reign of Hugh Capet, King of France at the end of the 10th century.

1.3 A 13th-century knight's equipment, consisting of a red tunic under a hauberk that extends over the head to form a hood, then a coat of chain mail (see detail above). A well-padded strip of material is placed on top of the hood, to support the cylindrical helmet, and the chain mail is covered with a coat of red silk.

The shield is still pointed, as in previous centuries, but is now much smaller and more manoeuverable.

1.4 A soldier from the beginning of the ninth century – the time of Charlemagne. His armour consists of flat plates of iron rivetted on to a base of thick leather. Below this is a skirt, like a kilt, of thick leather.

His helmet is made of four plates of iron, which form a protective edge at the temple. His breeches are made of leather, and strips of iron have been sewn on to them for extra protection. The brass-handled sword has grooves cut all the way along its blade, following a custom that persisted until the 13th century.

1..5 A 12th-century knight, carrying a shield made of painted wood that is long enough to protect his whole body. A long chain mail coat is worn over a long robe made from yellow and blue wool. He is also wearing leather gloves and shoes, gilded spurs and a helmet of painted iron.

2.1 & 2 Jakennes Loucart, one of the King's knights, with his insignia of a lion emblazoned on his tunic. Such insignia were popular, though they had not at this stage been formalized as coats of arms. His shield is padded and stitched round on the inside, and his gloves have a detachable thumb-piece.

2.3 Hugh de Chalon, wearing an all-enveloping mail coat and a tunic bearing his colours.

2.6 Philip of Artois with a shield bearing a formal coat of arms.

# SPAIN

THE 13TH CENTURY

THE PERIOD THAT SAW THE DEFEAT of the Moslems and the move towards unity in Spain marked a corresponding change in costume. Most nations, following the example of the French, shook off Byzantine influence and adopted clothing more suited to the ideals of the Middle Ages. Spain was no exception. It preserved some of the traditions left behind by many centuries of foreign rule, but aspired to a much greater simplicity in costume. The nobility wore little jewellery, and, in general, costume bore the mark of austerity.

Austerity was the keynote of the reign of Alphonse X, known as "the Wise". His rulings went as far as to prohibit the wearing of an under-shirt next to the skin.

His successor, Alphonse XI, continued with sartorial reforms, making laws that prohibited the embellishment of garments with pearls or silver and banned the Oriental-style luxury that still predominated in horses' trappings, with their lavish caparisons and bells. His success can be seen in 2.1.

1.1 A young lady wearing a tiara of fine, embroidered material, decorated with pearls and precious stones and secured on the head by means of a *barbuquejo* – a wide ribbon passed underneath the chin. Despite the edicts of Alphonse X, the height of such headdresses increased during the last years of his reign.

Her hair hangs down in thick curls over her shoulders; this was the popular style among young Spanish girls. She is wearing the cloak, or pallium, that was worn by both noblemen and women and beneath it a pair of robes: a *cyclas* and a *loba*.

The man sitting at her side wears the same garments. The servant, clothed in a tunic made of coarse, brown wool of Saracen origin, is handing him a sealed letter.

1.2 A group of soldiers, whose leader is wearing a white *loba*.

1.3 Two women offering a man a *faja* – a scarf with fringes. Their tiaras are similar to the horn-shaped hats worn by Venetian ladies. The woman on the left is wearing a *cyclas* that takes the place of a bodice, whereas the woman on the right has a long tunic.

2.1 (top) Examples of 13th-century Spanish furnishings: a wooden pitcher, decorated with bronze; a lamp on a stand; types of hanging lamps with vessels for oil and saucers, as used by Arabs; and a brass candlestick with extinguisher.

The item of clothing is an *aumusse*, worn by laymen when out of doors.

2.1 (bottom) Huntsmen. The horseman on the left is wearing an embroidered bonnet that comes down over his ears, a *quezote* – a sleeveless tunic lined with ermine – and greaves. The central character has a leather bonnet, greaves and a hat hanging down his back, and is hunting with a hawk.

The figure on the right is Alphonse X, wrapped in a *gonelle*, complete with a cape. This garment was always worn without a belt for hunting in the country.

2.2 Alphonse X, carrying a reliquary at the head of a procession. He is wearing a red pallium and an eight-pointed crown. Beside him, a bishop, wearing an embroidered cape, is blessing the crowd.

# EUROPE

## THE MIDDLE AGES – COURT DRESS

**A**S IN ALL COURTS, THE COSTUMES OF WEALTHY LADIES at the French court became more and more resplendent and ornate throughout the Middle Ages. Much of the emphasis was on extravagant headdresses, which probably owed much to the Middle Eastern influences that were assimilated during the Crusades. According to the historian Juvenal de Ursin, these headdresses became so large that "when they wished to pass from one room to another, women were forced to turn their heads sideways in order to get through the doors."

1.1 & 2 Two servants. The one on the right is wearing a *hennin* covered with a starched veil. The *hennin* is a pointed bonnet based on a Syrian fashion, which may well have been brought back to Europe by returning Crusaders.

1.3 Isabeau de Bavière, who became the wife of King Charles VI of France in 1385. This beauty caused a sensation on her debut in society, which came at the age of 14. Here she is wearing a sumptuous *hennin*, which is a compromise between the high-pointed and double-pointed versions of the headdress, both of which were the focus of some criticism at the time.

1.4 Jacqueline de la Grange, the wife of Jean de Montagu, Charles VI's Chief Minister. Her headdress consists of a bonnet over which is placed an *escoffion* – a contraption made from rings of varying sizes and shapes. The example here is of average size.
    Both the de la Grange and the Montagu coats of arms are emblazoned on her dress.

1.5 The daughter of Jean Juvénal and Michelle de Vitry, and so a member of the famous Ursin family. Her headdress can either be considered as a double-pointed *hennin* or as a large *escoffion*. It is richly decorated with embroidery and gemstones, and covered with gauze to soften the effect. Unusually, this lady's arms are completely covered; normally they were left bare.

1.6 Euriant, the wife of the Comte de Nevers, wearing a long veil from her headdress, as was the fashion between 1420 and 1430.

2.1 Marguerite de Beaujeu, the daughter of Edward, Marshal of France, who died in 1351. She is wearing a *mantel d'honneur*, a cape worn for ceremonial occasions, lined with fur.

2.2 A lady's costume from the 15th century.

2.3 & 5 Anne, who became the Dauphine d'Auvergne when she married Louis II, the Duke of Bourbon, in 1371, and her servant. Both ladies are wearing the dashing gown that marks them as married women. By convention, the coat of arms is only worn on one side of the gown.

2.4 Jeane de Flandre, the wife of Jean de Montfort, Duke of Brittany, wearing the costume in which she made her society debut at Nantes. A feature of this is the extravagant *hennin*.

2.6 Reputedly, Héloise, whose tragic affair with Abelard has passed into legend, and who died in 1163. The bag hanging from her waist is known as an *escarelle*, from the old French word *escar*, meaning "miserly".

## THE MIDDLE AGES – NEW STYLES

THE TIGHT-FITTING COSTUMES characteristic of the 14th century emerged in Northern France in about 1340, though they had been seen on the Mediterranean coast for some considerable time. A narrow, short camisole, called a *jaquette* replaced the long tunic, and a padded jerkin that opened either at the front or the sides served as a coat. This left the thighs exposed: they were covered with leggings that had a sole attached to the foot, so that separate shoes were unnecessary. In bad weather, however, wooden galoshes or iron blocks were fixed to the soles.

———— • ————

Eventually, fashion dictated that huge points, stiffened with whalebone, be attached to both shoes and boots. These were called *poulaines* (a corruption of the word *Polonaise*) in France, and Cracoves in England – both words showing the fashion's Polish origin.

During the 14th century, the *poulaines* became ridiculously large (3), and even influenced the shape of soldiers' iron boots.

At this time, shirts became more common, while lords and ladies took to wearing hose of two different colours: one leg would be white, yellow or green; and the other black, blue or red (3). Sometimes even the shoes were of different colours.

In a reaction to the new styles favoured by youth, ceremonial dress, as worn by men of letters and lawyers, stayed full and traditional. So much so, in fact, that it was common to talk of two different styles: "short" and "long" clothes. Fashionable "short" clothes, as worn at court, are shown in **3**.

14th-century costume did not yet include immense hoods, with their points hanging down the back, that later became so fashionable, nor exaggerated sleeve-ends that hung down to the ground. The man in **3.1**, for example, is wearing a conical hat over a short hood, though it is extravagantly decorated with a costly ostrich feather.

The *jaquettes* shown here only have short sleeves, while the sleeves of the doublets fit tightly over the arms for the whole of their length.

**1.1** Philippe, Comte d'Evreux, the son of Louis who kneels to his right. He is dressed in the same manner as his father, but has a larger belt. This is worn slanting down from right to left and is heavily decorated.

**1.2** Louis de France, the youngest son of Philipe le Hardi, who died in 1319. His hair is worn long at the back, but cut short at the front. It is held in place by a circlet consisting of a single ribbon decorated with pieces of gold and silver.

**1.4** A group of civic dignitaries. The figure at the front is holding a tall hat and is wearing a smock over his doublet; the third figure is wearing a *corset-sangle* whose sleeves have been let out. All three men are wearing tight breeches and *poulaine* shoes.

**1.5** Louis, the eldest son of Louis IX who died in 1260. His azure robe carries a *fleur de lys* pattern, and is topped by a false hood called a *rondeau*.

**2** A man playing a flute and other peasants from the reign of Charles V of France. The everyday costume of a peasant consisted of a jerkin over a tunic and hose, with a cape over the shoulders that could be drawn up to form a hood. A straw hat was usually worn on top of this.

To the right is a group of grape pickers. The man is wearing a sleeveless jerkin over a simple tunic. His breeches are tight-fitting, and his shoes are made of yellow leather.

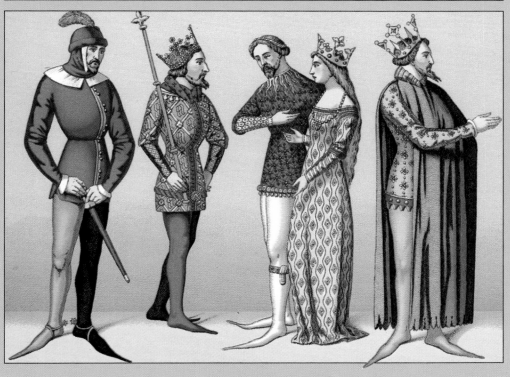

# EUROPE

## THE 14TH AND 15TH CENTURIES – ARMOUR

A S MILITARY TECHNOLOGY ADVANCED and new tactics evolved, chain mail started to give way to plate armour. However, this increase in weight gave rise to a new trend. Shock troops, such as the heavy cavalry, continued to wear heavy armour, but now some horsemen and the majority of foot-soldiers began to wear less armour, in order to increase their mobility.

**1.**1, 2, 4, 7 & 8 Helmets. 4 & 7 are English and date back to the end of the 14th century.

**2.**9 & 10 Men of the Grand Guard of the army of Charles VII. These guards took their name from the weapons they carried, and as they abandoned the mace and took up the bow and arrow, they became known as archers. The white cross was the French national emblem, as opposed to the red cross of England.

On his entry into Rouen in 1449, Charles VII was followed by his Grand Guard of archers and cross-bowmen. According to Mathieu de Coussy, they wore: "sleeveless *hoquetons* coloured vermillion, red and green, and decorated with gold, with plumes in matching colours."

**1.**12 A soldier from the second half of the 14th century. The use of leather combined with iron marks a transitional period, which follows the chain mail hauberk and precedes perfect armour plating.

**1.**13 Charles d'Orléans, who lived in the 15th century during the reign of Charles VII. The metal suit of armour completely covers the body, and greaves even cover the heels of the iron shoes.

**1.**14 A knight wearing a type of armour known as *xaintrailles* at the beginning of the 15th century. His iron helmet has a jutting edge that goes right the way round. This style of military headdress can be seen on Greek and Roman monu-

ments. In the 12th century it was made of leather; by the 13th century it was made of iron and worn over a hood of chain mail.

**1.**15 A soldier from the period of Charles V.

**1.**16 The armour of the Dauphin, the son of King John who became Charles V. The variety of armour in this period was a result of the rivalry between two methods of protection: plate armour and chain mail.

Armour plate had not yet been generally adopted. Chain mail persisted, though reduced to use in a small haubergeon as a compromise that included a cuirass covered by a padded surcoat.

**2.**3 A knight on horseback, part of the light cavalry that was developed in imitation of the Eastern fighting tactics met in the Crusades. Light cavalrymen were less encumbered than the traditional knight on horseback, and had greater freedom of movement.

**2.**4 & 5 An archer and a cross-bowman. The shoulders and legs of the crossbowman were not always protected by armour, following the adoption of the studded leather jerkin around 1320. Rules laid down by the Dauphin, later Louis IX, in 1474, dictated that crossbowmen had to have "doublet, breeches and a white hood under the sallet." This was to reduce the excessive amount of armour, both defensive and offensive, worn by some foot soldiers.

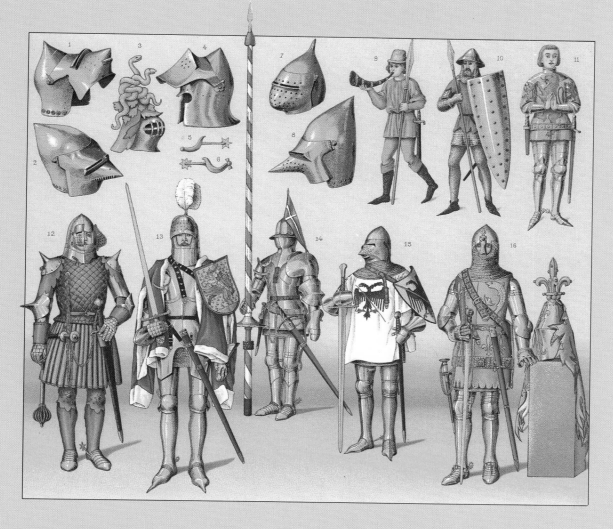

## THE 14TH AND 15TH CENTURIES – TOURNAMENTS

IN MEDIAEVAL TIMES, TOURNAMENTS were seen by the nobility as both sporting and political events. While they provided an opportunity for the combatants to display their knightly skills, they were also important in upholding the ideals of chivalry.

**1.2 & 2.1** These two pictures form one group. The figures with their backs turned in the foreground are positioned in the way of the Duke of Bourbon, the adversary of the Duke of Brittany, who is about to enter the tiltyard where he will take his oath.

This ceremony took place the day before the great tournament. In this joust the Duke of Brittany is the challenger and the Duke of Bourbon is the defendant, who accepts his challenge. The two knights, escorted by their followers, come from opposite ends of the field to swear that they will conform to the rules of the contest.

They do this in front of the judges who, in the original picture, are sitting on a platform next to the lords and ladies in the spectators' boxes.

Enter the Duke of Bourbon, in civilian costume, without armour, carrying a baton in his hand. Behind him is his banneret, though only the head of his mount is visible in this picture.

The Duke's route is lined with the heralds of the Duke of Brittany, wearing his coat of arms and ermine capes, a trumpeter – also wearing the Brittany arms – and other knights from different houses. The Duke is riding a charger harnessed with a steel chamfrain and a headstall topped by gold *fleur de lys*.

**1.1 & 2.2** Fashionable gentlemen from around 1488. They are wearing skullcaps called *bicoquets* under large hats with upturned brims, which are decorated with plumes that can either stand upright or lie flat. Their gowns are open at the front and trail along the ground. They have long sleeves, set far back on the shoulders to reveal nearly the whole front of the doublet beneath.

**3.** The rural population at this time always appears to have been decently and modestly dressed. Women showed good taste in their dress and peasants' costume never showed the degree of abject poverty that was evident in later centuries.

**3.1** A 15th-century labourer, wearing a straw hat whose shape is reminiscent of the *chapeau à bec*. A small cloak, or *sagulum*, is thrown over his coat and an apron-like garment, tied in a knot at the back, holds up his trousers.

**3.2** A man sowing corn, wearing a hat like a hemispherical cap and a jerkin over a blue cloth coat.

**3.3** A reaper. Daily labourers preferred short clothes and for some tasks, when the season permitted, they did not bother with certain items of clothing.

**3. 4 & 5** Gravediggers. The man on the left is wearing *gamashes* over his bare legs, and a doublet is visible beneath his sleeveless tunic. The sleeves of the doublet are short, revealing those of the under-shirt – these are long, but are rolled up to the elbow in order to facilitate digging.

The second gravedigger is wearing a peaked hat and a coat with long tight sleeves. His breeches are attached to the coat with aglets. These often snapped through the strain put on them when the labourer bent over to dig. The painter here shows the shirt tails hanging over the top of his breeches – no doubt the result of such an accident.

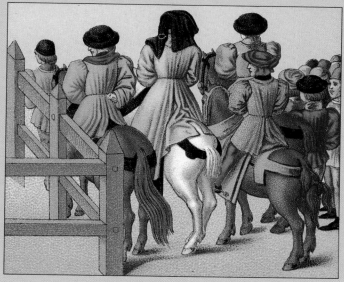

# EUROPE

## THE 15TH CENTURY – "SHORT" CLOTHES

THE TOP TWO ILLUSTRATIONS are taken from a manuscript on French law that dates back to the second half of the 15th century. The simplicity of the costumes is a result of the reforms initiated by Louis XI. Except for two magistrates, the characters are merchants, shopkeepers and minor officials. By this time, the "long" and "short" controversy had been largely settled in favour of "short" clothes – long robes were now only worn by lawyers, men of letters and the clergy, who believed them to be a mark of distinction.

———— • ————

The illustration of an interior is also from the 15th century. In keeping with the custom of the Middle Ages, the costumes are contemporary with the painter, who lived about the time of Charles VII. But the action represented took place in the 14th century, and is one of the incidents of the first phase of the Hundred Years War which began in 1340.

It shows the capture of the King of Navarre. He is seated at the table, dining with the Dauphin and other lords. The two kings, of France and Navarre, are recognizable by the golden crowns encircling their hats. The Dauphin is seated at the end of the row; he appears much younger than the others.

The guests are sitting along one side of the table as custom dictated, the table being small enough to enable the servants to wait from the other side. The long seat with a back and a foot-rest – the chair of honour – is normally found at one end of the great hall, often on a platform.

The dining table was not normally covered with wines and fine dishes. These were put on dressers and sideboards. Servants brought the silver and pewter plates to the table with goblets containing wine. The speed with which these dining tables could be laid and cleared suggests that they were made of boards placed on mobile trestles. Table linen consists of damask, often in two layers, with the cloth reaching to the ground.

Transport was primitive in Western Europe, even as late as the 15th century – especially when one considers that the Romans used sprung chariots.

A ceremonial coach, as in the top example, was constructed like a cart, with the frame of a semi-circular hood mounted on boards placed directly on top of the axles of four equally sized wheels. By contrast, the wood here is gilded and the pall and mantel are both rich.

The explanation of so backward a construction as this is that it derives from an entirely national, rather than Roman, tradition.

The lower illustration shows the simple agricultural cart that is at the root of this tradition. Its size was standard, so that a cart-load could be used as a unit of measurement. The poor state of the roads and the ideals of knightly conduct made riding a horse infinitely preferable to riding in a cart, and this mitigated against any serious progress in the design and construction of the latter. The only people who travelled in wheeled vehicles were the old and the sick.

———— • ————

1.1 Pierre de Dreux, known as "Mauclerc", who died in 1250. This illustration is taken from the stained glass windows of Notre-Dame de Chartres. He is wearing a mail coat, a hauberk with his coat of arms and an emblazoned shield.

Under Louis IX, knights had adopted the custom of shaving the tops of their heads, either through fear of being seized by the hair should their helmets fall off in battle, or in case the hair fell forward under the helmet.

1.2 Jean II, called the "Good", King of France from 1350 to 1364. He is wearing the costume that Philippe de Valois had chosen for the royal family: a crown decorated with gold *fleur de lys*, an overcoat worn under a cloak and a cape trimmed with fur.

1.3 Francois I, Duke of Brittany (1414-1450), wearing a ducal crown and a blue dalmatic. His cloak, which dates from the 14th century, is wrapped round the body and folded back over the left arm; it has a slit down the side and is worn with a fur cape.

1.4 Francois I in town costume, wearing a surcoat with slashes in its sleeves. In this period the sleeves of over-garments were frequently tight at the wrists.

1.5 Louis I, Duke of Bourbon, a 14th-century courtier, wearing a cloak lined with ermine, spangled with a band of jewels and decorated with his blazon.

1.6 A gentleman's costume from the 15th century. Jean, Duke of Bourbon, was captured at the Battle of Agincourt and died in England in 1433.

1.7 An ecclesiastical costume of the 14th century. The robe worn under the linen tunic served the same purpose as a cassock.

2.1 Louis II, son of Louis I, King of Naples. Louis II is wearing a *houppelande*, or greatcoat. During the reign of Charles II, this garment replaced the surcoat and the cloak.

2.2 & 3 Fashionable young men from the court of Charles VII.

2.4 Jean de Montagu, counsellor and chamberlain to the king, wearing a surcoat with open sleeves that are closed at the wrists and padded shoulders. He was beheaded in 1409.

2.5 Charles I, Duke of Bourbon, wearing an unbelted overcoat that reaches to the ground. His small black hat has an almost 19th-century shape, and his dagger appears to be hanging from a cord.

2.6 Jean de Montagu, son of the de Montagu in 2.4, who was killed at Agincourt in 1415.

3.1 The Duke of Cologne in outdoor costume during the reign of Charles V. His long robe is trimmed with fur and reveals the red collar of the surcoat.

3.2 A gentleman from the court of Charles V, wearing a small pleated bonnet and a doublet in gold coloured material, laced up behind and attached to his breeches. His shoes are *poulaines*.

3.3 A 14th-century lute player. Minstrels wore a similar costume to that of peasants: a surcoat, a cape that covered the shoulders, and leggings.

3.4 A sergeant of arms during the reign of Charles VI, wearing a robe with slashed sleeves over a blue doublet.

3.5 A 14th-century musician playing a bass stringed instrument called a dicord.

# POLAND

## THE 13TH AND 14TH CENTURIES

THE COSTUMES OF THE SLAVS – the Western branch of whom occupy Poland – have retained a considerable degree of uniformity, though there are certain small differences. Polish costume developed within the framework of the Slavonic tradition throughout the 13th century, and for a part of the 14th century. The most important documentary source for this period is a manuscript called *The Legend of Saint Hedvige*. This was completed in 1353; it shows the court of Prince Henri "the Bearded", as well as battles with the Tartars and scenes from everyday life.

Traditionally, the basic Polish garment was a long tunic, called a *joupane*. It was worn by men from all social classes up until the beginning of the 19th century.

The *joupane* was tight-fitting across the chest and did not have pleats round the bottom. The sleeves could be of variable width and it had a short standing collar.

The length of this tunic could vary, although it generally ended at the calf, and its colour and style depended on the wealth of its wearer. The oldest *joupanes* were grey, but over the years their colours changed to shades of red: sandalwood, lilac and crimson or scarlet (1). Only the nobility had the right to wear clothes of this colour; in fact, the word *karmazyn*, meaning crimson, became synonymous with the word "gentleman".

A fur-lined cloak was worn over the *joupane*, and attached to it either by emblazoned hooks or by a single hook on the right shoulder. It was often furnished with a hood (1.5) and in this form became the national costume – one that is still worn by peasants in many areas of Poland.

The costume of a noblewoman in the Middle Ages consisted of a long gown, at first with flared sleeves (from the 10th to the 13th centuries) and then with sleeves that were buttoned from the wrist to the elbow. She would wear a wide belt and a cloak fastened with an emblazoned clasp, or one decorated with diamonds. During the 14th century the gown became tighter at the waist and in general the costume became more lavish.

At this time the armour of Polish knights combined Eastern and Western influences: chain mail and metal plates were worn from the 12th to the 18th century. Helmets were usually pointed in the manner of early Slavic models.

2.1 Henri IV, who died in 1290.

2.2 An abbess from the Cistercian convent at Trebnitz in Silesia.

2.3 A young noblewoman.

2.4 A merchant.

2.5 & 6 Conrad, Duke of Mazovie, who died in 1237.

3.1 An abbot from the abbey of Oliva in 1307.

3.2 A bishop.

3.3 Boleslas V "the Chaste", who died in 1279.

3.4 Vladislas "the Brief", who died in 1333.

3.5 Leszek "the Black", who died in 1289.

3.6 Przemylas, Duke of Oppeln, who died in 1295.

# ITALY

## A 15TH-CENTURY WEDDING

THE ILLUSTRATIONS OPPOSITE SHOW civil and religious costumes from 15th-century Italy. The top panel is a study by an unknown painter of the wedding of Boccace Adimari and Lise Ricasoli, celebrated in Florence in 1420. The painting conveys a remarkably vivid impression of an episode of 15th-century Italian life.

———— • ————

The couple is leaving the Bigallo, the home of the Adimari, which is still standing some 450 years later, and the baptistry can be seen in the background.

The bride is dressed in black velvet robes, embroidered with gold, and a pointed headdress. She is giving her hand to the bridegroom, himself bareheaded. The musicians, sitting on the dais, have the ancient arms of the Florentine republic on their instruments – a red *fleur de lys* with red flowers on a silver background.

After the marriage service, it was the custom to receive attendants and guests at the front door of the house. The head of the family, recognizable by the long red tails on his hat, appears to be inviting two young noblemen to join the festivities.

The illustration in the bottom left-hand corner comes from part of a reredos painted by Francesco Pesello. It shows the Saints Come and Damian, two brothers who visited the sick and ministered to them.

The illustration in the middle of the bottom strip shows a piece of black velvet material with gold lamé and red satinwork, taken from a painting by Gentile da Fabriano in the 15th century.

The painting in the bottom right-hand corner shows Girolamo Savonarola, the famous Dominican monk, in his cell. The painting is after the school of Fra Bartolomeo.

Savonarola's cell has been depicted just as it was at the time of his death in 1498. The chair is authentic, and the desk looks as it would have done when he worked and prayed at it. The crucifix is the very one that Savonarola held as he went to meet his death at the stake.

Fittingly, the painting can be found in the convent of Saint-Marc in Florence, where Savonarola was the prior.

# EUROPE

## THE 15TH AND 16TH CENTURIES

ETWEEN 1485 AND 1510, THE MOST FASHIONABLE style of dress for the women of the court that was shown opposite – a long, lined garment, with a square-cut corsage revealing a flimsy chemise and sleeves that were loose all the way down. This outfit – or, more precisely, a uniform – was generally worn with a gold, silver or cord belt, whose ends hung down either at the front or at the sides.

The headdresses illustrated here show many different kinds of *templette*. Strictly speaking, the true *templette* was of the type shown in 3.2: this is shaped to go round the back of the head and come forward at the sides, and has a string of large beads across the top.

But there were many variations on this basic style. As in 1.3, some *templettes* were covered with what is almost a hood, made from thick material and placed the top and back of the head as well as coming down over the forehead. In other cases (1.1 & 5) the hood does not come out over the forehead but simply falls down the back.

Finally, a *templette* was sometimes covered by a turban, as in 2.3, 5 & 7, or by a crown (1.6).

## THE 15TH AND 16TH CENTURIES

WHILE THE TRADITIONS OF THE MIDDLE AGES persisted through the 15th and 16th centuries so far as women's costume was concerned, men's costume changed radically. This was mainly the result of Italian influences following Charles VIII's expedition to Italy. Some experts think that this was the most gracious and elegant of all the different ages of costume in France.

———— • ————

One striking change was that the doublet no longer had a collar, so that the top of the shirt could be seen. To compensate, the turned-down collars of coats and gowns became longer and longer, until they extended almost to the middle of the back (1.2 & 4). When a ceremonial coat was not worn, it was replaced by a collarless cape, put on over the doublet and left open at the front (1.5 & 6).

Men's headgear consisted of toques and *bicoquets*, worn separately or one on top of one another, and various types of bonnet. 1.2 & 4 show bonnets with rims at the front. Toques with small upturned brims can be seen in 1.5, 6 & 7, 2.1, 4 and 3.8. Another similar style of toque decorated with a plume, can be seen in 1.1. Many of the hats are worn over a decorative *bicoquet* and attached with long ribbons.

Metal clasps and heavy necklaces were favoured by the French nobility at the end of the 15th century, in one of the last vestiges of the Flemish influence that had originated with the Count of Burgundy. They were soon to be seen less often, however, as Italian styles gained in popularity.

Some Flemish styles were to be seen in French women's headdress, as well, and two are shown opposite. That in 2.5 consists of a hat adorned with a jewel, while in 2.7 the headdress consists of a metal frame to which a muslin veil has been attached.

# EUROPE

## THE 16th CENTURY – ENGLAND – FRANCE – ITALY

THE ILLUSTRATIONS OPPOSITE ARE OF historical figures and women of distinction from 16th-century France, England and Italy. They show not only how beauty was perceived in different ways in these countries, but also how the fashions of North-Western Europe drew heavily on those of Italy. The materials for dressmaking, such as damask, satin and velvet, all came from Italy.

———— • ————

**1.1 & 2** Diane de Poitiers (1499-1566), and Eléonore de Castille, second wife of Francis I (1498-1558). These two illustrations show clearly how the tendency was for French dresses to spread outwards from the waist to the hemline.

To achieve the required shape, the bust was flattened; to improve the cut, the dress was made of two pieces of material that spread outwards and downwards from the belt. The top of the dress looked rather like a funnel, with the top cut square in Italian style, showing a bare throat.

From the hips downwards the dress is bell-shaped; whale-bone corsets, which made the bodices end in a point lower than waist level, had not yet come into fashion, and would not do so until the reign of Henri III. At this time the corset or small doublet was still sleeveless, Made of strong material, it squeezed the bust inwards.

The *vertugale* – the under-skirt that gave the lower part of the dress its shape – did not originally include the padding for the hips that was to later give the garment its unique appearance.

This primitive *vertugale* was a petticoat made from coarse, starched canvas, which rich women would cover with taffeta. It was attached to the basques of the corset, its purpose being not to enlarge the hips but to increase the circumference of the hem.

The garment that was worn over this dress did not have any pleats. Only the front of the skirt was visible between the front opening of the outer dress.

**1.3** Marguerite of France, third daughter of Francois I (1523-1574).

**1.4** The beautiful Ferroniè, around 1540.

During the second half of the 16th century, women's headdresses became less voluminous. This was a result of Italian influence, as can be seen from the examples in **2**. Italian ladies increased their height – for height was considered a mark of distinction – by wearing platform shoes with high heels.

**2.1** A noblewoman from Ravenna.

**2.2** A noble matron from Naples.

**2.3** A married Neapolitan princess.

**2.4** A woman from Padua.

**3.1** Elizabeth de Valois, Queen of Spain, and the daughter of Henry II and Catherine de Medici.

**3.2** Anne Boleyn, born in 1500, Queen of England and mother of Queen Elizabeth I.

**3.3** Mary of England, born in 1497, the younger sister of Henry VIII. She married Louis XII, King of France, in 1514 when she was only just 16 and considered one of the most beautiful women of her age. Her sleeves are *à rebras* – that is, wide and pushed back a little up the arm, just allowing the decorative cuffs of the dress underneath to peep out.

**3.4** Jane Seymour, Queen of England, after Holbein. She is wearing the same style of headdress as Anne Boleyn and Mary of England.

## TIGHT CLOTHING AND RUFFS

AS THE INFLUENCE OF ITALIAN STYLES WANED, and low-cut bodices and slashed sleeves began to decline in popularity, a fashion emerged that aimed to cover all but the hands and face almost completely. First, for example, the collar became attached to the base of the neck; later it circled it entirely, and became tighter and more restrictive. Women affected this tight clothing in order to achieve what was called a "Spanish" figure. The *espoitrinement* of women (literally, the "imprisonment of women's chests"), in Henri Estienne's term, was carried to such an extent that some actually died, so Montaigne says, from the cuts they received from metal and wooden splints.

———— • ————

This adjustment of the shape of the upper body, common to both sexes, was first a characteristic of men's costume and was picked up by women later. The fashion of wearing the combination of close-fitting bodices and riding-habits has been attributed to the ladies of the court of Catherine of Medici, who followed her on horseback.

The nature of this costume made deportment an art. The essential items comprised: a ruff around the neck; a corset known as a *corps piqué*; a skirt with hoops; a long robe that hid the feet so that women could pretend to be taller than they were by wearing high heels; and a skirt tucked up so that petticoats could be shown on special occasions.

It was in around 1575 that such fashions reached their high point, as did the ruff. Generally, French ruffs were the largest, but individuals in some other countries were extravagant beyond the wildest fancies of the French.

Queen Elizabeth I of England, for example, had more than 3,000 dresses. All were decorated with the finest lace and spangled with jewels. Walpole said of one of her portraits: "It is as if one is seeing an idol of crowns and diamonds and a huge quantity of pearls."

A portrait of Queen Elizabeth is shown here (3), but in this example the open collar is a compromise between a circular ruff and a high collar in the shape of a fan.

Later, the ruff was replaced by the fan-shaped collar, which rose out of the corsage like a facing. More lacy than a ruff, but made from a single layer of material, it was held up by a linen frame.

A great deal of jewellery was worn in the 16th century, importance being given both to the size of the stones and to the new discovery of transparent enamelling. This innovation meant that jewellery could become brighter and more colourful than ever before.

It was fashionable to wear pearl earrings and pearls in the hair. The short necklace, or choker, which became redundant because of the ruff, was replaced by a single string of pearls or beads that hung down over the bodice.

1.1 & 2 Anonymous portraits.

2.1 Catherine de Bourbon in 1600.

2.2 Marie de Medici (1573-1642).

3 Queen Elizabeth of England (1533-1603).

## ECCLESIASTICAL COSTUME

UNTIL THE 9TH CENTURY, white was the sole colour considered suitable for ecclesiastical garments. This can clearly be seen in the *Lives of the Popes* by Anastase the Librarian, and also in the mosaics of the Roman Basilica at Saint-Paul. Only occasionally did bands of purple or gold break this tradition. After the 11th century, though, the Church authorized the wearing of the five colours that have persisted up to the 19th century. white, red, black, green and violet. By the 16th century, ecclesiastical dress had evolved to the point shown opposite.

———— • ————

1.1 A pope. When the conclave has proclaimed a new pope, he is dressed in the pontifical vestments: an amice, alb, belt, stole, cope, gloves, sandals and, finally, the papal headdress.

The red silk gloves with embroidered crosses date back to the 11th century. The sandals are also made of red silk; they are only worn on ceremonial occasions, the usual footwear being slippers in the Moroccan style.

The headdress is, in fact, a papal adaptation of the mitre, known as a tiara: it is a round bonnet made of gold-coloured cloth, encircled by three rings of precious stones and topped by a sphere and a cross. Like the mitre, the tiara is embellished with two small pendants that hang down the back. The Church refers to this ornament as a *regnum*.

1.2 A cardinal dressed from head to foot in red. This colour was not always the prerogative of cardinals; Boniface VIII ruled that red should be worn by members of the "Sacred College". However, until the 15th century, these are shown wearing blue, violet and grey vestments.

Their coats, which were really only cloth copes, became a type of cloak that had a large hood and were closed apart for openings for the arms. Here, the red silk hat, with a slightly upturned brim, has two long strings hanging from it, each of which ends in five tassels. Pope Innocent IV granted this mark of distinction to the cardinals at the Council of Lyons, in 1245. This cardinal is holding a purple

bag that would contain a chalice and a ciborium.

1.3 & 4 A patriarch and a bishop. The former is dressed in his formal vestments, including a chasuble. Until the 15th century, this was a long, sleeveless robe, but later it became less ample over the arms, adopted a curved hem-line, and, like the cope, came to be richly decorated. The only item of clothing that marks the bishop's rank is his mitre.

2.1 A Benedictine monk – an abbot, since he is carrying a crozier (outdoors, though, this was the mark of a bishop). No monastic order was as frequently censured as that of Saint Benedict; the lay brothers dressed in as many different ways as they had communities. Generally, though, their costume consisted of a black robe and scapular with a small cowl, their outer garment being a black cope with vast sleeves.

2.2 & 3 Canons. There are two groups of canon: the secular and the regular. The latter generally followed the rules of Saint Augustine. The costume of the two groups differs little, except in the cut of the stoles and the colour of the robes.

2.4 & 5 The figure on the left is a member of a congregation dedicated to Saints Valentine, Quirin and Anthony. The figure on the right is a layman – possibly an acolyte or a churchwarden – wearing a tunic and a coat with half-length sleeves.

# GERMANY

## THE LATE 16TH CENTURY

THESE WOMEN'S COSTUMES COME FROM the west of Germany at the end of the 16th century. Although later than those shown in the work of Titian, the great Italian painter, and slightly different from them – especially in details such as the long trains – we can nevertheless gain some information from the various descriptions that Titian left of German fashions. However, these prove that in many instances Titian was less well-informed than the Fleming, Abraham de Bruyn.

Although new fashion ideas did have their effect in Germany, they were far from being as influential as they were everywhere else in Europe. For example, the costume worn by the lady in **2.2**, is hardly in keeping with contemporary European styles. She has a tall hat, a bare throat, dropped shoulders, a long train of furs worn over a skirt that also has a long train, and plaited hair secured over her ears. This last fashion dates back to the Middle Ages, as does the loose hair of the unmarried woman in **2.1**.

In France, Italy, England, Spain and Flanders, women wore their hair in buns. They wore collars in fan-shapes, or turned down, with epaulettes and loose sleeves hanging from the epaulettes at the back. German women were slow to adopt these standard European styles.

The illustration here of a matron from Augsburg (**1.4**) brings to mind Titian's description of a middle-class Bavarian woman. As an outer garment both wear a coat of the type invented by Catherine de Medici – it is fastened across the chest, with sides that flare out over the skirt and leg-of-mutton sleeves. The coat described by Titian also has an upright collar supporting the ruff.

In the rest of Europe, collars had lapels. Here, the restrictive collars that rise from closed corsages are more in the style of the 14th and 15th centuries. Examples are seen in **1.1**, **2**, & **3** and **2.4**.

Titian tells us that coats were generally embroidered with gold thread or silk in the form of a band round the bottom of the garment. The coats here do not show this band of embroidery; by this time the style had gone out of fashion, since it tended to make women look smaller in an age when height was all-important.

The winter costumes of the two noblewomen from Augsburg (**1.2** & **1.3**) are similar to the costume worn by the middle-class woman in **1.4**. The corsage is closed, with the collar rising out of it to join a fluted ruff. The coat has lapels and a lining of a contrasting colour. As a sign of rank, it is longer than the coat in **1.4**, and by the same token, the noblewomen's coats have very short leg-of-mutton sleeves.

All three ladies wear white aprons, decorated with bands near the bottom, and carry gloves. The noblewomen are wearing chain jewellery over their corsages.

**1.1** This young lady has neither coat, nor apron. Her hair is drawn back over her ears and plaited down the back, while her toque is worn right on the top of the head and is discreetly plumed. Her décolletage is cut square, in the Italian style, and her throat is covered by a guimpe.

**2** The four costumes in the bottom strip are those of noblewomen from Nuremberg.

———— • ————

**1**.1 & 6 and **2**.5 & 6 Noblemen. There is a common thread running through these costumes (shared by the costumes of the ladies in **1**.3 & 6) – that is, that capes were becoming shorter at this time, following a long resistance to change *(see pp166/7)*. This trend followed the influences of both the French and Spanish courts.

As the movement developed, capes became so short they did not reach the waist, and so richly decorated that it was impossible to tell from what material they had been made.

**1**.2 and **2**.1 & 3 Burghers from towns in northern Germany. Men such as this were extremely wealthy, and their dress consequently often rivalled that of the nobility. Their dress is traditional, however; such men did not consider it necessary to be slaves to fashion.

The first man of this group is a banker: he is dressed like an aristocrat, and even carries a noble's sword. **2**.1 shows a tailor, carrying a coat over his right arm and a paper – probably the bill for it – in his left hand. The banker is wearing a traditional coat, known as an *aharzkappe*, that has large openings for the arms; the tailor's coat, known as a *puffjacke*, is similar, but is shorter and wider. The burgher in **2**.3 is a goldsmith, holding up an example of his work – a double-lidded, embossed goblet. This tall goblet appears to have

a glass at each end; in fact, it does, since it unscrews to make two identical drinking glasses. This was an ingenious way round the ancient custom of toasting an event by drinking from the same cup.

**2**.2 & 4 A nobleman and his page. The nobleman is wearing a sleeveless jacket with arm-holes and a large, turned-down collar, and breeches made of finely embroidered velvet. His costume is completed by silk hose and black shoes of a Spanish design, with a velvet cap decorated with feathers and a sword and scabbard inlaid with silver.

**3**.1 A horseman, heavily armoured in the Swiss style. From greaves to gorget, he is almost entirely clad in iron – with an over-garment attached to his corselet and a skirt vented at the back.

**3**.2 A huntsman, wearing a traditional costume that has only been modified in a few areas by contemporary fashion, to include a ruff and soft, long boots. A short, loose-sleeved shirt is tucked into his belt, and is worn with the collar shut. A fur hat replaces the traditional hood.

**3**.3 The son of a nobleman, wearing his first suit of armour.

**3**.4 An infantry drummer.

# ITALY

LEADERS OF EUROPEAN FASHION

FOR MUCH OF THE 15TH CENTURY, Italian fashions led the way for the rest of Europe. As new styles came into fashion, prospered and then waned in Italy, the women of France, Spain and England adopted them in their turn.

— • —

**1.1** A Milanese lady, in a costume that was current for many years before the time of this illustration. Dresses such as this were fastened at the back, and, depending on the wealth of the wearer, could be made of fabric containing gold and silver thread or of coloured silk.

Openings at the shoulders of the dress show the shirt worn underneath it, and coquettes would contrive similar arrangements so that the under-shirt could also be seen through the skirt. Here, the sleeves are made from strips of material that have been linked together and joined to the shoulders by silk laces.

The shirt itself was normally embroidered – often with pearls – as were the stockings, while the skirt has alternating vertical bands of gold and silver lamé. According to their social status, women would wear necklaces of pearls, gold or coral.

All women wore their hair long at this time, and curls did not become popular until the 1550s. Here, it is contained by a band and hangs down over the ears to fall down the back in a single plait.

**1.2** An unmarried girl. According to the custom of this time, she is wearing her hair long and loose and does not have a corset. Her tunic is long, wide and straight, but richly decorated. Thick-soled sandals can be seen beneath it.

**2.1 & 2** A headdress consisting of a net of gold thread (of which a detail can be seen in the bottom centre of this strip) edged with pearls and a band made of pink silk and decorated with jewels – a detail of one such jewel can be seen in the top left.

**2.3** A lady wearing a light hair-net, which is mounted on brass wire, and a blouse of clear muslin embroidered with red at the straight collar. She has a velvet dress with a short bodice and sleeves with long and short slashes that are held together with silk ribbons.

**2.4** A lady with a red velvet skullcap, criss-crossed with gold ribbons that have been embroidered with black and decorated with flowerets of pearls.

**2.5** A lady wearing a hair-net shaped like a crown that encloses the knot of her tied-up hair. Her transparent blouse is embroidered with white, and her bodice is embroidered with gold.

**2.6** A brooch in the style of the period.

**2.7** In the bottom left-hand corner, a child's skullcap. This is threaded with gold, criss-crossed with black velvet and decorated with rubies, sapphires and pearls.

## VENETIAN EXTRAVAGANCE

THE COSTUMES PAINTED IN THE LATTER HALF OF the 16th century by Veronese precede by a short time the descriptions which Bertelli and Titian have left us of dress between 1589 and 1591. In Veronese's time, the fashion for extreme elongation of the bodice had only just started – it ended up by changing the height of the waist, which itself was enlarged with the help of padding. Also not yet seen is the hairstyle in which the hair is crossed over on the top of the head and curled into points, or "horns" as women called them. The costumes in this picture are of an intermediary period, between 1550 and the time of the painter's death in 1588; probably from the 10 years following 1575.

———— • ————

Special magistrates enforced stern laws governing costume in Venice. One such law declared that black must be worn by everyone when in public. In the winter both rich and poor wore black wool, though in the summer months the nobility would substitute black silk.

Nevertheless, this law meant that the nobility were almost indistinguishable from lowlier citizens. It served as a safe-guard in case of a riot by the mob, and also meant that ostentatious extravagance was held in check.

However, in Venice, as in most places, there were periods of laxity when the magistrates neglected to enforce these laws strictly.

It is possible that Veronese has chosen one of these periods as the setting for the scene opposite. It shows six beautiful women attended by a high government official, who is wearing a red robe and gold-coloured stole, and a typical Venetian civil servant dressed in black.

Another theory is that the scene shows a group of courtesans. Such ladies were at the height of their power in the second half of the 16th century, and ambassadors and senior officials would think nothing of discussing the affairs of state in their boudoirs. After all, it was common for Venetian men to spend more time with their mistresses than with their wives.

In Veronese's painting it seems likely that at least two of the four seated women on the left-hand side are wives. Yet, ironically,

the gentlemen are paying attention, in a rather servile, obsequious way, to the two courtesans on the right of the painting.

The courtesans' costumes are less modest and more décolleté than those of the other women. One of them wears a small pointed bonnet, reminiscent of the *corno* of the Doge's wife. It is almost an allusion to her sovereignty.

The costumes worn here are similar to those that Titian shows noblewomen wearing at public feasts, where indulgence was permitted. One such reception, given to Henri III, was attended by 200 of the most beautiful noblewomen of Venice. The value of the costumes was reckoned to be 50,000 ecus: collars, bodices and sleeves glittered with precious stones, pearls and gold, while necklaces and golden hair-ornaments gleamed in the candlelight.

Titian tells us that all the robes were white on this particular occasion, but at other times the *podestaresses* and *capitainesses* wore robes of many different colours, made from brocade and silk and decorated with silver and gold. The hair was always blonde, whether natural or dyed.

Venetians women also attached a great deal of importance to their lingerie – so much so that the expression: "the chemise before the doublet" became a Venetian proverb. Lingerie was decorated with great care and in fine detail, embroidered with silken thread and trimmed with lace.

P. VERONÈSE

## NOBLEWOMEN AND COURTESANS

THESE ILLUSTRATIONS ARE TAKEN FROM famous paintings of noblewomen in the 16th century. As an interesting comparison, the bottom strip shows illustrations of Venetian courtesans. Although the costume of the latter is often as grand and extravagant as that of the noblewomen, it was, in fact, absolutely forbidden for a courtesan to wear any of the pearls that as a matter of course adorned the collar, bodice, sleeves, head and neck of noblewomen.

1.1, 2 & 3 A noblewomen with details of her costume, taken from a portrait by Bronzino. Her dress has a V-necked décolletage, slashed sleeves and epaulettes, and she is wearing a small ruff round the opening of her corsage and a string of pearls round her head. Her necklace and belt are also made of pearls (detail in **1**.1), and a jewel is fixed at the bottom of the V of her bodice.

In nearly all the portraits of noblewomen at the time, a piece of fur is placed over the lady's wrist – as is the case here.

1.4 A noblewoman, taken from a portrait of the period of Andrea del Sarto. Her headdress is made of black velvet with gold brocade, and shaped like a small version of the Venetian *balzo*.

1.5 A young noblewoman, taken from a painting by Tisi. She is wearing a type of *balzo* that is made of satin and decorated with a jewel. Her guimpe is pleated and the collar turns into a small ruff. Her dress is made of velvet with yellow satin trimmings.

1.7 Catarina Cornaro, Queen of Cyprus, from a painting by Titian. She is wearing a ducal crown with a veil of fine silk that falls down over her shoulders. Her satin dress is decorated on the bodice with pearls, while her *zimarra* is made of embroidered velvet, trimmed with gold.

2.2 A Venetian woman, taken from a portrait by Lorenzo Lotto. Her guimpe is made of gold- and silver-coloured material and she is carrying a fan made of feathers.

2.8, 9, 10, 11, 12 & 13 The Duchess of Urbin and details of her costume taken from a painting by Titian. She is wearing a velvet dress, decorated with small bows of gold brocade (detail in 2.8) and her guimpe has an open neckline that is edged with a chain of rubies (detail **2**.13).

2.11 shows a detail of the ornament attached to her long necklace. Her belt is made of knotted cord in which each knot is speared by a golden pin with a ruby head (detail 2.10).

2.14 A Venetian woman called "Titian's mistress". She is wearing a blue satin dress embroidered with gold, whose puffed epaulettes have slashes trimmed with velvet. 2.15 shows a detail of the chain that attaches her muff.

3.5 A flagellant. The back of his garment is left open so that he can whip himself more effectively.

3.6 A noblewoman from Rome, holding a pleated fan of the type that would eventually replace the fans made of feathers and cloth.

3.7 A Venetian courtesan. These two illustrations show the undergarments and exterior of the same costume. It can be clearly seen how the aim and the effect of contemporary fashion was to elongate the bust and lower the waist while increasing the height. The platform shoes, called *chopines*, were a Venetian specialty.

# FRANCE

## 16TH-CENTURY MILITARY COSTUME

LOUIS XII INSPIRED A RADICAL CHANGE in French military tactics in the first quarter of the 16th century by encouraging the nobility to fight alongside the infantry. The necessity of such a change, and the effectiveness of massed infantry, had been made clear by the Swiss victories at Morat and Granson. Louis formed the *Bandes de Piémont*, an infantry force that was bolstered by auxiliaries, such as Swiss and Italian mercenaries and lancers.

———— • ————

Even this proved insufficient, however, and in 1523 he increased his infantry strength further by making the old-established *francs-archers* separate units within the general army's muster.

Previously, the army had been divided into seven legions, each containing 6,000 men. This structure was dissolved after the death of Francois I, to be replaced that of the *bandes*. Each *bande* was made up of two groups of pikemen, one group of halberdiers and one group of arquebusiers. With every *bande* there were four men known as *payes royales* – these were gentlemen of reduced means who were guaranteed an income for life by the king in return for service.

At this time, uniforms had not yet been standardized, though there was a movement towards this in crack units, such as the Swiss Guards and the Scottish Archers.

1.1 A pikeman in 1548, wearing the standard infantry helmet called a *bourguingnotte*; a light corselet made of small strips of flattened iron laid in overlapping scales, called a *hallecret*; rounded shoulder guards; armbands; mail gauntlets; a long sword and a dagger.

1.2 A Swiss captain. Swiss mercenaries had formed the backbone of the French army for many years, but could not always be relied on. The Swiss soldiers wore doublets and breeches that were slashed in an unusual manner, and, distinct-ively, hats decorated extravagantly with feathers.

1.3 An arquebusier of 1548. These soldiers were lightly clad, since they relied on pikemen for their protection. Here, the arquebusier is wearing a type of helmet known as a *morion*, a leather tunic and mail sleeves.

1.4 A member of the Swiss Guards, who traditionally marched in front of the king, protecting him with their halberds. In time of war they wore *hallecrets*, but in peacetime they sported a black and white livery, shown here, that was ins-tituted by Henri II. The Guard's doublet and breeches are lined with silver taffeta, decorated with quarters of silver-coloured material and black velvet, and covered with slashes.

2.1, 2 & 5 An officer, an arque-busier and a halberdier from one of the many mercenary bands em-ployed by France.

2.3 & 4 A Swiss artilleryman and a gunner. Louis XI first realized the importance of artillery, and it played an important role in the Italian campaigns.

3 A group of soldiers from the army of Francois I, thus part of the legionary structure that was aban-doned later. 3.9 is a drummer; 3.10 a halberdier; and 3.12 is an arque-busier, wearing a iron skullcap, called a *secrette*, beneath his cap.

## COURT DRESS

THE COSTUME OF COURT LADIES differed from that of the rich gentry only in the extravagance of its decoration and materials. The ostentation of court dress was something to which all wealthy Frenchwomen aspired, as can be seen from the increasing number and specificity of laws passed to control excesses. When Henri II came to the throne, in 1547, a number of laws were passed banning *superfluités* in women's dress. The only ladies exempt from these regulations were the royal princesses and the ladies of Catherine de Medici's retinue. Most of the latter came from Italy, from whence they had brought rich materials and new styles.

———— • ————

Soon, Italian styles had completely eclipsed the native fashions of France, though the French ladies fought back hard, as can be seen in **1**. In doing so, they tended to ignore Henri II's laws, which had to be extended and re-enacted frequently.

The Wars of Religion, however, made them hard to impose – indeed, they were only ever effectively imposed during the reign of Charles IX. He made it illegal for French citizens to use imported perfumes, and for widows to wear silk.

Charles particularly wanted to outlaw the farthingale, whose vast proportions were especially wasteful of cloth. But this restriction was never enforced, after a petition to Charles by the women of Toulouse, whom it seems were unusually fond of the farthingale.

2.1 Catherine de Medici, wearing a typically innovative costume in which the corset matches the petticoat, and both are covered by a frock coat. This tight-fitting garment is closed high on the chest and and flows down to the ankles.

Her collar rises up to meet a ruff, in a reference to past fashions, but the main innovation lies in the width of the opening of her outer dress, over the opening of another dress. The outer garment is made in such a way that it appears to be part of an ordinary dress.

2.2 Marie Touchet, born in 1549, wearing her town clothes. She is not in mourning, since a blue under-skirt can be seen, so the black of her costume – set off by the white of her ruff – is entirely her own choice.

This costume is entirely closed, the skirt being raised on either side of her hips. Her sleeves are rather masculine, while her collar goes up into a ruff that it encloses and holds in place. Her small cap is of the type that was made fashionable by Eléonore, the second wife of Francis I – it just covered the ears.

2.4 The Duchess of Etampes, wearing the oldest of this group of costumes. There are a number of Italian elements here: the black dress is split from waist to feet; the sleeves have green slashes; and the shoulders are padded. A number of original touches are also present, however: the ruff, for example, embossed with braid, is held up by a jewelled collar.

# CATHERINE DE MEDICI

THE ILLUSTRATIONS OPPOSITE ARE PARTICULARLY good examples of 16th-century court dress. The richness of these costumes is not due to the influence of the King, Charles VI, who cared little for such matters, but to Catherine de Medici. Under her fashion leadership the most extravagant finery became *de rigeur*. Following the 18th-month reign of Francis II there was a period of mourning, but then styles became more and more outrageously expensive as the rich forgot their fears for an uncertain future in a pursuit of fads and fashions.

———— • ————

**1.1** Francis, the Duke of Alencon and brother of Francis II, Charles IX and Henry III. Francis was known for the near-femininity of his dress, and invented an all-green costume that became the height of fashion for a short while.

**1.2, 3 & 4** Jacqueline de Longwy, Jeanne d'Albret and Elizabeth of Austria. Despite the fact that these women are all of different periods, their costume is surprisingly similar. Elizabeth of Austria is wearing a band of jewellery in her hair, and the top of her bodice, from which hangs an expensive pendant, is also bordered with jewellery.

**1.5** Henry, Duke of Longueville, wearing a costume fashionable towards the end of Henri III's reign. His turned-down collar is decorated with lace and embroidered with gold.

**2.1, 3 & 5** Three costumes that bear the hallmark of Catherine de Medici's influence. The lady in 2.5 is wearing one of the fashions that was current during the reign of Henri III: a skirt that hangs down straight, leaving a gap at the back through which her richly coloured petticoat can be seen. Women would often wear up to three different petticoats, all of which were on display in this manner.

**2.4** Although Charles VI had little influence on fashion, his reign did mark one costume innovation. This was the development of a short coat with picked-out edges, called a cape. There were a number of variations on the basic style. Here it is sleeveless and has a turned-down collar that is wrapped round the chest.

**3.1** Charles XI, King of France, with a feathered cap on his head and a tight-fitting doublet – rather like a corselet – with a raised collar. Both the doublet and the padded breeches are gold braided.

**3.2** A counsellor at the Parliament of Paris, dressed in scarlet robes with black trimmings, and a square hat.

**3.5** A gentleman from the reign of Charles IX, with a turned-down collar, breeches padded out in a balloon shape, hose attached with aiguillettes and garters knotted below the knee.

## FARTHINGALES AND WIDE SLEEVES

THE FASHION FOR A FUNNEL-SHAPED BODICE with a long waist and front reached its peak towards the end of the reign of Henri III and the accession of Henri IV. By this time it had become almost impractical, as the effect of the pointed bodice was heightened by the addition of the farthingale – to which 18th-century fashion was to return, in the form of panniers – and huge sleeves, almost as wide at the top as the bodice itself.

These sleeves came in various different styles (3.1 & 3). Those in **3.1** are reminiscent of the Italian style, so popular in the early part of the 16th century. In this case, the sleeve was independent of the bodice and attached to it with gold buttons. The sleeves in **3.3** are also separate from the bodice, being attached under the epaulettes.

The surcoat, or over-gown, no longer had sleeves, but stopped at the shoulders in epaulettes, and the skirt of the surcoat was no longer open at the front.

Women wore long pants just like men's breeches (**1.2**) under their farthingales. They were attached to a garment similar to a man's doublet, which was worn over a quilted bodice. Silk stockings from Naples or Spain were attached to the pants with the assistance of aglets, or they were held up by garters. Stockings were always brightly coloured: red, violet, blue and green were popular.

Shoes were often white, and low-heeled French shoes were no longer fashionable – women preferred high-heeled Italian shoes.

The ruff was replaced by a high, fan-shaped collar that was supported by wire and decorated with lace or fine gold threads (**3.2**).

Women often wore a visible busk (**3.1**). This was sewn into the bodice.

**1.1** A widow in mourning.

**1.2** Henri III.

**1.3** A young noblewoman.

**1.4** A young noblewoman or widow in mourning.

**1.5** A middle-class woman in mourning.

**1.6** A lawyer.

**2.1** A doctor of medicine in ceremonial costume in 1586, wearing a four-cornered hat, a ruff, a red cope trimmed with fur, a fur cloak with openings for the sleeves and an ermine cape.

**2.2** A footman in royal livery, wearing a small beaver hat with pompons in the King's colours: blue, crimson and white. His collar is turned down and he has a long-sleeved yellow doublet.

**2.3** A young lady with hair that has been powdered, formed into a bun in the shape of a prickly-pear, and decorated with pins and a golden star. Her lace collar is supported by wire and her bodice has a round décolletage and billowing, Italian-style sleeves. Small mirrors suspended from golden chains hang over her upper robe.

**2.4** A courier from a great house, armed with a baton and wearing a red velvet bonnet decorated with feathers
in Italian style.

**2.5** A royal page, wearing a small ruff, a long-sleeved yellow doublet, an open-sleeved tabard belted at the waist and round hose.

**3.1** A noblewoman.

**3.2 & 3** Middle-class women.

**3.4** A young lady in her dressing gown.

## PEASANTS AND SOLDIERS

THE ILLUSTRATIONS AT THE TOP of the facing page show the costumes worn by working people in 16th-century France, during the reign of Henri III. The bottom two plates are illustrations of French infantry uniforms from the same period. Some experts have argued that these costumes in fact belong to Flemish soldiers, but there are enough similarities between the uniforms of the French and Flemish infantry for the details given below to serve as an adequate description of both.

———— • ————

1.1 A peasant from the neighbourhood of Saumur, wearing a felt hat with a turned-down brim, a *sayon* that goes down as far as mid-thigh level and a blue jerkin. He has a country-style coat, called a *balandras*, and is wearing *gamashes* to protect his legs from mud.

1.2 A wine seller in 1586, wearing a red-trimmed felt hat and a loose jacket with long basques that is gathered into the waist by a leather belt from which hangs a money bag. His breeches are narrow and his stockings are held up beneath the knee by garters. Men such as this wandered the streets of Paris in the mornings, offering wine to passers-by.

1.3 A shoeblack, wearing a large smock with a cape and stockings made of coarse wool. His huge leather bag is carried by means of a shoulder-strap.

1.4 A shepherdess from Anjou, wearing a cloth bonnet with a raised crown, a loose-sleeved blouse with a fluted collar, a blue bodice, braces and a woollen skirt.

1.5 A rich peasant woman wearing a décolleté blouse with a large, high collar, a bright blue surcoat, a white coat and a black apron.

1.6 A servant girl going to market in Paris in 1586. Her bonnet is covered with a cloth hood that hangs down the back as far as the belt, and she has a blouse with a high collar and a red bodice that is laced up at the front and trimmed with black velvet.

1.7 A chambermaid from Saumur wearing a bonnet from Anjou, as in 1.5, and a blouse that is gathered into the collar.

In 1574 and 1579, Henri III ruled that only infantry company commanders could wear tabards and breeches made of gold and silver material or silk on silk. Apart from this, and their possession of a baton, there was nothing to distinguish officers from men.

There was no rigid uniform, and it was considered quite permissible to mix colours, with stockings of one colour and breeches of another. Infantry soldiers often sported as many as eight or 10 colours.

While ladies wore busks in order to flatten the stomach, soldiers of this period wore devices known as *panserons*, which had the opposite effect. This gave the flamboyant French and Flemish soldiers the appearance of bully boys – apparently felt to be desirable at this time.

The doublet, with or without sleeves and slashes, was adjusted to fit over the *panseron*. Breeches could be tight or baggy going down to just below the knee, but codpieces were now not worn.

A puckered collar or ruff rose out of the doublet. Headgear consisted of a toque or a Spanish-style sombrero with a plume.

Soldiers wore sashes as a personal token, but their rallying point was the company's flag. This was made of silk, and was often so large that it had to be held up to prevent it from dragging along the ground. Drums, too, were enormous and awkward to carry, but military cloaks were surprisingly small, barely going past the knees.

# ENGLAND

## AN ELIZABETHAN INTERIOR

THE ILLUSTRATION OPPOSITE SHOWS the interior of Speke Hall, in Lancashire in the late 16th century, as reconstructed under the direction of Joseph Brereton in the 19th century. Some parts of the building date from before the 16th century, but this room can be dated precisely through the inscription above the doorway that commemorates Sir Edward Norris, who had the room constructed in 1598. Brereton's restoration has made it is one of the most perfect examples of an Elizabethan manor house, although the original moat has been filled in and given over to gardens.

At the end of the 16th century, the French, Spanish and Germans began to revert to classical traditions. England, however, stood apart from this trend, in an attempt to create her own renaissance. This became known as the Elizabethan style.

The dining hall at Speke is the epitome of this style. It is a beautiful and spacious room that, together with the large entrance hall, is a testimonial to the wealth of its owner. One can easily imagine Sir Edward entertaining his fellow noblemen to dinner here, or receiving his richer tenants.

The ceiling is particularly notable for its moulded joists, which criss-cross to form a coffered surface. The beams themselves are decorated with scrolling patterns of intertwined hop stalks, which provide a delicate, embroidery-like relief, without spoiling the pattern of the beams.

Oak panelling covers the walls from floor to ceiling, and the chimney's wide mantleshelf is also made from carved wood. Above it are what appear to be carved portraits of Sir Edward and his two wives, with their children below.

Part of the scene's attraction lies in the charming window recess, vastly superior in architectural terms to the more dour building style of the Middle Ages. The recess is made of wood, and light streams through small leaded panes in the windows.

The whole scene is very northern European in character, but with differences made necessary by the cold, the damp and the fog that are so common in Britain. The windows, for example, are designed to let in as much light as possible while protecting those indoors from the elements.

The style of the windows makes this recess typically English. Similar examples are found everywhere, jutting out from houses like glassed-in balconies. They are a particular feature of the black and white checker-boarded buildings of beams and plaster found so often in Cheshire, Shropshire and Lancashire.

An 18th-century French traveller once remarked in connection with this distinctive style: "Every Englishman who builds wants to be his own architect; a fantasy that probably derives from their freedom as a nation".

# FRANCE

SOBER ELEGANCE

IN THE 17TH CENTURY, FRANCE once more came to lead European fashion, having been equal in terms of influence with Italy and Spain in the previous century. Lace became an obsession in dress from around 1620 – so much so, in fact, that within a few years every conceivable item of clothing was decorated with it. This fashion was taken to such extreme lengths that eventually, in 1634, a law was passed forbidding it. Henceforth, all frills, fringes and fripperies were prohibited and costumes became the essence of sober good taste. Buttons replaced ribbons, and clothes became dark or neutral in colour.

1.1 A women sitting at a harpsichord, wearing a Dutch costume. The skirt is made of satin and the shawl of delicate linen. The outfit is of the more sober style that spread through Europe following the 1635 regulations in France.

1.2 A group of musicians, taken from a fragment of a painting by Adrian Van de Venne that shows a fête held to mark the 1609 truce between Austria and Holland. A scene from Plato is visible on the raised lid of a spinet behind the musicians to the right, who have put their hats and instrument cases on the ground.

The collars shown here are rounded; they did not become elaborate, as in **2** until around 1634.

**2** A French interior of around 1635, a charming scene of a musical soirée. On the left, a gentleman is holding a music score in one hand and beating time with the other. He seems to be dressed for hunting, with a splendidly plumed hat, spurs and red hose.

Such a costume did not necessarily mean, though, that he was on his way to or from a hunt. A red costume might be a hint that his pursuit is more amorous than equestrian. Hats were low at this time, and made of felt or beaver fur, with their wide brims circled with two long feathers. Long, thick hair was very fashionable, so men often wore wigs; they would also detach a single lock – called a *moustache* – from their hair and tie it with a piece of coloured ribbon, as the young boy second from the right has done.

Lace was still very much in vogue, and collars had become much more elaborate than in **1.2**. The new style was helped by the demise of the ruff and the high-necked collar, both in the case of women and men. Boots had also shortened to about calf-length, and were covered with lace where they turned down.

If boots were not worn, gentlemen were expected to wear silk stockings. At first, these were lined with wool to keep out the cold. The result was somewhat unsightly, though, and soon several layers of silk stockings were worn instead. The cellist at the right of this illustration is wearing stockings held up with garters and decorated with rosettes.

# EUROPE

### THE 17TH CENTURY – GERMANY – FRANCE – ENGLAND

THE COMMON ELEMENT IN THE ILLUSTRATIONS opposite, which draw on English, French and German styles, is that a shawl is worn round the shoulders to cover a low-cut bodice edged with lace. The Puritan influence is apparent, and although the lace is of the highest quality the style of dress is fundamentally very simple, jewellery rarely being seen.

———— • ————

1.1 & 3 Englishwomen wearing the autumn and summer styles of 1641.

1.2 The Lord Mayor's wife.

1.4 A woman dressed in the indoor clothes of 1647.

1.5 Autumn wear from 1644.

1.6 A woman of Anvers in 1644.

1.7 An English lady dressed against the cold in the winter in 1641. The black velvet mask attached with a white chin strap is worn partly for warmth, and partly, no doubt, to be coquettish. The fur of the King Charles Spaniel on the table beside her has been styled into a mane.

2.1 & 7 Englishwomen, wearing the spring fashions of 1644 and 1641.

2.2 A lady from Cologne.

2.3 An Englishwoman in the summer fashions of 1641, holding an ivory fan of Flemish design.

2.4 A portrait of a young girl, probably by the Dutch painter Van der Helst.

2.5 An Englishwoman dressed for the winter of 1641.

2.6 A portrait of a women – probably French, since she has unusually long hair that falls in corkscrew curls down each side of her head, rather than the usual ringlets. Her small cap, called a *rond*, is tilted at a fashionable angle at the back of her head.

3 All the women in this strip are wearing a type of martyr's bonnet known as a *gibeline*, which was fashionable among the middle-classes after around 1613, and was particularly popular in Spain. Some *gibelines* are small, showing most of the hair; others have a feathered plume at the front.
  As time went on, *gibelines* became less and less like caps, resembling more round, flat mushrooms on the forehead, from which plumes sprouted forward. The plume worn by the lady on the far right is practically horizontal.

3.1 A woman from Cologne.

3.2 A married woman from Cologne, around 1634.

3.3 A woman from Cologne dressed for a walk, with a large, frilled ruff around her neck. It was fashionable at the time for women to drape the ends of their trains over their arms and hold their plumed hats in their hands.

3.4, 5 & 6 Noblewomen from Cologne, between 1642 and 1643. Although sombre colours dominated clothes at this time, petticoats were brightly coloured.

# HOLLAND

A 17TH-CENTURY SALON

THIS INTERESTING PICTURE IS is the joint work of Dirck Hals, who painted the people, and Van Dalen who painted the architecture. It represents one of the *salons de conversation* that were popular in 17th-century Flanders. These salons were held by fashionable women, and became places in which young people, intellectuals and members of society could meet and exchange ideas. Both men and women were free to dress and talk as they wished, according to individual taste – though this would be tempered by the desire to please, whether with the latest, innovative fashions in dress or with fine conversation.

The woman and the centre of the painting, and the one at the far right, are both wearing a unique item of costume. This is a corset with a wide ruff made from only one layer of material.

DIRCK HALS — VAN DALEN

# A PRINCE'S FUNERAL

THE REMARKABLE ILLUSTRATION OPPOSITE is a record of the funeral procession of Frédéric-Henri-Friso, a Prince who died at The Hague in 1647. It comes from a collection of similar pictures, drawn by Post, engraved by Nolpe and published in 1651 in Amsterdam by Van Ravesteyn. The Prince was a Protestant, so neither candles nor Catholic clergy are seen in the procession. In fact, there are far fewer religious personnages than would normally figure in a solemn and formal ceremony such as this.

———— • ————

Because of the Prince's status, this funeral procession has retained much of the form of a procession of the Middle Ages. One can see, among other details given in the original captions, that as in the Middle Ages the weapons, emblems and horses used in tournaments head the procession, behind a herald, a cornet carrier and a standard bearer. Next come the weapons and horses that the Prince used in battle.

This custom must have been firmly fixed indeed to be still observed in mid-17th-century Holland, suggesting that it was a tradition followed in all Christian countries.

Accounts given in the 14th, 15th and 16th centuries show that the details of such processions varied a great deal. For example, although the guards carry javelins and muskets, there are no shields held up high, as Jean de Troyes tells us was the custom at royal funerals.

Certainly the uniformity of costume would not have been so closely observed in in previous centuries. The number of horses pulling the funeral coach was also variable. At the burial of King Charles VII of France there were five horses, but here the carriage is drawn by eight.

1 Guards.
2 Servants.
3 Tambour players.
4 Trumpet players.
5 A herald.
6 The cornet.
7 A standard bearer.
8 A page carrying a plumed tournament helmet.
9 A page carrying a tournament breast-plate with its emblem.
10 The Prince's horse.
11 The great standard.
12 A herald and banner-carrier.
13 to 32 Horses with caparisons and banderoles bearing coats of arms.
33 A herald with blazon.
34 & 35 Standard bearers.
36 The battle charger.
37 A standard with the Prince's arms.
38 The ceremonial horse.
39 A banner carrier.
40 to 43 The four degrees of nobility: Leval; Staelbergen; Coligny; and Nassau.
44 The helm.
45 The shield, with full coat of arms.
46 & 47 The Prince's sword and his insignia.
48 A ceremonial horse.
49 The insignia of the Order of the Garter carried on a cushion.
50 A cermonial guard.
51 The Prince's crown.
52 A herald.
53 to 72 Mourners: princes, knights, counsellors, magistrates and clergy (72).
73 Civil guard.

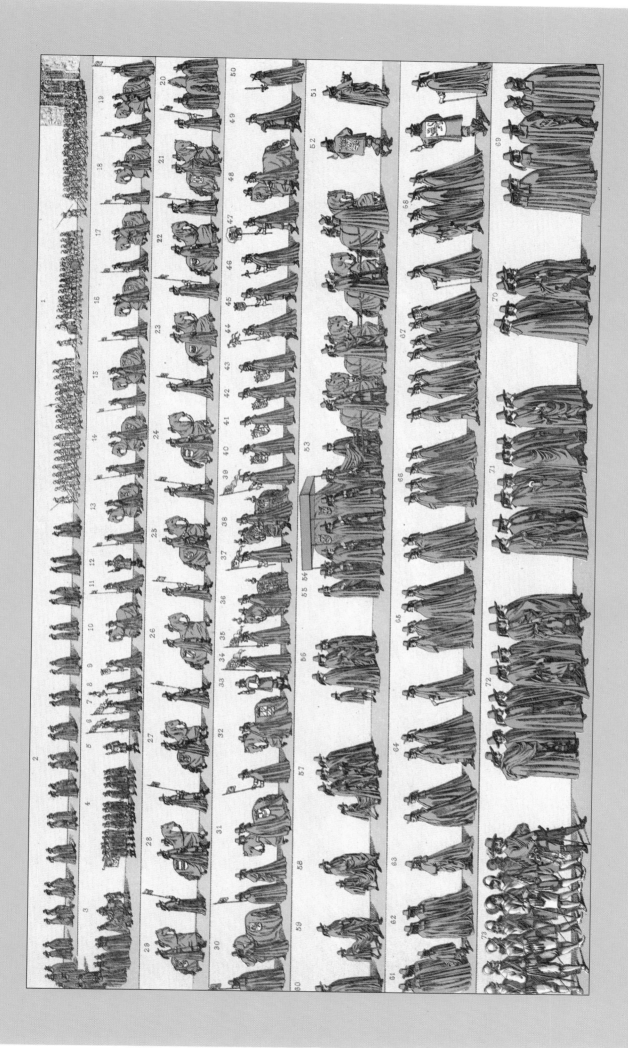

# A SEPARATE TRADITION

HOLLAND IS NOT JUST DISTINCT FROM the rest of Europe in a geographical sense, but in a social sense, too. Its customs and traditions are very different from those of other European countries. The differences have been illuminated by the great Dutch artists, such as Van der Helst, Dirk Hals, Peter de Hoogh, Van der Velde and Collaert, who have given us a superb vision of 17th-century Dutch life through their pictures of outdoor scenes and salon interiors.

Most of the figures opposite come from the upper classes of Dutch society. Three different aspects of women's costume are shown. First, the ladies in **1.2 & 6** are dressed for a walk in town. They are still wearing high ruffs, thick and starched, at this late date, as well as farthingales under a type of open cloak. These clothes, made from rich materials, are complemented by straw hats. Also worn by Englishwomen, these straw hats are reminiscent of the hat like an upside-down bowl, to which Titian refers.

The next style is worn by the women in **1.1** and **2.8**. The first lady is wearing a town outfit and the second a ball gown. These ladies have made more of a concession to fashion, and, in fact, are dressed in a style current in France between 1634 and 1635.

The neck is free from clinging collars and the skirt can be seen beneath a gown that opens at the front. This has wide sleeves that are slashed down their length and gathered in halfway down the arm and again at the cuffs.

The first of these ladies wears her hair in a coiled chignon – still fashionable in 19th-century France. The second simply wears her hair loose over her shoulders with a plume of feathers in the same colours as her skirt.

The third style can be seen in **1.4**. In the original painting, this woman is walking in an Amsterdam square – strictly speaking, the costume belongs to an earlier period than the previous two types, but this style was still seen in Holland up about 1660.

A number of different styles of male costume are also shown opposite. The man in **2.7**, playing the violoncello, is dressed in a satin doublet that has slits around the chest and sleeves. A collar trimmed with guipure is folded down over his doublet.

This man has all the appearance of being a member of the rich middle classes, who led the life of great lords without ever quite emulating their dégagé air or lofty bearing.

The man in **2.9**, however, is quite different. His costume and whole appearance reek of refinement. His plumed felt hat *à la Bassompierre*, his slitted doublet and his baggy red silk trousers, knotted at the bottom with wide ribbons – all mark him as a gallant, ready to dance opposite a lady decked out in an equally elegant costume.

The horseman in **2.10**, with a large felt hat decorated with a feather, a white doublet covered with hide and boots with spurs, is typical of the robust, brave Dutch soldiers so often painted by Van der Helst.

The figure in **2.11**, though, is later in date, and has a less military appearance. In fact, he has more in common with the young beaux of Amsterdam, whose long tresses would float out behind them as they walked, hat in hand, in public places, or bowed graciously before a young lady (**1.3 & 5**).

These last two figures are wearing the same costume as was worn at the French court during the years of splendour in the reign of Louis XIV.

# GERMANY

## THE INFLUENCE OF FRANCE

IN THE 16TH CENTURY, the Reformation gave German costume a rather austere character. From the early 17th century, however, this austerity began to be tempered by the influence of French fashions. Clothes started to become elegant and light; but this trend soon degenerated, among the lower classes at least, into vulgar ostentation.

———— • ————

The illustrations opposite show quite clearly that the traditional stiffness of Germanic clothing was not totally overpowered by the casual elegance of French costume – despite all the efforts of the followers of French fashion. The portrait of the future Duke of Brunswick (1) is an excellent example of this.

Men were generally the innovators of new fashions, women preferring to cling to elements, at least, of more traditional costume. In 10, for example, a woman is wearing a modern-style dress and fichu popularized by Anne of Austria, together with a *pelzkappe* – a traditional fur hat that could be of almost any shape and size.

1 Ferdinand Albert, who became Duke of Brunswick-Bevern in 1666, wearing a costume that was fashionable in about 1650. It consists of a short doublet with open sleeves that show his undershirt, and a tall felt hat.

2 A somewhat baroque character, drawn from life by Hollar in 1646. Everything about his appearance makes him look suspicious and untrustworthy. A thick, hide garment on his chest serves as a cuirass, and his stiff leather breeches are cut wide so that he can sit down.

3, 4, 5, 6 & 7 Women from Augsburg, whose raised headdresses must have their origins in the 15th century. The lady in 3 has a high curved bonnet, a small apron, a cloak trimmed with striped braid and a lacy cape. The woman in 4 is wearing a very broad-brimmed hat over curled hair and a hair-net.

The huge headdress in 5 has a solid frame and its wearer has a ruff that covers her shoulders. The headdress in 6 is similar to this, but covers the hair completely.

The lady in 7 is wearing a small conical-shaped bonnet with a veil. Her hands are hidden in a pocket in her belt.

8, 9, 10, 11, 12, 13, 14, 15, 17, 18 & 19 Costumes from the Rhine basin. These women are wearing *pelz-kappes* and small jackets known as *kittels*. The lady in 14 shows a good example of French influences at this period: open sleeves reveal the fine quality of her chemise beneath a tucked-up cloak and muff.

16 A gentleman whose appearance has much in common with that of the gallants at the court of Louis XIII, particularly as regards the plumed hat, lace collar, funnel-shaped boots and breeches held with aglets at the bottom of the doublet.

20 A Protestant minister, wearing a small round hat, a ruff and a doublet with puffed sleeves. These sleeves can just be seen emerging from openings in the cloak.

21 A portrait of the famously virtuous Lady Barbara.

# ITALY

ECCLESIASTICAL COSTUMES

THE 17TH CENTURY IS AN IMPORTANT PERIOD in the history of ecclesiastical dress. For many years, the immutability of the ideals of the Church had been reflected in the permanence of the costume worn during religious services. However, the spread of Protestantism and Nonconformity across Europe in the 16th and 17th centuries led to a marked divergence between the costumes of the different clergy. In England, for example, Queen Elizabeth I's Act of Uniformity, passed in 1559, marked the start of a reaction against the outward symbols of the Catholic Church, such as ecclesiastical vestments and the tonsure. In countries such as Italy, though, which remained Catholic, vestments survived, often becoming even more elaborate.

1 1.1, 2 & 4 A nun, the chaplain and the abbess of the Order of St Etienne in Florence, whose symbol is a red cross.

The two women are wearing white under-tunics, scapulars and black veils over white linen wimples.

The chaplain is wearing an ankle-length cassock, which opens at the front, an embroidered, lace-hemmed surplice over the cassock and a short, hooded cape called a *mozetta*.

1.3 A sister from the order of St Dominique, wearing a white habit underneath a scapular, a black veil and a white linen wimple.

1.5 and 2.2 Benedictines, the woman wearing a black habit over a white tunic with a low, square-cut neckline.

1.6 A priest of the Order of Humility, wearing similar robes to the chaplain in 1.4, but with a cape instead of a surplice, a scapular and a soft, pointed cap.

2.1 An Augustine nun, wearing a white habit with a particularly full cope and a veil of fine black gauze.

2.3 & 4 Black robes were traditionally worn at masses for the dead and at Good Friday services. The figure on the left, however, is a penitent, with portraits of Christ and an instrument symbolic of penitence and self-punishment.

2.5 A secular canon, wearing a *biretta*. Traditionally, a canon's *biretta* was black, and a cardinal's was red.

3 Styles worn by various religious orders in Rome. The hats are particularly interesting – especially those carried in 3.9 & 11 and worn in 3.10 & 12, since they appear to show a Nonconformist influence.

3.1 A pupil from the College of the Greeks wearing a chimere – a sleeveless gown in black or red, made from either silk or satin, worn by Anglican bishops and doctors of divinity.

3.2 A pupil of the College of Nazarenes, wearing a similar costume to 3.1.

3.3 A member of the College of Salvation, wearing white robes.

3.4 A member of the Scottish College.

3.5 A member of the College of Matthew, showing a distinct lay influence in his dress: breeches, hose, leather shoes and a coat can be seen beneath the chimere.

3.6 A priest, wearing a form of white surplice over his cassock.

# FRANCE

17TH-CENTURY FOPPISHNESS

THE SECOND QUARTER OF THE 17TH CENTURY in France was the age of Cardinals Mazarin and Richelieu. It was a time of duels and intrigue, as immortalized by Alexander Dumas in *The Three Musketeers*. Men may have appeared foppish, but both their costume and their gestures made it obvious that they were always ready – and often anxious – for a fight.

1.1 A nobleman wearing a hat of beaver fur, decorated with an extravagant feather plume. His doublet has small epaulettes and bouffant sleeves, and his shoes are decorated with a cluster of ribbons gathered into a rosette shape.

1.2 A noblewoman wearing an enormous headdress, consisting of a wire base covered with tulle.

1.3 A man dressed in an extravagant costume frilled with lace and ribbons, who is walking in the affected manner of a gallant.

1.4 A gentleman wearing a long jacket in the manner of an overcoat – slung over his shoulders and held on with his left hand.

1.5 The Comtesse de Saint-Belmonte, an aggressive and rather masculine woman, who liked nothing better than to wear men's clothes, ride astride a horse and fight duels.

2.6 It was considered stylish for a gentleman to sling a cape casually over one shoulder like this, leaving the spare hand at the hip ready to draw the sword. This gentleman is wearing matching collar and cuffs, and a doublet slashed behind and pulled in at the waist with a belt made of ribbons.

2.7 A horseman, dressed in military style and twirling his *moustache* – a long lock of hair from his wig – with his left hand.

2.8 This gentleman has his cape draped over his shoulders and pulled across his face to conceal his identity. It was usual for a gentleman to do this when entering a crowded room – he would survey the gathering for potential enemies without being seen himself.

2.9 Having drawn his sword, a gentleman would use his cape like a shield during a duel.

2.10 & 11 Noblemen, wearing similar costumes to those in 1.1.

3.1 & 6 Two wealthy ladies, each wearing an over-dresse known as a *modeste*. This was really a type of long jacket, worn open at the front and thickly gathered behind. Tightly drawn at the waist, the skirts fall in long, luxurious folds and trail along the ground. Two under-skirts were worn – one known as a *friponne* and the other as a *secrete*.

3.2 A courtier wearing a wide-brimmed hat with a thick plume. His doublet tapers to a point in the front, and his breeches are tied with a bow.

3.3 & 4 Louis XIII and the Marquis de Gesvres, taken from an engraving that commemorated an occasion at Fontainbleau in 1633.

3.5 A soldier from Louis XIII's army – probably a reserve as he has no gorget, nor any ribbons in his sleeve to show his rank. His sleeveless leather jacket, called a *buffe*, replaces the earlier breastplate, and is worn above a doublet.

## THE COURT OF THE SUN KING

SUCH WAS THE GLAMOUR OF ROYALTY during the reign of Louis XIV of France that the influence of the King's court over the great figures of the day nearly eclipsed the traditional power of the Church. The King became the absolute arbiter of style and taste, and a prosperous national industry emerged to produce items that had become *de rigeur* following an initiative by the King. It seemed as though everything that the King did, and every habit that he developed, had an important implication for some area of French life.

———— • ————

The King acquired a taste, for example, for holding receptions in the morning before he was fully dressed. The result was a fashion for sumptuous dressing gowns, embroidered with gold and silver, and short morning wigs.

As an alternative to this short wig, a cap would be worn – men had to shave their heads in order to wear wigs and were therefore reluctant to expose their bare heads.

Eventually, caps became luxury items. Made of linen, silk or velvet, and sometimes even quilted or fur-lined, they were covered with the most elaborate jewellery. Their use became such a part of 17th-century life that brides-to-be would make special caps for their husbands – some examples are shown in **1**.

The fashion spread to other countries, too. **1.3** shows a Venetian marriage cap of the 18th century, covered with emblems showing love crowned, and bearing the symbol of fatherhood, the pelican. The cap in **1.8** has a motif of entwined hearts.

**2.1** A gentleman who is imitating the costume of Louis XIV – a blue sash runs underneath his jacket, but over his waistcoat. The hand in the pocket of his breeches allows us to see that they are laced up at the side.

**2.2** A priest, wearing a long robe with a small collar. During this period, priests were among the most elegant of all the members of the court. This one has expensive cuffs and ribboned shoes, and is wearing the red trousers of a monsignor.

**2.3** A gentleman wearing an unusual coat for the period, in that it does not carry any braiding.

**2.4** The Duke of Maine, wearing a sash in the same way as Louis XIV and with a winter muff hanging by a ribbon from his belt.

**2.5** The Queen of Denmark, wearing a costume decked in lace – a fashion set by Madame de Maintenon, the King's mistress. The distinctive raised and pleated trimming of her skirt was of gold and silver, and her ribboned muffs were just becoming a new fashion.

What really makes her costume typical of the period, though, is the shape of her feather-bordered hat.

**3** The style of every item of clothing was considered important by courtiers: the dressing of the wig; the colour of a necktie; the length of the coat; the decorative bordering on sleeves; the height of shoe heels; the angle of the sword; even the length of the sword belt that was hidden beneath the waistcoat was considered to be of critical importance.

A number of variations on the basic themes are shown in this strip.

## A MEETING AT FONTAINEBLEAU

THE SCENE OPPOSITE, TAKEN FROM A GOBELINS TAPESTRY based on the drawings of Lebrun, marks an important moment in the early part of the reign of Louis XIV. Cardinal Chigi, nephew of Pope Alexander VII and his legate in France, is shown meeting the King at Fontainebleau on the 29th of July, 1664. He had come to put an end to the series of disputes that had bedevilled the relationship between France and the Vatican since 1661, when the followers of Duke Créqui had insulted Rome.

The Cardinal was welcomed with much ceremony: "He received under a dais the respects of the superior courts, of the town militia and of the clergy; he entered Paris, heralded by the firing of canon with the great Condé on his right and the Prince's son on his left," says Voltaire in *The age of Louis XIV*.

This exceptional audience was held in the King's bed chamber. The room, built during the reign of Charles IX, had remained almost as it had been constructed until Louis XIII had it decorated in about 1642: the furniture and hangings depicted here are from this period. In 1713 Louis XIV had its size increased by about one third and completely redecorated it.

In 1664 the King of France was just 26. As a Voltaire says, "This was a good time, when Louis XIV, through leading such a gay life, would appear to have made his kingdom the happiest in the world."

Mazarin was dead and the edict of 1660 that had obliged the nobility to remove the fine braid and lace from their garments had already been forgotten. Not only did this encourage the expansion of the French lace-making industry, but also caused the migration of hundreds of lace-makers from Flanders and Venice to Paris.

This year – 1664 – marked the introduction of the "royal jacket" as an institution. The object was not to do away with luxury, but to make it a mark of privilege. The jacket could only be worn by those who had received the royal warrant, signed by the hand of the King himself.

Louis, in the full flush of youth, loved splendour and naturally exercised a great influence over the new fashions. To begin with, these consisted of simple modifications that tended towards the effeminate. The doublet was very much shortened and the sleeves almost disappeared, the under-shirt becoming more and more apparent.

Louis XIII's breeches were replaced by breeches that looked rather like streamers, tied above the knee with ribbons. Called *rhingrave*, these came from Maestricht in Holland.

The transitional costume shown here characterizes the first part of Louis XIV's reign: seams were trimmed with narrow strips of lace; collars were cut square and turned down; and every kind of lace and an infinite number of ribbons in shell shapes, clusters and ruches decorated clothes from the shoulders to the shoes.

At this stage Louis XIV did not wear a wig and his long thick hair was natural, but a majestic wig that looked like a lion's mane was already popular among the nobility. Hats were decorated with two rows of feathers. A blouson was worn over the doublet and over the blouson, a baldric, from which hung the sword.

"This fashion," said Voltaire, "became the fashion throughout Europe, with the exceptions of Spain and Poland. Already fashion-conscious people every - where hastened to imitate the splendour of the French court."

# THE FASHION LIONS: MONTAURON AND CANDALE

TWENTY YEARS AFTER THE DUKE OF BELLEGARDE had set the fashion for the royal court, two other men ruled style. These were Montauron, in 1644, and, later, Candale. They were last of those whom the English called "the lions" – that is, individuals who on their own were able to define and name fashions and persuade others to adopt them. However, after 1648 the caprices of costume were no longer named eponymously and innovations in fashion were taken from the king. With the disappearance of Candale the reign of the "lions" was over.

**1.1** An officer to the guards in 1685, "to" being the correct designation in the case of the French guards. His uniform is turquoise, lined and trimmed with red, and his breeches and stockings are scarlet.

**1.2** An officer of the militia in 1688, wearing a grey jerkin with blue trimming at collar and cuffs.

**1.3** An officer in 1660. At this time officers were just beginning to wear special uniforms; before it, an officer could only really be distinguished by his lance and his high collar.

**1.4** A general in 1694, with a hat decorated with white feathers, and a red, gold-braided jacket.

**1.5** An officer in winter costume in 1685, with a hat decorated with white feathers and a scarlet cloak.

**2.1, 2 & 5** Costumes from the the Montauron period, around 1646.

**2.1 & 5** A characteristic of the Montauron style was the way in which the doublet became so short that underclothes could be seen at the waistline. By the same token, the sleeves were left open to show off the under-shirt.

The gentleman to the far right is wearing similar clothes, though of a different colour. In this case, however, the cloak has taken on a more military aspect.

**2.2** A gallant, wearing the short, puffed breeches that were fashionable during the reign of Henri IV.

However, details such as the baldric, silk stockings and small boots date this costume back to the reign of Henri III.

**2.3 & 4** The wife and niece of the Marshal of Guébriant. The former is wearing a very décolleté dress, and her open neck is covered by a white fichu ready for a trip to town. This is attached to a large collar turned down over her shoulders like a cape. The black gown shows that she is in mourning.

Apart from the absence of a widow's mantle her niece is similarly dressed, except that her costume is rich and colourful.

**3.1** Louis XIV in 1660, and **3.3**, Louis in 1670. In the first illustration he is still cultivating the appearance of casual undress of which Candale was the principal instigator. The doublet is exaggeratedly short and the belt has been lowered, so the underclothes can be seen hanging out above the hose. Children in the street used to shout: "Look out, sir, your trousers are falling down!".

The first costume, worn when Louis was only 22, shows the influence of Mazarin and his regulations – there are no gold or silver trimmings. Neither trimmings, nor the "royal jacket" – blue with a red lining and magnificent embroidery – could worn by others without a royal warrant.

**3.2** Maria Theresa of Austria in 1660. The top of her dress is trimmed with a strip of gauze or linen, and decorated with beads and precious stones.

# FRANCE

## THE LATE 17TH AND EARLY 18TH CENTURIES

THE COSTUMES ILLUSTRATED OPPOSITE are all from the latter part of Louis XIV's reign, that is, the end of the 17th century and the beginning of the 18th. Madame de Maintenon, the King's mistress, had imposed a somewhat starchy, disciplined approach to costume, but, nevertheless, women's costume was still ornate and meticulous – especially as regards headgear.

Between 1680 and 1701 women wore headdresses *à la Fontange*. The variety of these can be seen in **1**. Lace, hair, ribbons and iron frames were used in their construction, and each style had a different name: "duchess", "solitary", "mouse", "firmament", "10th heaven" and so on.

Women wore very heavy make-up, with foundation and rouge, and stuck pieces of silk or velvet on their faces. These were known as *mouches*, or flies, and were considered an indispensable part of a woman's costume. Men also wore *mouches*, but the designs tended to be more discreet.

**1.1** Madame de Maintenon

**1.2** The Dowager Princess of Conti.

**1.3** The Duchess of Bourbon.

**1.4** Elisabeth-Charlotte de Bourbon, called "Mademoiselle de Chartres", the sister of the Regent.

**1.5** The Countess of Egmont, née Princess d'Aremberg.

**1.6** The Duchess of Chartres.

**2.1 & 5** Noblewomen in winter costume, wearing taffeta scarves like capes to cover the head and shoulders when out of doors. These women are also carrying muffs, which were becoming more and more fashionable at this time and were made from a variety of animal skins, such as wolf, fox, bear, tiger, and sable.

**2.2 & 3** The Loison sisters.

**2.4** An abbot wearing a short cape and a *soutanelle*. This garment distinguishes him from lesser clergy; essentially, it is a *soutane* cut down for wear in the country.

**2.6** A nobleman in summer costume. This outfit, with ribbons on the right shoulder and at the wrists that recall the old *galands*, dates from before 1690.
  Despite such frivolities, there is a certain formality and starchiness about the nobleman's costume that smacks of the austerity of the final days of the old regime. The jacket is really a morning coat, cut narrow and straight with two or three buttons, showing the silk jerkin underneath.

**3.3** All the ladies in **3** have similar costumes, to which this one description can apply.
  This lady's headdress is in the *fontange* style. Her bodice is long and tight and pointed at the waist. The half-length sleeves are trimmed with lace from Alencon or Valenciennes, and she is wearing a single string of pearls, long gloves and a tie on her bodice called a *squinquerque*.
  The over-skirt worn here was, in fact, referred to as a cloak, because of the way in which was gathered so as to only fall down one side. The silk skirt itself is decorated in two ways: first, with a flounce where the material is ruched at the bottom (a device designed by Langlée); and, second, by golden threads applied lengthways.

# THE EARLY 18TH CENTURY

THESE EXAMPLES OF MEN'S HEADGEAR are taken from an engraving by Bernard Picart, itself based on a work by Baron Eisenberg in 1727. At that time there were only a few variations on the basic design of the three-cornered hat: the triangular brim could sometimes curve upwards and sometimes lie flat; and its height could be altered. Decoration, however, had more possibilities. Feathers and braid trimmings were used extensively, and sometimes the braid crossed over the crown of the hat to alter the angle of the brim.

———— • ————

**1** Folio wigs, with long, flowing, loose hair, did not fall entirely out of favour with the leaders of fashion until after the death of Louis XIV in 1715. But since the start of the 18th century there had been a gradual reaction against the inconvenience of such quantities of hair.

The movement started with a trend to part the hair at the back, tying the two strands in summer and leaving them loose in winter. Little by little the knotted wigs took took over from the loose type. Next came wigs with tails and the purse wig – both were variations of the old-style flowing wig that was divided into three sections, with two sections at the sides (the *cadenettes*) and one down the back (the tail).

As can be seen opposite, this tail could be worn in many ways: tied with a ribbon formed into a rosette with long ends (6 & 14); fastened half-way down with a clip (9 & 10); or twisted round into a long spiral (1, 2, 3 & 17). This last style was known as a "rat's tail".

The purse wig was a new way of wearing the tail. The purse itself was a small bag of black taffeta, decorated with a rosette of the same colour, that enclosed the lower section of hair at the back of the head. From 1710 the majority of the military, officers and soldiers, wore their hair thus.

Purse wigs were first adopted by civilians, and eventually worn in smart circles – where they were known as *"perruques à la régence"*. In fact, military men abandoned wigs fairly soon, and began to grow their own hair.

Wigs persisted for rather longer in court circles. Eventually, though, all that was worn was a hairpiece over the forehead, disguised by a coarse powder called "spinach grain".

The horseman is wearing a typically short costume of the period. His seat on the horse marks him as a member of the Franco-Italian equestrian school: the seat varied between nationalities and from period to period.

**3.1, 3 & 4** Middle-class costumes from 1730 to 1740, as drawn by Leclerq. The middle classes dressed in coarse materials, such as ratteen. Nearly all of their various articles of clothing were of matching colours, mainly in the range of tints between dark red and and light brown. From around 1750, though, black started to become the standard ceremonial colour.

The man in **3.3** is wearing a travelling costume, with a buttoned up jacket and belt, and long gaiters (worn by dragoons at that time) with spurs. These leather gaiters were indispensable to the horseman.

**3.2** This luxurious outfit was called "The Complete European Costume", and was kept in the Museum of Dresden. It was made from gold thread, and worn by a knight of the White Eagle, an order instituted in 1705 by Auguste II, King of Poland.

The jerkin is open down one side, in order to let the sword pass through, and the breeches – lacking buckles and gaiters – are gathered in under the stockings.

## FROM AUSTERITY TO EXTRAVAGANCE

THE ILLUSTRATIONS OPPOSITE show costumes from the reign of Louis XV (1710-1774), whose once austere court eventually became famous for its extravagance. So much so, in fact, that his reign led to a decline in respect for the institution of the monarchy.

———— • ————

1.1 Ulrique-Eléonore, Queen of Sweden and sister of Charles XII – for whom she gave up the throne in 1719. This illustration is taken from an 18th-century painting in the Museum at Versailles.

Noted for the masculine appearance that she affected, Ulrique-Eléonore is here wearing Polish costume, complete with a sword. It consists of a fur bonnet decorated with a feather, and a blue, frogged *kontousch* with a fur collar adorned with a silver brooch.

Her sash is white, and she is wearing a large sleeveless cloak fastened across the chest. Her jacket and breeches are red, and her white stockings end in low-fronted shoes.

1.2 & 4 Two ladies, each wearing a *casaquin* – a slight variation on the *casaque*, or over-blouse. In the 18th-century, this jacket with its long basques was known successively as a *casaquin*, a *pet-en-l'air* and a *caraco*.

The lady on the left has a type of gauze headdress called a *marli*, in which the ends are folded back and fastened with a pin. She also has a lace choker and her *casaquin* hangs down over a skirt supported with panniers. The other lady is wearing a *casaquin* whose waist is gathered in with a belt, and a headdress of the same type.

1.3 A middle-class woman. During the first part of the reign of Louis XV, middle-class costumes tended towards the austere. This costume is a good example: a full dress is adjusted over the bodice, so that it flows out behind and her pagoda sleeves are folded back. Her head is covered with a mantilla, whose ends are knotted under the chin and fall down the chest.

1.5 An everyday outfit of 1730. The hat is trimmed with a cockade of ribbons and the man has a purse wig, a cravat, a shirt with a jabot, and a waistcoat that is only buttoned up as far as the belt. His coat hangs gracefully, with pagoda sleeves and red trimming, and the tails of the coat are puffed out as if supported by panniers.

2.1 & 4 Two ladies wearing mantillas – very much the fashion in spring and autumn. A mantilla was a small scarf, with pointed ends like a very long fichu, that crossed over the bodice to be tied at the back.

2.2 A man wearing a coat with pagoda sleeves – these opened out in a funnel-shape, and were then turned back up to the elbow.

2.3 and 3.2 & 4 In the early part of the 18th century, clothes could either be graceful and flowing or stiff and cut to fit close to the body.

In 1729, though, it was the fashion to wear coat tails puffed out, as a reference to the use of panniers by women. Pleats were moved behind, to the right and left of the central opening, while the waistcoat was worn open to the waist.

As a result, the under-shirt and cravat could be seen.

Sometimes a black ribbon was tied at the throat to replace the white cravat, and the under-shirt had a jabot, to take the place of the ends of the linen cravat. Breeches were tucked into the stockings until 1730 – a clue to the dating of these illustrations.

3.1 & 7 Examples of the *bagnolette*, a winter headdress, worn by women of all ages and classes.

## THE SPIRIT OF THE AGE

THE ILLUSTRATION AT THE TOP of the opposite page is a reproduction of a sketch by Joseph Vernet, from a series of 12 pictures of the ports of France. Léon Legrange said of this artist: "If he had not been considered primarily as a great painter of sailors and seascapes, he would have been famous as a recorder of fashion. He has an extraordinary appreciation of the spirit of costume, and by costume he clearly understands what it is that should be understood: not only the form and colour of clothes, but the way of wearing them, their way of re-shaping the figure and, indeed, the manners and morals of an age."

In an age in which fashion exhausted itself with variations on such unrewarding themes as the whalebone corset, the dress that floated out behind, large panniers and high-heeled shoes, the form of the human body disappeared under contrivances that distorted and confused it more and more.

It is a relief, then, to find a portrait that reveals the figure and the face of a women who meets the exigencies of fashion in the mid-18th century. The picture at the bottom left, of a lady at her toilette in around 1760, is just such a portrait.

The artist is Baudouin, the son-in-law of Boucher and one of the most stylish painters of the period. According to the brothers de Goncourt, he "possessed a tasteful indecency" that we can sense here.

At this time, the idea of female beauty had been considerably affected by a decline in moral standards. The new ideal was that the face should have what was called *physionomie*. True beauty was disparaged; irregularities, far from being unpleasant, were thought to offer a greater opportunity to create a whimsical prettiness, a fashionable face, and a worldly appearance.

The best compliment a woman could be paid followed the idea implicit in this passage from Bachaumont: "Even if she is not quite beautiful, her graciousness will make her so".

As the brothers de Goncourt remarked, "fashion makes a woman's face". In order to achieve an eye-catching face – a face that was something more than merely pretty – a woman needed the following: large eyes – "for the most beautiful eyes in the world are large expressionless eyes"; "a fine noble nose with an almost imperceptible flaw that would animate the face"; or a retroussé nose – "with a delicate upward tilt"; finally, "the mouth should not be small and the complexion not too pale".

The heroine of the picture is very much in the de Goncourt mould. She has a fine, slender body, a gracious posture and a face that appears somehow spiritual.

Her maid is adjusting a bodice that is laced up at the back. This bodice is long and tight, so taken with the large panniers worn underneath the skirt, the overall impression is that of an orange tree in a box.

Her curly hair is worn without a headdress in a simple flat chignon, giving a natural look in the Greek style that was fashionable around 1760. The young man sitting so casually in an armchair, his jacket hanging over one side, is about to proffer a bouquet of roses. He looks like a typical gallant, with probably as many vices as debts.

The picture of Grandval next to this scene is by Lancret. It was painted in 1742, before the change of attitude towards standards of morality and behaviour.

The title "philosopher" is in fact one of ridicule. It mocks the serious expression and furrowed brow affected by some gentlemen in the first half of the 18th century.

# STANDARDIZATION IN UNIFORMS

DURING THE 18TH CENTURY, MILITARY UNIFORMS were becoming standardized, a trend formalized by decrees of the 1789 National Assembly. Different colours on lapels and cuffs had previously indicated the origins of different regiments, but these were abolished. From this point, the whole army wore blue, and differences in uniform, which were confined to the use of red and white on lapels and cuffs, came to indicate only the various military occupations.

In theory, the same uniforms were worn by reserves and volunteers. But in time of war, complete uniforms were often not available, so volunteers would fight in striped, rather than the usual white, trousers.

1 Headgear varied according to the soldier's specialty: infantrymen wore tricorne hats; grenadiers wore bearskins until 1793, when they changed to the tricorne hat, though in their case it was distinguished by a red plume. The heavy cavalry wore helmets made of a lightweight, shiny felt.

After 1791, every soldier had to wear a standard rosette on his hat, made of red, white and blue. These were the colours that had been adopted by the National Guard of Paris after the storming of the Bastille. The precise order in which they were used on flags was laid down in 1794: blue next to the flag-pole; white in the middle; and red at the edges. In battle, this flag would be carried by a sergeant (1.2).

1.8 shows a drum-major, wearing a splendid uniform of the 1790s: his breeches are made of suede; he has fine-turned-down boots; an officer's tail-coat; a soldier's sword; a plumed hat; pistols at his belt; a drumstick case on a chain; and a cane tipped with steel and decorated with catgut.

2.1 & 2 The French Revolution led to a complete change in the personnel of the army, as senior officers with Bourbon sympathies were weeded out and juniors took their places.

The officer, on the left of this pair, is wearing the same costume in 1792 as would have been worn by his predecessors. The rating, however, is wearing the more casual style that quickly became popular. It consists of a blue shirt with a large, turned-down collar, a loose-fitting jacket and trousers striped with the national colours.

2.3 & 4 An officer and soldier of the Coastguards, wearing the distinctive green of their service.

2.5 A rating in 1786, wearing a jacket and trousers made of a material called *estamète*.

2.6 A naval surgeon.

2.7 & 3.1 A soldier and an officer from the Brest Regiment of Marines. Formed in 1772, their uniforms kept the same colours of royal blue with red collar, cuffs and lapels until 1789.

3.2 & 3 An admiral's flag-guard. This body was formed by Louis XIV as an independent corps of gentlemen. Its members wore a royal blue coat lined with scarlet serge and decorated with scarlet trimmings.

3.4 A rear admiral, with a blue coat trimmed with gold braid, a red waistcoat and red breeches. The standard officer's epaulettes have been replaced by gold braid.

3.5 A vice-admiral, wearing the standard uniform with scarlet lapels and decorations. Both standard and dress uniforms had gilded leather buttons, each stamped with the shape of an anchor.

## LUXURY AND FRIVOLITY

FASHIONS WENT THROUGH two distinct phases of evolution during the reign of Louis XVI (1774-1793). The first was characterized by excessive luxury and frivolity. It marked the explosive finale to the carnival of dress that had started in the first quarter of the century. Panniers, for example, became ridiculously large – some were almost 15ft in circumference – and headdresses became gargantuan. The second style was a complete contrast. Simplicity was the keyword, and women adopted children's styles, with shirt-waister dresses, cambrics and lawns.

The illustrations opposite are all from the first period: the period of extravagance. At this time, some panniers were not as large as those described above, but cut-off. In this style, thick, broad panniers were worn with a shortened skirt that fell down straight, to show off the feet and high heeled shoes.

The headdresses, however, were always huge. The framework that supported such a headdress was so high that the wearer's head appeared to be as much as two-thirds of the size of the body; it was certainly something of a feat of engineering.

On top of the framework, the hair might be gathered up, back-combed, lacquered, curled or sprinkled with white powder. A cap of ribbons and feathers would crown the edifice, or a *pouf* might be worn. This was a piece of gauze interwoven with strands of hair.

1.1 & 4 The epitome of the exaggerated style. The material of the clothes is laden with decorations of all types: knots, shells, branches, bouquets, balls of gauze, pearls and gemstones.

1.3 A lady whose costume is almost bare of decoration, showing that it comes from the start of the age of simplicity.

2.1 An example of cut-off panniers, worn to display a coquette's shapely ankles and dainty high-heeled shoes.

2..2 A young lady of high birth, wearing formal clothes with an elegant *pouf* and a large, full headdress. Her dress has a low neckline and fits tightly on the upper body. It is trimmed with sable-coloured material, has straight pleats and is decorated all round with gathered-in bands of yellow. The pleats are cross-cut by two bars of eight puffs, the head of each puff being covered by two bands of yellow.

She has a pearl necklace attached by two gold ties, and her headdress – in the style known as *à la victoire* – incorporates a double olive branch and two ostrich feathers.

## EDUCATION AND EQUALITY

ACCORDING TO THE GONCOURT BROTHERS, a woman's smile should come from the soul, rather than the mind. This was one of the changes of emphasis that marked the beginning of the age of simplicity, which was triggered by the first pregnancy of Queen Marie-Antoinette. Women started to favour simple, white materials, and later turned to an affected parody of a rustic, peasant style. Later still, they began to adopt a style of dress that reflected women's new attitude towards themselves. Now, following the ideas of philosophers such as Voltaire and Rousseau, the emphasis was on learning and knowledge, and, inevitably on a degree of equality between the sexes. In consequence, women's costume began to adopt certain traditional elements of masculine dress, as can be seen from this series of fashion plates from the last years of the 18th century.

———— • ————

13 A man in autumn clothing, with a coat of puce-coloured material with white braid on its edges. (This was innovative, because previously the waistcoat alone had carried the braid.).

The waistcoat is of red moiré with violet stripes; his thigh-hugging breeches are of cashmere and his silk hose are striped in blue and white. The waistcoat has two pockets, each of which holds a watch. From one pocket hangs a simple black cord with a gold key at its end; from the other hangs a gold chain bearing several charms.

His gloves are made of a light, yellow chamois leather and he is carrying a bamboo walking stick, decorated with a black silk cord and tassels.

15 A gentleman in an outfit made for spring, with a lemon-coloured coat and jacket with green stripes and lilac sleeves. The narrow breeches are made from black silk and the shoes have red heels.

17 A lady wearing a frock coat and an under-coat, both made of dark blue taffeta. Sometimes the under-coat matched the coat, as here, but it could also be made from taffeta of a contrasting colour, such as white, pink or scarlet.

Her pink corset is cut in the style of a man's waistcoat and matches a pink taffeta petticoat, glazed with white and lined with a small slip of the same material.

This lady's costume is the last word in the fashions of the day. Essentially, she is dressed like a man – her waistcoat, the cut of her frock coat, her low-heeled shoes, and even watches and bracelet charms are all borrowed from male costume.

21 A woman wearing a shirt-waister dress made of foulard and trimmed with black ribbon. The dress is held in by a broad black belt, which is knotted at the back, and her bust is covered by a wide scarf made of white gauze.

Her headdress is in the style known as *à la bellone*. This was first seen in public at the theatre, where it caused such a sensation – so the story goes – that the play was quite forgotten as the audience craned for a better view.

Its peak, of yellow satin with black spots, is pulled down almost over the eyes, and the puffed-out bonnet is made of light blue satin.

24 A young man in a tail coat made from a bourbon cloth that carries a pattern of sea-green scales. The cloth is unusual, but the style is traditional – even to the gaiters that go down below his knees.

26 A lady dressed in mourning for the death of the King of Portugal. She is wearing a dress of black taffeta, with matching shoes decorated with black ribbon frills, and a scarf of white Italian gauze.

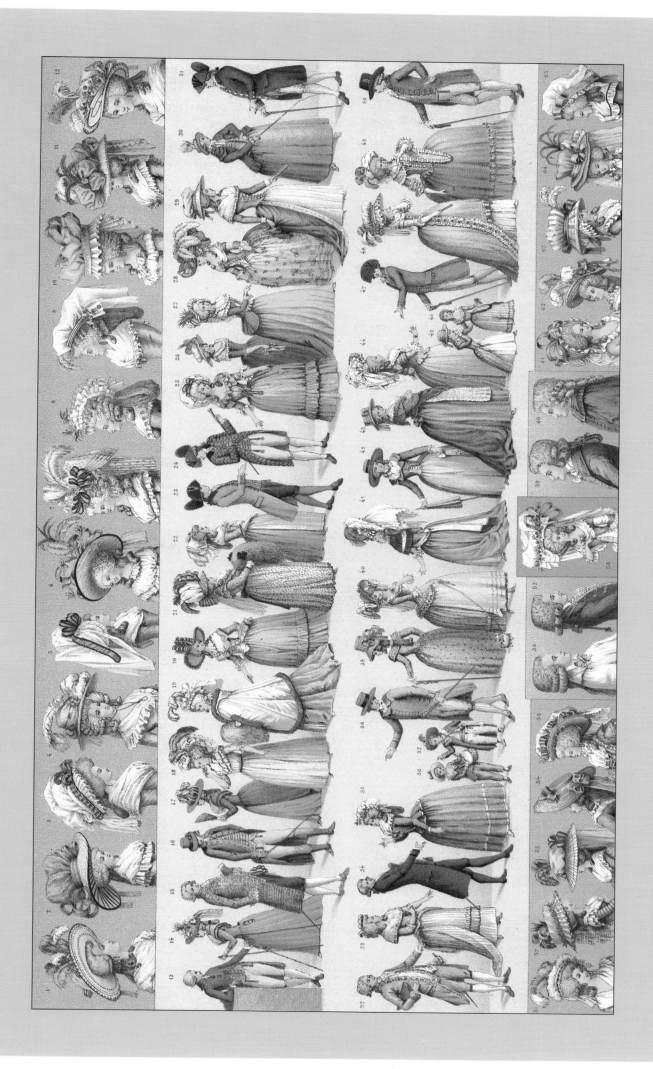

## TOWARDS THE TURN OF THE CENTURY

WOMEN'S COSTUME DID NOT CHANGE MUCH between 1790 and 1794. The bust continued to lengthen under the pressure of a whale-bone corset and, in one innovation, a large linen fichu began to be worn across the bodice to make it look larger. Crêpe de Chine scarves and loose blouses could also be also worn over fichus. The only real change was in the type of material used. This was often striped, and simple lawn and linen tended to be preferred to silks.

Hair was still worn in ringlets with a chignon hanging down the back, in the style that Marie-Antoinette had popularized in 1785. In 1794 large bonnets became the height of fashion and upright hats with tall crowns fell out of favour. This last style had entered France from England in 1786, having been borrowed from men's fashions.

But after these few years in which fashion idled, everything changed very quickly – except for the arrangement of the hair. By 1796, whale-bone corsets, elongated busts and fitted dresses had disappeared. Padding was worn with false fichus, and clothes became predominantly pale in colour. Ribbons served as belts and dresses were gathered at the neckline.

There were two causes for this change. The first was the influence of Marie-Antoinette, who had a natural affinity for white clothes and encouraged a cult of youth. The second cause was the influence of the medical profession, who had been agitating for many years to release women from the bondage of their corsets. But good sense and fashion never walk hand in hand for long. This comfortable costume with a belt worn at reasonable height was soon replaced by a low-necked dress with a belt worn high up under the bust.

Hair was still worn down over the neck – though one fleeting fashion was for it to be cut off at the neck as an expression of sympathy for the victims of Madame Guillotine. Generally, though, full wigs with a chignon falling low over the neck and back were still popular.

Sometimes hair was worn loose with a circlet on top of the head and ringlets at the sides, but most women followed the advice reported in a retrospective article of the *Journal of Ladies and Fashions* in 1812: "a blonde wig in the morning and a brown one in the evening."

Later, in one last reference to the Greek and Roman fashions of the past, wigs were discarded and hair came to be worn short and curly, with all the headbands and twists of hair that the Athenians loved. Dyeing was still common, though, and straw hats were usually worn.

2 and 3 show women's costumes between 1794 to 1800. They come from fashion magazines of the time, and show the number of modifications in dress – mainly involving the length and decoration of the bodice – that were made in a short period of time. The early fashions of the First Empire show a movement towards a revival of the costumes of ancient Greece. This is most noticeable in the second group of figures, taken from the last two years of the century.

# EUROPE

ORDERS AND DECORATIONS

IN 17TH- AND 18TH-CENTURY EUROPE, the most common orders of Knighthood were no longer the ancient orders, such as those of the Templars and the Knights of Malta, which were at the same time religious and military. Instead they were orders of recent creation, of which membership was granted by the sovereign as a means of paying off services rendered to the State: a method of giving away rewards and ribbons rather than money or other payment in kind. As Montaigne said: "This was a fine invention. Both we and our neighbours conferred knighthoods which were established only for this purpose." The illustrations opposite show a variety of orders and costumes from the 17th and 18th centuries.

———— • ————

The insignia of an ordinary knighthood was worn in the form of a jewel, hung from a ribbon of a fixed colour. Eventually, a ribbon alone, as in **1.5** where it is fixed on the inside of the coat and emerges through a buttonhole to the outside, took the place of the insignia in everyday costume, and its colour indicated the order.

The fashion of wearing the complete insignia on the left side was adopted in some quarters (**2.5**), but the earlier examples of knights of the orders of Malta and Saint-Louis, (**1.2** and **2.2, 4 & 6**), show that the insignia was formerly worn much lower. How low depended on personal taste, as did the garment to which it was attached, but it is clear that the insignia of the oldest orders was always worn at waist level.

As a reminder of a tradition which went back to the Middle Ages, the particular signs of certain orders of military knights were still worn on the clothing; they were embroidered like coats of arms, as **1.1 & 6** and **2.3** show.

Possibly this was a result of a desire to make a show of marks of distinction, as with the knight of the Hospital of Aubrac (**1.6**). This was an ancient hospital, served by monks and nuns and protected by armed knights. It is not clear why the decoration is worn, since the order was abolished in 1693.

**1.1** A knight of the Star in France.

The costume dates from the second half of the 16th century.

**1.2** A knight of the Royal Military Order of Saint-Louis, whose costume dates from the beginning of the 18th century. **1.5** and **2.5** are also knights of the Order of Saint-Louis. The first is dressed for a Paris morning in 1784; the second is in the formal costume of 1787.

**1.4** A knight of the Order of Two Swords (a French order, similar to that of Saint-Louis); the costume dates from the time of Louis XVI.

**1.6** A knight from the Hospital of Aubrac, wearing a costume from the beginning of the 18th century.

**2.1** A knight of the Royal Military Order of Saint-Louis; the costume is contemporary with the foundation of the order in 1693.

**2.2** A French knight of the Order of Malta in a costume of 1678.

**2.3** A knight of the Axe (a Spanish order), in a costume from the beginning of the 17th century.

**2.4** A Knight Commander of the Royal Military Order of Saint-Louis, wearing formal dress dating from 1693.

**2.6** A Knight from the Order of Malta, and a page to Louis XIV.

## FRANCE – GERMANY – ENGLAND

DURING THE FRENCH REVOLUTION, no fashion journals were published. However, within a few years French style was once more influencing all Europe. Carricoli's *Cabinet de la Mode* was published in 1793, and his *Galerie de la Mode* appeared in London in 1794. At about the same time, almanacs reported his ideas in Berlin, Switzerland and Leipzig. The majority of the illustrations opposite come from these sources; they make up a picture of a period of European fashion that ended with the beginning of the 19th century.

The French Revolution caused a temporary hiatus in fashion developments in France, and new styles really only began to appear after 1794.

The typical costume of the revolutionary period is shown in 3.29 – a woman from Frankfurt who is wearing a milkmaid's bonnet and a loose blouse. The women in 1.5, 7, & 11, 2.16 & 27 and 3.32, 35 & 37 are all wearing false fichus and English-style bodices – all with elongated busts and tight sleeves. The dresses are cut to resemble coats, with patterned blouses and straight skirts.

After 1794, luxury took hold once more. Fashions were set by French women who had sought refuge from the revolution in London and returned to France having grown used to English opulence, As a result of this, "anglomania", as it was called, led European fashion – the bonnet worn in 1.7 is a good example.

The gowns, belts and colours that came into vogue were all somehow reminiscent of childhood. Head-dresses became lower and the hair was no longer powdered. Blonde wigs were worn instead.

The German women in 1.8 and 2.17 & 25 are wearing costumes from the period between 1799 and 1804. This period marked the disappearance of classical hairstyles and the development of hairstyles said to be *à la Antinous*.

Next came the reappearance of clothes made of silk, muslin, gauze and percale. Most European women followed the fashions set by the new French court – of the consul, now, not the king.

Surprisingly, these changes were more obvious in men's costume than in women's. The well-dressed men of 1790 had abandoned Swiss-style hats, shown in many of these examples, to military use. Hair, whether it was powdered or not, was topped by a round hat with a high crown and encircled with a silk cord called a *bourdalou* (1.2, 12 & 14, 2.15 & 20 and 3.31 & 33).

Coats with long basques and semi-square frock coats – as in 1.12 and 3.32, 33, 34 & 37 – disappeared, being replaced by tail coats. These tails tapered into points like those of a cod, and the coats were decorated down the front by two short lapels.

A lace cravat was tied in a large knot at the throat. Breeches were made of suede or cashmere and fitted in equestrian style, going down as far as the calves where they were fastened with bows over long striped stockings. The outfit was completed by elegant boots with turned-down tops, or by low-heeled shoes with bows.

The appearance for the first time of advertisements for braces in the journals of 1792 tells us that proper trousers were beginning to develop at this time. They could either be loose or tight-fitting.

All the men opposite display the various attitudes common at the time. One was of confrontation and militarism; another, by contrast, was of foppishness, which reached its zenith in the appearance of the precious gentleman known as the *incroyables*. Many of these are illustrated opposite – notably in 1.9 & 10 and 2.18 & 19.

## FOLLOWING THE LEAD OF FRANCE

IN THE 17TH AND 18TH CENTURIES, the German court – in common with most of the other courts of Europe – followed the lead of France so far as fashion was concerned. Naturally, innovations took a little time to become established and once part of the costume tended to take longer than in France to lose their popularity.

1.11 & 12 The imperial drummer.

1.13 Frederick III, Elector of Brandenburg, who was crowned as King Frederick I of Prussia in 1701.

1.14 Frederick-Sophie-Wilhemina, Princess of Orange and Nassau, wearing a costume that unites both masculine and feminine elements of dress: a plumed hat and a frock coat.

2.2 Joseph II, Emperor of Germany, who abolished serfdom in 1781. Joseph was a very serious-minded monarch and a true philosopher king. He was said by one member of his court to have the bearing of a soldier but the wardrobe of a second lieutenant.

2.3 Maximilian, Archduke of Austria, with a tricorne hat decorated with gold trimmings and tassels. His white coat is edged with gold braid on the outside and red braid on the inside and he has a black scarf, white breeches and boots.

2.4 A dragoon guardsman, wearing a helmet of varnished felt with his regimental number engraved on its leather decoration.

3.1 Prince Henry of Prussia, the brother of Frederick.

3.4 Frederick II of Prussia, seen towards the end of his reign – he died in 1786. He is wearing the same uniform as his guard: a blue coat with a collar, red facings and silver buttons.

# ENGLAND

PURITANISM AND AFFECTATION

T HE TWO ENGRAVINGS OPPOSITE show two very different types of costume, reflecting different times and contrasting areas of society. The engraving at the top is by Hogarth, and is taken from a series that illustrated Butler's satirical poem *Hudibras*; it was inspired by drawings of around 1710. At that time, as many as 180 different religious sects co-existed quarrelsomely in London. Many of these groups laid themselves open to the particularly English form of mocking humour: this plate shows a strict sect of Puritans called "The Holy League".

Although most people laughed at the idea of Puritanism in the 18th century, descendants of the Roundheads still existed, clinging to their particular faiths. Such people wore simple, plain clothes and were fond of robustness in all things – in their food, their hunting and their furniture. It was a great contrast to the lifestyle enjoyed by the apparently feeble and pleasure-loving upper classes.

The Puritans scorned affected manners, which they considered to have been imported by foreigners, and would let visitors find their own seats and never declare themselves either one's servant or one's friend. Yet when they shook your hand, they would nearly shake you off your feet, squeezing until you were on the point of shouting for mercy.

Their wives were a far cry from those women for whom only French materials and fashions existed, and who would never have consented to wear a ribbon or even a thread that had been made in England. Such women would walk in St James Park in the morning, wearing a simple cambric apron and a small straw hat, with a single servant for company.

Gradually, the influence of the Puritans began to dominate English society, until around 1755 the point was reached when gracious manners, smart clothes, fine jewel-

lery, perfume, beauty spots and cultured accents – in short, all the affectations picked up from Parisian dandies – had completely disappeared.

Englishmen began to pride themselves on being unique, and London noblemen started to dress in coarser clothes than their servants. It amused them to be mistaken for porters, whose manners and speech were even mimicked. Their clothes were those of the mob: short, unpowdered wigs, coloured neckerchiefs and sailor's jackets.

Later this practice – itself an affectation – began to become less popular, as England's prosperity grew and the Jacobites and the Holy League fell into decline.

The bottom illustration shows a family scene in a middle-class home of 1766. Although inferior in quality to the Hogarth, it nevertheless has a naive charm that is in marked contrast to Hogarth's harsh, satirical style.

This seems to be a merchant's house – his family crest appears above the door. The family would take their morning tea in this large ground-floor room, and the drawing exudes a strong sense of family life : the children are playing with the dogs; an anxious grandmother sits at the left; young people sit politely at the table; and the master of the house takes his ease.

## FRENCH MANNERS AND ENGLISH STOLIDITY

WILLIAM HOGARTH WAS ONE OF THE FEW artists of his time who managed to leave a lasting impression of the England of his time. A particularly English satirist, in the tradition of Defoe and Richardson, he had a power of observation and skill of expression that is truly memorable.

The top illustration is one of the six scenes from Hogarth's *Marriage à la Mode*, published in 1745. The scathing French title suggests that the high society manners of the day, which Hogarth was attacking, were very much modelled on those of France – a hint of this can be seen in the *fleur-de-lys* above the lady's bed. At that time, it was almost part of an Englishman's patriotic duty to loathe the French, and Hogarth seems to have done his duty.

The theme of *Marriage à la Mode* is that of a marriage between the son of an impoverished nobleman and the daughter of a grasping merchant. The groom is hopeless and feeble; the bride robust and lively. After they are married, the young man becomes spiteful and obstinate, and the woman becomes capricious and flirtatious. Not surprisingly, war is declared between the two.

Sitting in front of her dressing-room table, the young lady – who could be French from her clothes – is being attended by her wig stylist. A good-looking young man, who could be a lawyer to judge by his black clothes, is talking to her. The husband looks on, with curlers in his hair.

They are being entertained by musicians – the singer is the famous Carestini, dressed richly in clothes picked out with gold braid, and the flautist behind him is Weidemann, a German contemporary of Hogarth's. An African servant is handing out hot chocolate, and in front of him a lady is visibly overcome by the music. Her husband, to her left, applauds in a cynical manner, with his fingers apart and thumbs sticking out.

The lower illustration shows a scene from a middle-class home. It is not clear what is happening, but there is a definite sense of the Englishman in his home, dignified and serious even in front of his own family.

He is one of a race who, at this time, were said to have had an innate belief in their own superiority. So, even though this family is wearing clothes that testify to French influence, and though even the furniture harks back to a French style, the general demeanor of the father and mother is particularly English: strong, proud and upstanding.

Towards the end of the 17th century, the English gradually shook off all foreign influences, having depended on France for fashion ideas for nearly 100 years. They developed a strikingly original style of dress, which found its way back to France in the movement known as "anglomania". In the end, one French writer claimed that the French "thought, played and died *à la Anglaise*".

# FRANCE

### THE CRAZE FOR SHAWLS

THE SHAWL BECAME AN IMPORTANT PART of women's dress in France around the turn of the 19th century. Shawls came from Asia, where traditionally they had been wrapped around the head. The illustrations opposite show the types of shawls popular between 1802 and 1814 and the different ways in which they were worn.

Although all shawls were basically of the same shape, they could take on an almost infinite variety of styles and forms, according to the ways in which they were folded, draped or tied.

Rectangular or square, they could either be folded into four or two, or folded diagonally into a triangle. Alternatively, as worn by the lady on the far right of **1**, or her neighbour, who is holding a small girl's hand, they could be folded diagonally into two unequal parts, so that two embroidered parts were visible. Some were knotted in front (see the girl on the bottom right of **1**), and some had tassels at the corners, but all were worn with an air of studied carelessness.

Shawls were made in many different sizes and were worn for all seasons. The materials used included cotton, wool, silk, cambric, muslin and lace, and the colours were equally various: canary, green white, poppy-red and blue were all the favourites.

It was the advent of cashmere, though, that really made the shawl popular. This soft, rich material, made from the pelt of a Tibetan mountain goat, had first been seen in 1755, when it had generally been rejected at court. But later it reappeared with a vengeance.

So much so, in fact, that the *Journal des Dames et des Modes* commented in 1815: "Ladies (and also, of course, their husbands) will recall the time when cashmere shawls were the height of fashion. The things ladies would have to do to obtain these precious pieces of material! They would invent 1,000 reasons why they had to have one. The richest only needed to say that it was the fashion; the middle-class women needed to look like everyone else; and the poorest women claimed that cashmere would be good for their health and would last longer than anything else. Even if there was no other reason, women would resort to the refrain that a cashmere shawl was the only acceptable proof of true love."

When the craze for shawls first started, women refused to be parted from them. They were worn at all times – even for dances, when they would be draped in a classical fashion around the shoulders, or simply folded over an arm.

Some shawls were long and thin, like scarves (**2.3**). This style used the shawl more as an accessory than a covering, swathing the bare neck.

The shawl was a fitting garment for an age that revered and imitated classical times, and it reached the height of its glory when a dance – the Dance of the Shawl – was dedicated to it. In this dance, an important part was played by a delicate silk shawl – similar to the one worn by the lady in **1.6**.

## A PROMENADE IN THE BOIS DE BOULOGNE

WHILE IT WAS THOUGHT IMPORTANT that a male aristocrat should look intelligent, it was considered vital that a noblewoman should be beautiful. This concept is fundamental to an understanding of the costumes worn in the early years of the 19th century. This scene, showing society men and women strolling in the Bois de Boulogne, shows that men had begun to abandon their brightly coloured plumage, leaving women alone to show off their figures.

———— • ————

Men would wear sober-coloured, tightly buttoned jackets, with frock coats and close-fitting breeches made of heavy material. Women, on the other hand, wore diaphanous dresses made of linen or fine lawn, but no petticoats; the necks, arms and chests were often left bare.

The difference betwen the clothes of the two sexes was so marked that it looked as if they were dressed for two different seasons. In fact, the harsh winter of 1802 took its toll on many of these scantily clad women.

All the men are either wearing or carrying large, semi-circular hats, called *chapeaux claques*, and short tail coats in dark blue, green (the most popular colour) or dark brown, with shiny round buttons. Their breeches either reach to the knee, where they are met by white hose, or are wide and tucked into knee-length boots.

The style of bonnets and hats changed constantly, as can be seen from the strip at the bottom of the main illustration. In addition, women wore wigs of every colour imaginable, changing them with their moods.

A special language of fashion grew up in France at this time. It described the cut of different garments: a dress would be *à la Philomele*, for example, *à la Romaine* or *à la Psyche*. This last phrase described a low-cut bodice, short sleeves and a full skirt with a train behind.

This was all part of the classical revival that affected not only France but the whole of Europe at this time, and not only costume, but also architecture, furniture and jewellery. The classical look had a fairly broad definition, however, since it included elements such as long shawls, pearls and even turbans.

239

# SECTION FOUR

# TRADITIONAL COSTUMES OF THE 1880s

THIS LAST SECTION of the book has perhaps the most confusing title of all. Racinet tells us that he is describing the traditional costumes of different European countries, without ever telling us how he defines such costumes. In fact, there is no consistent answer: the definition changes from country to country.

In some cases — Brittany, for example — he describes costumes that are traditional in the sense that they were worn in the 1880s for feast days and festivals. In the case of Poland, however, Racinet takes us on an historical tour of Polish costumes and shows how a costume still worn by peasants in his time had developed. In the case of England, he uses illustrations from the second quarter of the 19th century — drawings of London characters and tradesmen, probably because in this, and in many other cases, there is really no specific costume that can be labelled as "traditional clothes". After all, this was the era when "traditional" costumes were being invented, as part of the Gothic-Romantic revival. Scotland provides a good example: the design and attribution of specific tartans to specific clans had only recently taken place, as had the development of what we know today as traditional Highland dress.

Another area of confusion in this section derives from Racinet's use of political and social divisions that no longer exist. The pages on the Ottoman Empire, for example, were originally included by Racinet under the heading of "Turkey". At the time, Turkey's empire (the Ottoman Empire) included much of Greece and the Balkans, and Racinet did not attribute costumes individually to these countries.

Again, Racinet's confidence in his material allows him to give us more wry asides and comments: he considers the Spanish bull-fighter, for example, who thought that bull fighting was a sport for all the family until he was gored to death; and the Billingsgate fish seller, whose cries failed to convince him of the freshness of her produce.

# SCANDINAVIA

### SWEDEN – NORWAY – FINLAND – LAPLAND

SCANDINAVIAN COSTUMES ARE MUCH INFLUENCED by the extremes of temperature over the region. To the north, the hardy Lapps have to dress to cope with the sub-Arctic conditions of the Barents Sea; to the south, the Danes have a temperate summer, but cold winters. Costumes from Sweden, Norway, Finland and Lapland are shown on this and the following pages.

**1.33** A woman merchant from Sodermanland in Sweden, wearing a winter overcoat made of sheepskin and held in place with a belt. Her bonnet is of a traditional design – made of fringed wool, it completely hides her hair.

**1.34 & 36** A family group from Dannemora, in Sweden. This is a mining area, but the group here are free peasants, called *Dannemen*.

The man is wearing a type of frock coat, with broad epaulettes held at the belt to show off the waistcoat. The woman wears a low bodice, laced up at the front, and a quite short, striped skirt. The child's bonnet is cut in the shape of the unmarried woman's traditional bonnet: open at the nape of the neck to let plaits through it.

**1.37** A young woman in summer clothes, having her hair dressed. The hairdresser is arranging her hair in a circular plait that will lie on the top of her head, following the line of the front of her linen bonnet. Her bodice, not yet done up, would normally be made of black silk or velvet and trimmed with broad ribbons.

**1.38 & 39** A peasant couple from Dannemora in their Sunday best. The man's costume is appropriately sombre – his coat and waistcoat are dark, and his trousers are made of dark buckskin.

**2.40** A Lapp in summer dress, wearing a thick smock whose open top hangs down over a belt that supports a woollen purse.

**2.41** A reindeer sledge, the traditional method of transport. The leather bridle is fringed with different coloured pieces of wool, but some bridles are made of red leather and finely embroidered with thin threads of metal.

**3.43 & 44** A couple from Karasjok in the north of Norway in wedding dress. The bride is wearing a coat made from reindeer skin, and the groom a bearskin coat. In fact, bearskins are such a common and essential item of clothing that the people of this region are often known as "white bears".

Here, contrary to the general practice in Europe, it is the bride-groom who wears white. He really does look like a bear, with fur gloves, coat and hat.

**3.45** A woman and child from Swedish Lapland. The child is lying in a cot that has been hung from the roof of her tent. Her blouse is open at the front, showing the edges of her *silfverkrage*: a type of stiff false collar, whose edges are embroidered with metallic thread.

**3.47** A Lapp hunter armed with a large spear.

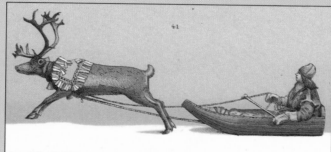

**1.**1 & 2 A Lapp couple from Finland, wearing summer clothes made of wool. The two costumes are similar in style, but vary in details. The man's robe, for example, has a straight collar, while the woman's does not. In both cases, though, bands round the shoulders give the impression of a wide sailor's collar.

The woman is wearing a type of *chatelaine* belt, of a red material embroidered with black designs, from which hang various kitchen utensils. Unusually, both the man and the woman sport white cotton neckerchiefs.

**1.**3 A Lapp woman in her tent, probably making coffee. She is certainly not cooking, because in Lapp society this is a man's task. Women are kept too busy making shoes, gloves, and harnesses and saddles for the reindeer.

**1.**4 & 5 Two Lapp women from Sweden, both wearing *silfverkrages* with gold and silver embroidery. The mother's belt is laden with useful household items.

**2.**1 & 2 A wedding couple from Scania, at the very south of Sweden. The man is wearing a short jacket decorated with embossed silver buttons, placed so close to each other that they form a band, as do his waistcoat buttons.

His trousers and waistcoat are made of wool, and his riding boots of supple black leather. His collar is high, flared and severely starched, and he is carrying a soft felt hat in his hand.

The bride is wearing a number of skirts – at least five – and, unusually, a woollen bodice; normally, this is made of silk. Her belt, though, is made of red silk, and its long ends hang down over a wide white apron.

Her jewellery is somewhat rustic in design. It is made of gilded silver, without any gemstones, and the large, cross-shaped pendant is fashioned from pieces of metal that clash together when she walks.

**2.**3 A peasant in winter clothing. The colour of his outer-garment, made of coarse cloth, can either be black or white, depending on the region from which he comes. He is wearing typical large leather apron, which is held in by a belt. Very much dressed for work, he has a thick, hide coat, lined on the inside with sheepskin, and strong shoes with a double sole.

**2.**4 & 5 A bride and bridesmaid from Buren, in Sweden. Both are wearing stiff-collared blouses with a thin neckerchiefs and chain necklaces. The bride's headdress is traditional in design, and is a sign of virginity; this style is not seen often nowadays.

**3.**1 A Scanian peasant girl at harvest time, wearing a dress called a *hoste sarken*, or "Autumn shirt".

**3.**2 & 3 A farmer and a girl, both dressed, up for an important occasion. The man is wearing a light coloured coat with white buttons embroidered with black wool.

**3.**4 A mother and child in winter clothing. Her headgear is that of a married woman – an embroidered woollen bonnet, trimmed with lace, that entirely hides her hair; in the summer, the same style of bonnet is worn, but it is made of cotton. Unmarried girls show off their hair, and decorate it prettily with brightly coloured ribbons.

**3.**5 A bridegroom with a stove-pipe hat. The collar of his shirt is straight and heavily starched, and his red jacket is lined with white and decorated with buttons.

**1.1** A bride from Trondheim, in Norway, wearing a crown-like headdress made of gilded brass. The Church authorities give these headdresses to brides whose virtue is known to be above suspicion.

The other specifically bridal part of her costume is a beautifully decorated cape. Made of wool, this is attached at the neck and covers the bust. It is decorated with silk and with ribbons laid over broad, patterned lace-work that goes round the neck and serves as the cape's border. The triangular design in its centre has a red base and is almost entirely covered by metalwork, jewellery and coloured stones linked by chains.

The rest of her costume is dark and simple: a long, full skirt, and shoes with silver buckles.

**1. 2 & 3** A wedding couple from Scania, in Sweden. The bride's metalwork embroidery is of traditional design, but the man cuts a rather more dashing figure than is usual, as a result of his adaptation of a horseman's outfit.

His short jacket with epaulettes is similar to Spanish dress of the 16th and 17th centuries; embroidered on its back is a vividly coloured flower.

**1.4 & 5** An engaged couple from Sodermanland, in Sweden. The man is bare-headed, but his hat would have been made of beaver, with broad edges turned up at the end, and would have been decorated with velvet and a silver buckle, set at the front.

His over-garment, made of unbleached linen, is of the type known as a *walmar*. This is a summer coat, and has a small, straight collar of black velvet, but no buttons. He is wearing a knitted waistcoat, narrow trousers and white stockings with leather shoes. The girl's dress is a special engagement costume; it is not the same as the outfit worn for the actual wedding. Her high cotton bonnet is rather like a mitre – it completely covers the top of her head, allowing her hair to fall down her back.

Her blouse has a turned-down collar, bordered with lace, and she is wearing a type of black woollen shawl with sleeves. This covers the bodice, and is attached at the collar by a broad metalwork clip. Her high waistband is fastened on top of her silk apron with another metalwork buckle. A skirt of scarlet wool and buckled leather shoes complete the outfit.

**2.1 & 2** Inhabitants of Dalarne, in the mining district of northern Sweden. This peasant couple are wearing the local wedding costume.

**2.3 & 4** A clockmaking family from Mora wearing work clothes.

**2.5 & 6** A family from Leksands in central Sweden, dressed for church in the traditional costume of the region.

**3.1 & 2** A bridesmaid and a bride from Hardanger, in Norway.

**3.3 & 4** A wedding couple from Satherdalen.

**3.5** A rich peasant from Scania.

# HOLLAND

FISHERFOLK – FRIESIANS – BATAVIANS

THERE ARE SEVERAL DISTINCT GROUPINGS among the working people of Holland, so far as costumes are concerned. First, there are fishing folk, often from coastal islands, whose isolation from centres of population and simple lifestyle mean that styles of dress change very slowly.

Then there are the Friesians, Scandinavian by influence, whose relative isolation leads to a general conservatism. Third, there are the Batavians, from the two islands of Zeeland. These lack the originality that Friesians display in their costume, but they wear clothes of a considerably more modern vintage. Among the men, for example, one sees jackets, waistcoats, narrow trousers and buckled shoes: certainly not part of any traditional costume. The women, too, wear clothes of a modern cut, and adopt fashionable hairstyles.

---

1.1 A bride from Marken, an island that was cut off from the west coast near Amsterdam by a storm in the 13th century. The inhabitants' costume has changed little since that time, and is now unique.

The girl is wearing a fine linen bonnet in the shape of a mitre, bordered at the top with a ribbon of red silk. The sleeves of her blouse, which can be seen between shoulder and elbow, end above the wrist in an embroidered border. The skirt – usually dark blue – covers as many as seven underskirts, worn as a show of wealth.

1.2 & 3 Provincial Friesians, dressed for a festival. The man is wearing a brown serge jerkin and a large pair of breeches in the same material, tied at the knees by knotted ribbons. The woman is wearing a printed calico jerkin, vented at the front, and a damask skirt stretched over rings.

1.5 & 6 The wife of a rich Friesian and her servant. The servant is smartly dressed for market. She has two headscarves: one is white, and is held up under the chin by a gold clip; the second is red, and is knotted at the back like a small shawl. Her headdress is made entirely from lace.

2.1 & 2 Islanders from the Ijsselmeer. As in Marken, isolation has preserved many traditional customs. The man is wearing a type of woollen skullcap, knitted in very tight stitches. He has a dark blue jacket, bordered with red braid, a red waistcoat with silver buttons, generously cut red trousers and clogs.

The woman, dressed in the same style as generations of her ancestors, is here putting braid on the seams of clothes.

2.3 & 4 A peasant and his wife from the Gouda region.

3.1 & 2 A servant and a milkmaid from Rotterdam. As is customary, the milkmaid is wearing a large straw hat with a turned-up brim, large earrings and a pearl necklace.

3.3 & 4 Zeelanders from Walcheren, dressed for an important occasion. Zeelanders are noted for the elegance of their clothes. Here the man is wearing a fine beaverskin hat, and a blue and red chamois leather waistcoat over a shirt, which is closed at the collar by a gold button.

3.4 A fish-seller, from the town of Scheveningen.

1.1 & 2 Two Zeelanders from the Island of Zuid-Beveland. If Walcheren is considered the garden of Zeeland, then Zuid-Beveland is its vegetable patch, its granary and its orchard. This is because the land is so rich in natural fertilizer, having been reclaimed from the sea.

Here the man is shown carrying a spade, as a symbol of the region's abundance. He is wearing a yellow damask waistcoat with a floral pattern and a row of silver buttons. Two gold buttons close his collar, and on the belt of his trousers are two large convex silver buttons, with matching smaller ones, to close his fob.

Above the knees, his trousers are held in place with black straps, clipped tight with silver buckles, and there are also silver buckles on his shoes. In addition to this impressive collection of silverware, he is sporting a silver watch and watch-chain.

In the country regions, peasants wear their hair long over the nape of their necks to form a semicircle over the collar. At the front, it falls low over the forehead. The peasants are very attached to this hairstyle, which they consider a symbol of their freedom.

The lady is dressed for making social calls in her village. Her youth and unmarried status are indicated by the fact that her *hoofdnaald* - a flat piece of metal – is worn diagonally across her forehead, slanting down from left to right. If she was married, it would slant in the opposite direction: from right to left.

Her straw hat is attached over a bonnet that holds her hair in, with only the iron jewellery worn in her hair allowed to show. Her costume consists of a large piece of painted calico, which veils her body from beneath her chin to below her bust. Two more pieces of calico serve as covers for the sleeves of her bodice; they are held above the elbow by gold buttons.

The bodice is made of black damask with a design of white flowers, and is crossed by a silken ribbon, embroidered with silk and floral patterns. Below, a silver clip holds up a wide apron of red check cloth.

1.3 & 4 Two fishermen's wives from the north of Holland, dressed in their best clothes. The lady on the left wears a headdress made from a fine piece of gauze, embroidered with flowers and held in place with a ribbon knotted at the back of the head. The gauze sits on a black skullcap, and is attached by a broad gold clip that ends in two buttons over the ears. The front of the bonnet is attached to each of the buttons by a gold, pearl-headed pin.

The lady on the right wears a much simpler costume, with basic jewellery. Her linen bonnet is turned down over her head and edged at the front with lace. her necklace is made of red coral, and her shoes are simply decorated with a knotted ribbon.

2 & 3 Even though Dutch costumes are now throroughly European, the tradition of wearing iron jewellery in the hair still persists, as these illustrations show. Only the lady in 3.6 is dressed in the traditional style: her arms are bare below the tight, short sleeves; her bodice is held in by a belt and almost entirely covered by a sash; her headgear is tight around the hair, hiding her ears; and she is wearing a high collar made of pearls.

# SCOTLAND

TARTAN AND THE CLANS

THE MOST DISTINCTIVE ELEMENT of traditional Scottish costume is the material from which it is made: tartan. This may have originated as a type of camouflage for use when hunting; certainly it blends in well with the colours of the heather-clad landscape in which the Highlanders live. The tartan pattern is referred to as a *breacen* – possibly a suggestion of the way in which tartan deceives the eye, breaking up visual impressions to enable a huntsman or warrior to escape detection.

The colours used in tartans are not arbitrary, but have been determined by a tradition that allocates different patterns to different clans – originally so that they could be identified in battle. Also by tradition, the various ranks of society are allowed to wear different numbers of colours: one for ordinary clansmen; three for chieftains; and seven for the royal family.

**1.1** A warrior from the clan of MacDougal of Lorne, wearing the traditional kilt and sporran.

**1.2** A Ferguson clansman, the leafy twig on his helmet being the clan emblem. He is wearing a saffron-coloured shirt – this colour is popular in Scotland, especially among gentleman.

**1.3** A warrior from the Macmillan clan, wearing a kilt and brandishing a small claymore with a basket-guard.

**1.4** A MacInnes clansman, armed with an *aseth* – a spear that was thrown at the enemy, then retrieved by means of the strap to which it is attached. He is wearing a fur jacket and a mail coat that covers his flannel coat.

**1.5** A piper from the clan Mac-Cruimin, wearing the traditional bonnet that carries the clan's symbol. The piper was an important figure in the royal household. He is dressed accordingly, in a fur baldric and laced buckskin boots, and is carrying a small claymore.

**1.6** The laird of MacDonald of the Isles and one of his barons, hold-ing audience on the *tom moid*, or "mount of law". His helmet is decorated with a circle of precious stones and surmounted by an eagle's wing, the chieftain's insignia. His mail coat goes almost down to his knees over a leather doublet and his arms and legs carry the MacDonald clan colours.

**1.8** An archer from the Maclaurin clan, wearing a conical helmet and a silk doublet underneath a coat of chain mail.

**1.12** An archer of the MacQuaaries clan, wearing a doublet that has been slashed at the shoulders.

**2.14** A laird of the Skenes clan, dressed in the style of the time of James VI of Scotland (later James I of England). His doublet is decorated with braid in the Spanish manner – a fashion that persisted in the Highlands long after it had died out elsewhere.

**2.16** A Scottish gentleman of the Robertson clan, who lived at the Court of Louis XV, managing to successfully blend French influences with Scottish plaid.

**2.19** A gentleman of the Macintosh clan, dressed for the court in a lavishly embroidered velvet coat.

1.27 A Highland gentleman of the Ogilvie clan, wearing white plaid – fashionable in 1745 – over a doublet.

1.28 A Davidson clansman, wearing his plaid as a hood. This was a popular style in the inhospitable weather of the Western Highlands.

1.29 Charles Edward Stuart – "Bonnie Prince Charlie", figurehead of the '45 rebellion – wearing the Stuart tartan and carrying a velvet bonnet with a white rosette.

1.30 A Buchanan clansman, wearing a small flat bonnet that carries the clan's emblem of a tuft of leaves.

1.31 William, Duke of Sutherland, who raised a regiment in 1759. He is wearing the regimental costume.

1.32 A shepherd of the Macmachtans clan, turning his head into the wind. His flat bonnet is is tipped forward to shield his face.

1.33 An 18th-century costume of the clan Macintyre, which shows that despite the Prohibition Act of 1746 the Highlanders managed to preserve their traditional dress.

2.2 A lady from the Sinclair clan, wearing a blue skirt made from mixture of wool and cotton, and a long scarf in the clan tartan that covers her head. At one time it was the custom to pin this scarf to the chest with a brooch made from silver, bronze or copper.

Going barefoot, as this lady does, is a common practice in the Highlands, and should not be taken as a mark of poverty.

2.4 A Colquhoun clansman of the 18th century, with a flat cap that carries the clan's emblem. His tunic is decorated with brass buttons and his full-length plaid is worn crossed over at the chest and attached at the shoulder by a silver brooch. His trousers, or trews, carry the same tartan as the plaid.

2.6 A dairymaid from the MacNicol clan, wearing a *tonag* – a square of tartan worn as a small shawl. The silver brooch used to hold this in place is usually a treasured family heirloom, handed down from generation to generation.

2.11 A Farquharson warrior after the Battle of Culloden in 1746, wrapped in a large plaid and carrying a large, hatchet-tipped pike.

3.13 An Urquhart clanswoman draped in an *arisaid* – a large plaid of sufficient size to cover the wearer from head to toe. Her hair is worn in plaits.

3.15 A woman and child of the Matheson clan. The woman is wearing a striped yellow *arisaid*, held at the chest by a large brooch and gathered at the waist by a belt, whose end dangles down over the plaid.

The bodice is made of scarlet material, embroidered with silver and decorated with buttons set with precious stones.

3.17 A horseman from the MacNeil clan, wearing trews. His jacket is held tightly at the waist by a belt, and needles made from deer bones keep his flat cap turned up and hold its plant badge in place.

# ENGLAND

## THE UNIFORM OF THE INDIVIDUAL

ENGLISH TRADITIONAL COSTUMES tend to vary according to the trade and occupation of the wearer. Indeed, it was often possible to tell a man's or a woman's occupation at a glance by the style of their clothes. Fishermen, onion sellers, shoe-blacks and judges all had distinctive costumes, and were fiercely protective of their right to wear them. As a result, the English streets were a riot of individualism, with the harsh cries of the street sellers and a wealth of variety in costume. These illustrations are mainly taken from the end of the 18th century and the early 19th century.

**1.1** An almanac seller.

**1.2** A street hawker, who collects fat from kitchens makes candles.

**1.3** An old woman, carrying a barrel of black pudding.

**1.4** A quack, selling elixirs that are guaranteed to cure illness and revive the spirits.

**1.5** An onion seller.

**2.6 & 7** Draymen, who drive brewers' carts, called "drays". This job requires a good deal of brute strength, and draymen are doughty characters whose constitution is under constant assault from the hospitality offered by grateful customers.

**2.8** A waterman at a coach stand. His job is to water and feed the horses during a short coach stop, and to open the coach doors for passengers.

**2.9** John Clancey, an Irish sailor who was shipwrecked off the coast of America and lost his legs through frostbite. He lived off public charity, and became a well-known London character.

**2.10** A cattle drover, who drives the cattle to market.

**2.11** A fish seller.

**2.12** A postman.

**2.16** Henry Thrale, a shoe-black who worked in the Strand.

**2.18** A chief fireman, wearing a uniform that denotes his membership of an organization set up in the days of Queen Anne, and with a metal badge of rank of his arm.

**2.19** An agricultural labourer from the outskirts of London, wearing a smock of simple, unbleached linen, which has a slit in the side to facilitate movement.

**3.2** A milkmaid, carrying her heavy load in tin pails supported by a wooden yolk.

**3.3** A fireman, differently dressed from the chief fireman above. This man is wearing a helmet made from thick, black leather and decorated with metal bands. He is dressed in blue, and carries an axe.

**3.4** A match seller.

**3.5** A newspaper seller. When there is important news, these men announce the fact by blowing loudly on a metal horn; a taste of the news is written on a placard attached on the hat.

**3.6** A watchman, who would walk his beat every half-hour, calling out the time.

———— • ————

**1.1** A barrow woman, probably selling fruit.

**1.2** A young woman selling shrimps, and carrying the net in which they are caught.

**1.3** A fish seller at Billingsgate Market, at which, according to the ancient rules, all fish coming into the City of London has to be sold. Unfortunately, women such as this are unlikely to be able to afford the best fish, and the cries of "best fish here" are usually lies.

**1.4** A baker. Bakers are the only tradesmen whose profits were limited by law.

**1.5** Washerwomen. These women line the river bank and wash their laundry by beating it when wet with a wooden spatula, then soaping, rinsing and beating again.

**2.1** A London alderman, wearing his official costume of a scarlet robe bordered with fur. Originally, an alderman was the senior magistrate of a county. Later the title came to denote a municipal magistrate. In London, there are 26 aldermen - one for each Ward.

**2.2** A lady in the style of summer dress that was all the rage in 1814. Such clothes would have been worn for a morning promenade in London or one of the seaside resorts.

**2.3** A judge, wearing a red robe trimmed with ermine.

**2.4** A bishop, as he would dress for the House of Lords.

**2.5** A Chelsea Pensioner from the Chelsea Hospital for old soldiers. Building of the hospital started under Charles II and was finished by Queen Mary. The uniform consists of a red tunic with a blue jacket and trousers.

**2.6** A Greenwich Pensioner. The Royal Hospital at Greenwich was founded by King William in 1639 as a refuge for old and crippled sailors. Both the ordinary pensioners and the officers wear red, but the latter are also allowed a thin gold stripe.

**3.7** A dustman. At this time, dustmen were employed by entrepreneurs who purchased the right to collect ashes.

**3.8** A fisherman from Hastings, whose shirt and small hat recall the dress of Normandy fisherman.

**3.9** A church beadle, whose principal duty is to ensure that no misdemeanours are committed in the vicinity of the church and to check that every inn-keeper keeps his doors shut during services.

**3.10** A pupil of Christchurch Hospital, the "bluejacket" school.

**3.11** The Speaker of the House of Commons. When the House is sitting, the Speaker wears a long wig and a black robe.

**3.12** The Lord Mayor of London.

# GERMANY

FRANCONIANS AND BAVARIANS

THE LAND THAT WE KNOW AS BAVARIA contains a variety of different people. Strictly speaking, the real Bavarians inhabit the south-eastern region up to the great River Lech; beyond it are the Serbs. The Franconians, who are mixed descendants of the Franks, occupy northern Bavaria and are noted for their grace and the elegance of their costume. The people of southern Bavaria are more influenced by their near neighbours, the Italians.

In the regions of Bavaria where the population is divided between the two main religions, the Catholics and Protestants can be told apart by their costume. In general the former prefer bright colours, while the latter opt for colours that are darker.

A Catholic's hat will be decorated with yellow and green ribbons; the Protestant's with black. Young Catholic peasants still tend to wear red jackets, which the Protestant now consider to be unfashionable.

Women's hats and headdresses, however, do not vary according to religious belief. The *pelzkappe*, for example, a round cap of otter-skin, decorated with a little piece of embroidered material (**1.7**) has been worn by German women for many years.

Another type of headdress consists of a small bonnet with a curved base, fastened by straps under the chin (**1.1 & 17** and **2.25**). A variation of this is the Phrygian bonnet, either with wings (**1.2 & 16**) or simply decorated with ribbons (**1.11**).

The women in **1.4** and **2.24** have both framed their faces with a pieces of material, but have tied them differently on their foreheads. The lady in **1.9** is wearing a bonnet that sticks out at the front of the head; similar types of bonnet, in **2.22 & 23**, have visors made from tulle.

The Serbian woman's bonnet in **1.14** is also similar but for the crown, which is made of em

broidered silk rather than cloth. Some women from southern Bavaria wear a piece of dark material on their heads that they turn into a type of bonnet, as in **2.20**.

Beneath their chemises, which have half-length sleeves, Bavarian women wear corsets – generally with a V-neckline. These are worn with fichus made from printed cotton, normally with a red background and a flowered pattern.

On feast days, these are replaced by finely embroidered white handkerchiefs (**2.22 & 23**). Fichus can either be knotted tightly or loosely at the nape of the neck (**1.4, 7, &** **17** and **2.20, 24 & 25**).

Jackets are brightly coloured with padded, puffed sleeves. Dresses are tightly pleated and normally mid-calf length. Again they tend to be brightly coloured, as are the aprons: bright red, carmine, green and blue being popular. On feast days silk aprons are worn, decorated with lace and ribbons.

Normally peasants dress simply in a jacket without cut or tails, but on Sundays they wear a dark blue morning-coat with an upright collar and silver buttons. The waistcoat, which is normally bright red, is decorated with coloured silk in between the metal buttons.

In fact, the metal buttons are coins and on a night of revelry will be cut off the morning coat or waistcoat as payment. Many men now wear trousers, though there are some who still adhere to the traditional *lederhosen*.

## THE TYROL

LIKE BAVARIA, THE TYROL CONTAINS many different types of people. In the east, the population consist of Germans and Slavs, while in the west it is made up of Germans and Latins. The beauty of the Tyrolians' mountain environment, their appealing costume, their hunting skills and their songs and traditions all combine to charm and delight visitors to the region.

———— • ————

**1.1** A mountain dweller from Zillerthal. His hat is made of black felt with a wide brim lined with silk, and is decorated with a plume of wild cock feathers. He is wearing a *brutsfleck*, a bright red waistcoat, trimmed round the neck with silver braid, as well as *lederhosen* and white stockings.

**1.2** A young German girl from Auherzen in summer clothes, with long plaits tied with white ribbons. A thick petticoat made of hay makes her woollen skirt stick out.

**1,3 & 4** Women from the Black Forest. Their large and remarkable headdress consists of a black silk bonnet, the top of which is made from velvet, decorated with metal objects. A semi-circular plume fixed on an iron frame rises above the head and four wide black ribbons, attached to the velvet, fall down the back, leaving spaces wide enough to reveal long plaits tied with red ribbons.

**1.5** A student from Heidelberg, who cultivates a typically romantic appearance with long hair and a huge porcelain pipe.

**1.6** A woman wearing a broad-brimmed felt hat and a laced bodice with braces.

**1.7** A peasant dressed for a feast day, in morning coat and a felt hat.

**1.8** A woman wearing a white chemise attached to braces. Her woollen corselet is fastened with silver hooks and silk laces.

**1.9** A young German from Kladau, whose felt hat is decorated with flowers and a ribbon with black silk tassels.

**1.10** A woman from Darmstadt, with a headdress whose ribbons frame the face and fall down over the chest and back.

**1.11** A peasant from the Inn valley. A road runs through this valley, and the influences it has brought have added woollen trousers and a fitted coat to the traditional costume.

**2.12** A young Wend girl wearing a skirt with sewn-in pleats. A Catholic, therefore: Protestants wear skirts without sewn-in pleats.

**2.13** A fruit-seller from Hamburg wearing an Indian bonnet.

**2.14 & 17** Women from Saxe-Altenbourg, who generally wear dark colours with bright decoration.

**2.15** A peasant from Oetzhal wearing a remarkable hat with a bell-shaped rim. His *joppe*, or jacket, is made of dark brown cloth.

**2.16** A peasant from Passeyer wearing a cotton headdress and a *niederleibel*. This is a jacket of violet cloth, trimmed at the neck and cuffs with crimson silk and fastened at the front with coloured ribbons and a silver buttons.

**2.18** A young girl from Coburg with a small cap on her head, decorated with glass beads. Her chemise has puffed sleeves and her skirt is tightly pleated.

**2.19** A young peasant from Sarnthal in feast day costume. His *joppe* and his *brustfleck* are made of bright red cloth and his damask braces are bright green. His garters, worn over white stockings, are also bright red.

# SWITZERLAND

BRIGHT COLOURS AND RIBBONS

IN THE EARLY PART OF THE 19TH CENTURY, clothes were bright and gay throughout Switzerland. This is not surprising, because the Swiss have always loved to dress in bright colours. There is always something jolly and blooming about their style of dress.

———— • ————

**1.1** A woman from the canton of Lucerne, wearing a costume that can only be described as coquettish against a background of tranquil countryside: a straw hat; a chemise fastened tightly at the throat with three-quarter length sleeves (showing some bare arm is traditional among women from every canton); an embroidered bodice; and a pleated skirt that stops at the knee, revealing white stockings.

**1.2** and **2.**1 & 3 Women from the canton of Friburg. Nearly all the women have the same coiffure: they plait their hair and wear big straw hats decorated with lace.

The first figure is from the French community, while the other two figures are from the German part of the canton. These wear ribbons around their necks, from which hang small purses of a type called an *Agnus Dei*.

**1.**3 & 4 Peasants from the canton of Zug in their Sunday best. Sundays and feast days give these peasants the opportunity to dress up in brightly coloured costumes.

The man's ballooning *chausses* are reminiscent of of the costume of Henri IV, while his pleated chemise is from Louis XIV's era.

Young girls wear hats highly decorated with ribbons and flowers, and short tight skirts of blue or green material, normally with red tights.

**1.5** and **2.5** Married women from the canton of Bern. The top figure has a chemise with leg-of-mutton sleeves and a black satin cap. Her hair is plaited and twisted on the top of her head – by convention, unmarried women wore their plaits long.

The other woman is a milkmaid from the valleys. She is wearing a velvet cap and a large apron over a long, brightly coloured skirt.

**1.6** A peasant from the canton of Schwitz, wearing a frogged jacket and an open waistcoat.

**2.2** A young girl from the canton of Schaffouse, wearing a short-sleeved chemise, a laced corsage and a short skirt.

**2.4** A young girl from Valais, wearing a straw hat with a curved brim. A fichu covers her shoulders and chest and the sleeves of her corsage are decorated with lace. Her skirt is short and her apron made of silk.

**3.1** A woman from the canton of Bern. *For fuller details see p266.*

**3.**2 & 6 Women from the canton of Appenzell. Their pretty and original headdresses of black gauze look like butterfly wings rising above their heads.

**3.3** A bride from the canton of Friburg. This girl is from the German part of the canton, where the old traditions are better preserved than in the French sector.

**3.4** A woman from the canton of Lucerne, wearing a black velvet bodice with a plastron – a pleated chemise that covers the upper chest – an open blouse with loose sleeves and a ruched bonnet.

# REGIONAL VARIATIONS

SWISS TRADITIONAL COSTUMES OFTEN DIFFER from region to region. Generally they are duller and darker coloured in flat land and brighter and more jolly in high country. But costume does not just reflect the character of a region: it also has an influence on regional customs and behaviour.

— • —

1.2 & 4, and p264 3.1 Costumes from the canton of Bern. Nowadays, as in many other European countries, the traditional costume is only worn as a matter of course by servants and peasants.

Most women follow foreign fashion, particularly that of the French – as can be seen from the illustration here of a servant carrying a basket.

The example on the previous page is square-cut. The breast and throat are covered by a white pleated chemise with leg-of-mutton sleeves and there is a velvet cravat around the neck. Silver chains attached to the corners of this cravat hang down each side of the bodice and run to the belt.

1.4 A different headdress from that in the first two examples. Here it consists of a pretty cap with a tuft of red material at the top.

1.1 & 3 Women from the cantons of Uri and Unterwalden. The costume is a full skirt of brown material, a red belt and blue stockings and elegant shoes.

A distinctive feature is a wide, high plastron, crossed over by a fine chain with filigree pendants hanging from both sides. There are signs of Italian influence here, especially in the fichu under the laced bodice.

2.1 A woman from Underwalden, wearing a closed bodice and a cravat. The bodice is made of black material at the back and different colours of material, such as red and green, at the front.

2.2 A woman from Saint-Gall.

2.2 and 3.3 Women from the canton of Bern. The first illustration shows a young girl from Simmenthal, with a closed Italian-style bodice made of black velvet and trimmed with a wide strip of velvet.

A white chemise reaches up to the throat and a fichu is tucked into the bodice. The sleeves are puffed to the elbow, then run tightly along the forearm. The skirt is black, trimmed with colour and worn under an apron.

2.4 A woman from the canton of Valais, which, according to Rousseau, boasts some of the most beautiful women in Switzerland. The costume is primarily French, the only article of traditional costume that remains being the hat.

2.5 A woman from the canton of Zurich.

3.1 A girl from the canton of Zug. This agricultural canton is the smallest and one of the most charming in Switzerland. The girls love to borrow ideas for their costume from the flowers of the fields. Here, the collar of the girl's chemise is frilled like an ox-eye daisy, and her apron is the colour of the blueberry; a corolla has inspired her hat.

3.3 A woman from the canton of Lucerne. Some say that Swiss costume attains near perfection here, with its calf-length skirt showing red stockings. The simply cut bodice is often decorated with a profusion of ornaments.

3.4 A woman from Little Basel. There is a sad, sombre atmosphere here, and this is reflected in the neat, severe costume.

# RUSSIA

## SLAVS AND MONGOLIANS

NO EMPIRE IN THE WORLD CAN BOAST such a diversity of races as that of Russia, and, naturally, this variety is evident in the costumes. Without documentary evidence we cannot be sure what was worn in ancient times, but it appears that the mainly Slavic population, along with the Finnish and Mongolian elements, followed the general traditions of their race, with certain changes due to the different weather conditions in this vast country.

Russia did not just take religion from Byzantium, but an entire civilization. The Byzantine costume was first adopted by court circles and gradually spread to all the upper echelons of society.

From the original, relatively short clothing that was open from the belt down, male costume changed to the long, closed Byzantine robe, with borders made from strips of coloured material. Even more than men, women hastened to follow the new fashion, until interrupted in the 13th century by the Mongolian invasion.

The closed robe was then replaced by the Mongolian robe. This was buttoned over the chest, but then allowed to hang open. It stayed in fashion until the reign of Peter the Great, and even longer than that in certain regions.

In the 16th century, male clothing consisted of a basic wide, short shirt with a small collar – a triangular piece of red, embroidered silk was sewn in between the shoulders. Large trousers were gathered in at the waist and tucked into knee-length boots. Over this went a narrow coat, called a caftan, which was not normally longer than the knees but had long sleeves.

Next came a *ferez* which, like a caftan, could be cut in a variety of ways. For outdoors an overcoat was also worn, made of woollen cloth, velvet and satin.

Women's costume was very similar to men's, except that it was larger. Women never wore the caftan, however, but they did wear large bonnets made from satin or damask. Married women put their hair up on the tops of their heads while young girls let it tumble down over their foreheads and plaited it down their backs.

Four examples of this type of costume are shows here:

**1. 2 & 5** Two views of a cossack wearing an open-sleeved caftan.

**3.1** Boris Godounov, attired in a type of short smock or demi-caftan over which is a *ferez*.

**3.8** Tsar Ivan IV wearing either a caftan or a *ferez*.

The finery of the clothes shown opposite is due to the fact that they are worn on feast days.

**2.1, 3, 4 & 8** Women wearing the *sarafan*. This headdress is a type of metal diadem, decorated with stones or glass and fixed on a bonnet called a *volosnik*.

**2.4 & 6** and **3.2 & 4** Married women from Torjok, all wearing a pointed headdress called a *kokoschnik* (literally, "a cock's comb").

**2.7 & 8** Young unmarried girls from Torjok, wearing a variation of the *kokoschnik*.

**3.2 & 4** Winter costume as worn in Torjok. The fichu is made from white taffeta fringed with golden material which covers a *kokoschnik*.

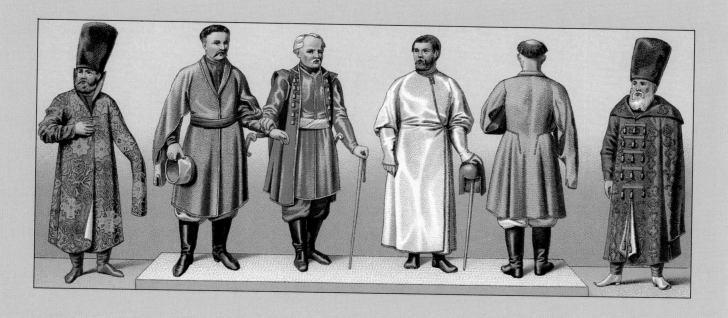

1.1 Peter the Great, Tsar of Russia from 1682 to 1725, wearing a sailor's costume while *incognito* in Holland to study boat construction. The material is a coarse woollen cloth lined with taffeta.

1.2 A young upper-class girl from the the time of Peter the Great. She is wearing a long *sarafan* of white silk, embroidered round the edges and down the front, with silk-covered buttons. Her belt is also made of white silk and is embroidered with flowers.

1.3 This prince's caftan is made of velvet and his cloak is made of blue satin with a zibeline lining. He has a red silk belt and a hat trimmed with fur.

1.4 Peter the Great wearing a Polish-style caftan, so called because of its vertical opening down the front. The Russian caftan was normally fastened obliquely across the chest.

1.5 Prince Pierre Repnine in a dark pink smock decorated with pearls. Over it he is wearing a *ferez* lined with green silk. The stiff upright collar attached to this, called a *kozir*, is richly decorated.

1.6 This *boiar narischkine* is wearing a caftan made from Persian material, gathered in at the waist by a belt of the same provenance. His *pelisse* is lined with black zibeline.

2 & 3 Women from Torjok. The standard item of dress is a straight garment gathered in with a belt of Asiatic origin. It is sleeveless, so the sleeves of the under-garment, called a *braverie*, can be seen.

De Rechberg says that in general the long dress, with an opening at the front, is fastened with metal buttons. He also says that the wives of the better-off shopkeepers and peasants wear a type of short cloak and a bonnet called a *tche-petz*, with silver and gold embroidery and sometimes decoration of lace or a skein of fine pearls.

Torjuk is essentially an agricultural region. The peasants wear short clothes made from coarse cloth. 2.4 is an exception, as she is wearing a loose-fitting, sleeveless robe gathered in at the waist.

These peasants had to wear many layers of clothing as well as extremely thick stockings and large shoes to ward off the cold. Far from hiding these rather ungainly items, though, the ladies in 2.1 & 3 have relatively high hemlines.

2.2 A Tartar woman, whose costume is strikingly different from those described above. Both her over- and under-garments are made from striped silk. The former, a type of enveloping veil, is slashed so that the embroidered sleeves of the under-garment can pass through. Tartars wear baggy pantaloons. Poor women would wear the same type of clothes as in our example, but they would be made from nankeen rather than silk.

3.1 An unusual costume, perhaps a wedding outfit. According to one source, the large transparent veil, embroidered with small flowers and edged with silk, is a worn as a protection against the mosquitoes.

3.2, 4 & 5 Working women, wearing large aprons with the tops of their bonnets covered with a pieces of material that are wrapped around their neck. Even the little boy in his mother's arms is wearing this headgear. The short cloaks are sometimes worn without sleeves with just an opening for the arms (2) or with sleeves that are the same length as the garment itself (5). More usually, (4), they do not have sleeves at all and resemble capes.

## SLAVES AND SIBERIANS

THESE HEADDRESSES ALL BELONG TO RUSSIAN SLAVES. They are borrowed from the costumes of European dignitaries and show variations of the *tschepatz*, the bonnet worn by the wives of peasants and tradesmen. The primitive styles of headdress are likely to be the most ancient; such decorations can be found in the portraits of rulers as far back as the Middle Ages.

———— • ————

**1.3** and **2.2** Hats richly decorated with rubies, topazes, sapphires and large pearls. The first differs from the second in that the red crown of the *tschepatz* has coloured ornaments sewn into it, as well as having fluting over the forehead like **1.1**.

**1.2** A girl from Bielozersk.

**2.1** The crown of this bonnet is made from woven cloth. It is decorated with silver filigree and beads in the shape of rosettes. The trimming over the forehead is also made of beads. The collar of the chemise is decorated with *piqué* and fastened with a sapphire. The earrings are beads, fashioned to look like bunches of grapes mounted on gold.

**2.3** A hat of the same character, but placed more upright on the head and down over the forehead, with a fringe of beads. It has a very Asiatic appearance and is decorated with silver leaves. The necklace is made from rows of beads.

**2.2** A woman from Oustioug-Jele-zepolski, in the Novgorod region.

**3** Siberians, from the lower regions of the Irtich and the Obi in the provinces of Tobolsk, Berezov and Sourghout. Their clothes are made from animal skins.

Men wear a leather garment that just about reaches to the knees and fastens both at the back and front. In very cold weather a second, larger garment is added. This has a hood that keeps the head and neck warm and small bags attached to the ends of the sleeves to serve as gloves. In **3.2 & 3** the hood and over-garment are made of wool.

Siberian women, who bear the burden of all the domestic tasks and are often treated like slaves, wear clothes made of fur. These have openings down the front and are fastened with belts. In winter they wear leather leggings and a hooded garment.

**3.1** A Koloche, or Hinkite – an Indian from Alaska sold to the Russians by the Americans in 1867 and since then known as the "Russian American". His cloak is made of leather with *appliqué* and is fringed with strips of the same material as his apron. These skins are so well treated that they look like velvet.

The light, almost transparent shirt is impermeable to water, being made from the intestines of sea animals. The legs and feet are covered with material that is also impermeable, made from seals' gullets.

**3.4 & 5** The former is a Toungouse from the town of Nertchinsk and the latter is a Toungouse nomad. The Toungouses are a different race from the Tartars and Mongolians, having originated in Manchuria and spread out through China and Russia.

The nomad is dressed from head to foot in leather on to which decorations have been sewn, such as pieces of metal. The town-dweller wears a hat made from woollen cloth and fur. His over-garment is made from woollen cloth lined with fur and decorated with designs in braid.

# POLAND

NOBLES AND PEASANTS

THE BASIS OF POLISH NATIONAL COSTUME is an over-garment with slashed sleeves called a *kontousch*. This garment first arrived in Poland from the Persia towards the end of the 15th century, though it was not frequently seen until the end of the 16th century. By then it had been more widely adopted among the nobility and also by the the bourgeoisie, but the original style had been modified in accordance with Polish taste.

The *kontousch* was put on over an under-garment called a *joupane*, and had a neckline low enough to show the latter, with its row of six buttons. It crossed over slightly at the belt and was smooth at the front, while at the back there were large pleats from the waist down.

The sleeves were wide from the shoulder to the elbow and then narrowed towards the wrist, being slashed their whole length at the front to show some of the sleeve of the *joupane*. The arms could easily be slipped out of the sleeves, which could either hang down at the sides (**1.4**) or be thrown back over the shoulders (**1.6**).

Sometimes the *kontousch* was buttoned up to the neck (**1.2**) and it had gold and silver frogs as well as buttons. It was trimmed with material in the same colour as the garment itself or with gold or silver. The lining of was always the same colour as the *joupane*. The collar was sometimes upright and sometimes folded flat around the neckline (**1.4**).

The Polish nobility never wore anything other than bonnets on their heads. Either these were made entirely of fur, or decorated with pieces of fur to give the same effect. In the early years of the reign of the last sovereign the *konfederatka* appeared. This was made from four rectangular pieces of material, which enlarged almost imperceptibly towards the square crown (**1.6**).

The *konfederatka* is often confused with the *krakouska* (**1.5**). This is also square, but it is flat and is only worn by peasants, being particularly popular in the neighbourhood of Krakow, from which it derives its name.

**2** Polish women tend to follow foreign fashions and adhere less than men to their national costume. However, the 17th century saw the revival of the old *amicula*, shown on Trajan's Column. This was a fairly short overcoat, trimmed with fur (**1.3**).

Women also wear an over-garment similar to the *kontousch* called a *kontusik*. This has slashed sleeves and is nearly always trimmed with fur as in **2.1**.

**3.** A great soldier. His bonnet, or *kolpak*, is made entirely of fur and is decorated with a plume. He is wearing a white *joupane* and a brocade *kontousch* buttoned up to the neck. His large cloak, lined with fur, is called a *deliura*.

The traditional peasant's costume consisted of short tunics, long trousers, a long overcoat or cloak made of sheepskin, and boots or shoes made from woven strips of bark. Peasants' hats were either conical with narrow brims or round with low crowns.

This style persisted until the end of the 15th century. Towards the end of the 18th century, however, regional differences began to grow, though what is thought of as the national costume contains references to the majority of these variations.

## MILITARY COSTUMES

DURING THE EARLY YEARS OF EXISTENCE Poland did not have a regular army and the sole defenders of the country were groups of mounted noblemen. Boleslas the Great organised the first national force by forming an army of horsemen of between 150,000 and 200,000 men. However, the permanent regular army only dates back to 1562, in the reign of Sigismond-Auguste. He ruled that one quarter of the royal revenue should be set aside for the maintenance of a regular defence force. As a result, it was known as the *woysko-kwarciane* or "quarter army". Traditional Polish military costume has been strongly influenced both by the use of foreign troops and by the Asiatic origina of many of Poland's enemies.

———— • ————

The regular army was never very large, even during the periods when Poland flourished. Etienne Batory fought his campaign against the Russians with only 40,000 men, and Charles Chodkiewicz did not have many more for his Chocim expedition. When Sobieski assembled the European army under the walls of Vienna, he had only 30,000 Poles.

Under Sobieski, the military school financed by the kings of Poland consisted of 600 foot soldiers, 600 cavalry and 200-strong regiment of infantry.

At the siege of Vienna, Sobieski's entourage were astonished to see another Christian king advancing towards them with a similar escort. Sobieski was worried that his janissaries would refuse to fight their fellow countryman, so suggested that they avoid this duty by attacking the rear of the enemy formation. To a man, the janissaries stood by their Polish king.

The continual wars against the Tartars and the Turks meant that Poland was always in contact with the Asiatic world, and it is not surprising that their influence is evident in all traditional military costumes. The cavalry was recruited from the nobility, as is apparent from their fine costumes and beautiful horses.

1.1 A *billiepassi*, a captain commanding the musketeers of the king's guard, wearing a plumed hat, a *kontousch* and a *joupane*. He is carrying an officer's baton.

1.2 A Polish general wearing a fur *kolpak* decorated with golden brooches, and a gold-decorated cuirass. He has a large cloak lined with fur, called a *deliura*, and is armed with a short, wide-bladed sword. The commander's baton was not used in battle; instead the general would be accompanied by a rider brandishing a lance with a horse's tail tied to it. This was known as a *boutschouk*.

1.3 An *ottopasch porrutschnik*, a lieutenant of the janissaries in the king's guard, wearing a headdress like a turban.

2.1 A *jeschemek*, a corporal of the janissaries. He is wearing a *kulah* – a high felt bonnet decorated with an immense plume – a Turkish jacket and baggy breeches.

2.2 A *jeschemek*, clasping a type of halberd that has a curved blade and a small flag blowing in the wind.

2.3 A *wartapssi-consqui*, the flag-bearer of the janissaries.

2.4 A janissary of the guard in front of the king's palace.

2.5 A *beuraktar-courougi*, an ensign-bearer of the janissaries, wearing a turban adorned with a plume. His belt, worn over a *kontousch*, is made of cord, and he is carrying an axe – always a popular weapon in the Polish army.

## BUTTONS AND BOOTS

IN THE 16TH CENTURY, the under-garment and the *joupane* worn by Polish nobles were of variable lengths. Their buttons were generally made from gold or silver, and either decorated with small precious stones or enamelled. Sometimes the buttons were made of silk or braid, but the most expensive types were fashioned from precious stones and given the appearance of small dog roses. Quite often the *joupane* was fastened by frogs made of silk, gold or silver, and sometimes the buttons were replaced by small hooks hidden under the edges of the clothes.

———— • ————

Trousers were very loose-fitting, though not as baggy as Oriental pantaloons, and were made of satin or damask, the most popular colour being blue or lilac. The lesser nobility made do with cloth.

Trousers were tucked into boots and allowed to hang down a few inches over the boot-tops. Indoors, nobleman wore boots made of black leather. In public, however, boots were always either red or yellow – only one colour was allowed, and the decorations shown on **2**.1, 3 & 5 are incorrect.

Heels were reinforced with iron and sometimes even with silver. This was partly done to increase wear, and partly so that they made a sharp clicking sound when dancing the *mazurka*, the national dance.

The overcoat worn by the man in **1**.7 and by King Batory in **2**.1 is a sleeveless fur-lined garment called a *chouba*. Another type of *chouba*, worn tight at the waist, can be seen in **2**.5. The coat shown in **2**.3 is of yet another type, called a *déelia*. All these fur-lined coats are kept for formal occasions.

Two types of a garment of Hungarian origin, known as a *bekiécha* and introduced into Poland during the reign of Etienne Batory, are shown in **1**.3 & 4. The *bekiécha* narrowed a little more at the waist and was a few inches longer than the *joupane*. It was either fastened across the chest by means of silk frogs or by pieces of gold and silver passed through silken loops.

In the 16th century and later, a gentleman rarely went out without carrying an *oboukh*. This was a cane with a pear-shaped metal ferrule at the top and a steel tip at the bottom. One half of this tip was like a hammer and the other like a falcon's beak or an axe head. Though it was carried for show it could, if necessary, be an effective weapon.

**1**.1 & 2 Lithuanian peasants.

**1**.3, 4 & 5 Noblemen in the last quarter of the 16th century.

**1**.6 A peasant from the neighbourhood of Kalisz.

**1**.7 A gentleman at the end of the 16th century.

**2**.1 Etienne Batory, King of Poland (1576–1568), from a portrait of the period.

**2**.2 An alderman from the town of Kazimierz in the 16th century.

**2**.3 Stanislas Zolkiewski (1547–1620) from a portrait of the period.

**2**.4 The daughter of a great lord.

**2**.5 Roman Sanguszko, Marshal of the Lithuanian camp, from a 16th-century portrait.

# HUNGARY & CROATIA

## MAGYARS – SLOVAKS – RUMANIANS – CROATIANS

HUNGARY AND CROATIA ARE POPULATED by several races, each with their own distinct customs and languages. The Magyars, or Hungarians, live mostly near the Danube, while Saxons of German descent live in Transylvania with the Magyars and Rumanians. Slovaks, the main group of Slavs, are scattered throughout Hungary and Croatia, along with a smaller group of Slavs called Ruthenians. Poles live between Galicia and Silesia, and Rumanians – a mixture of Valaks and Moldavians – occupy the Danube Valley and Transylvanian Alps. The Croatians, the most isolated of the peoples of Hungary and Croatia, live in the hills.

——— • ———

1.1 A Ruthenian girl with a cap cocked jauntily on the side of her head. An embroidered leather jacket, fronted with fur, covers a close-fitting skirt and leather boots.

1.2 A Polish girl from Krakow, wearing a low, square peasant cap called a *Krakouska*. Her necklace, made of coral and coins, rests on a high-necked blouse and a small embroidered apron covers her skirt.

1.3 A Saxon girl in her wedding dress. Her sheepskin coat has been painstakingly embroidered; her headdress of black velvet is attached to long, multi-coloured ribbons behind.

1.4 A Croatian wearing a black felt hat with yellow border. His long white jacket is embroidered with gold thread.

1.5 A typical long-haired Ruthenian peasant from Marmaros.

1.6 A young Valak girl from Orsova with a headband.

1.7 A Ruthenian woman with a typical tall headdress, embroidered at the front with a knot of ribbons.

1.9 A Slovak with a small hat covered in ribbons, feathers and flowers. The cut of his trousers is characteristic of Hungarian costume.

2.10 A young Kaposvar Magyar sporting a felt hat topped with ribbons and fresh flowers – obviously dressed for a festival.

2,11 A Banat woman, whose long hair falls from beneath an embroidered cap on to a vest that resembles a breast-plate, but has intricate, swirling designs.

2.12 A girl from Neutraer, wearing a lace-trimmed bonnet with a ribbon tied at its side.

2.13 A girl in Bekeser costume, with her hair plaited with ribbons and wearing a coral necklace.

2.14 A nobleman wearing a velvet and sable hat – a *kucsma* – set off by an eagle-feather brooch.

2.15 A costume similar to that worn by the Empress of Austria, comprising a white satin robe, an apron of fine lace and a red velvet cape trimmed with sable.

2.16 A Tartar. Mountain-dwellers, these people wear goat-hide jackets for warmth and thick linen shirts, fastened with copper or tin brooches.

# THE OTTOMAN EMPIRE

TURKEY – GREECE – BULGARIA

UNTIL RECENTLY, THE OTTOMAN EMPIRE – in effect, Turkey and its dominions – held sway over the whole of Greece, Bulgaria and the lands of the Serbs, Croatians and southern Slavs. Over the past 100 years or so, Turkish influence has waned: Greece, for example, has become independent. Turkish influence over costume, though, persists to this day.

1.1 A peasant from Baidjas, whose hair has been lengthened by the addition of flax and laden with sequins and glass beads. She is wearing a small fez wrapped round with a piece of wool that is knotted under the chin. Her chemise – hidden here – is embroidered and the belt is made of felt.

1.2 A Bulgarian woman from Roustchouk. Her headdress is a simple piece of material wrapped around the head with the ends falling fetchingly over the shoulders. Her chemise is made of embroidered wool and she is wearing two belts, one of which is holding up the apron. Her coat is sleeveless and lined with fur with facings made from fine skins, and her costume is completed by woollen stockings and shoes with curled-up toes.

1.3 A Bulgarian woman from Ali Tchélebi wearing stockings of striped wool and leggings, pleated so that they billow outwards until they reach the feet.

1.4 A Greek woman from Hasskeui, wearing a headdress called a *bachlik*. From it hangs a piece of material similar in style to a veil or a *mantilla*. Her beads are made of glass and she is wearing a V-necked jacket, a coat, an apron and two belts, the uppermost being of silver and fastened with hooks. Her stockings are striped and she is not wearing shoes.

1.5 A Greek peasant from Bitola, with an astrakhan headdress. His jacket, trousers and gaiters are made of felt, and his shoes are Moroccan.

2.1 A farmer's wife from Scutari. Her headdress consists of an embroidered brimless hat with a covering for the back of the neck. Her loose-fitting linen chemise comes down lower than her skirt and has wide sleeves that are not gathered into cuffs. Her sleeveless jacket is made of felt and a woollen apron is attached to her silver belt.

2.2 An inhabitant of Sofia, with clothes made from wool and decorated with silk braid. His woollen belt is wrapped round his body many times.

2.3 A Bulgarian Christian from Widdin, with a headdress made from the skin of a black lamb. He is wearing a short cotton robe and a woollen belt. His *pelisse* is also made of sheepskin turned inside out and decorated with pieces of coloured wool, cotton and silk braid. His shoes are made from animal skins.

2.4 A Greek peasant from Bitola. The material of her headdress is painted, and made from two pieces: one in the style of a fichu and the other like a veil that falls prettily over her shoulders.
    Her chemise is made of coarse linen and the sleeveless jacket of felt. The apron is made from a carpet material. Two belts are wrapped round her waist, one of them almost long enough to reach the ground. Moroccan shoes protect her feet.

## TURKEY – GREECE – BULGARIA

SLAVIC TRADITIONS ARE SHOWN AT their most ancient in tapestry clothing and in embroideries in coloured silks. *Appliqué* designs, however, originated in the custom of disguising the seams of clothes made from skins. Such designs are hardly ever seen in early pictures.

**1.2** The costume of this peasant woman from Malissor is made from tapestry. Twenty-nine separate pieces can be counted. They make up the *gueuchluk*, or tight-fitting bodice; the *dubliten*, or striped skirt without pleats; the apron; the *terba*, or work-bag; thick, strong stockings that go up to mid-thigh level and normally take the place of shoes; and, lastly, a belt made entirely from the finest wool and decorated with embroidery and fringes.

Small chains spangled with sequins cover the forehead, and the head itself is veiled with a large *bachlik* embroidered with gold, which falls casually over the shoulder.

A *oustrougha*, or cloak, is draped over the other shoulder. It has fringes, but is simpler than the *bachlik*.

**1.3** A Christian woman, who like the Muslims wears billowing pantaloons.

Her headdress is a simple piece of cotton embroidered with silk and wrapped round with thick braid. The earrings are made of silver filigree, as is the necklace, which has a crucifix attached to it.

**1.1 and 4** A Muslim woman, with a headdress made from material woven with threads of gold and topped with a plume of gold plate that is screwed on to a thick plaque of finely wrought silver.

Her chemise, or *bourundjuk*, is transparent.

**2.1** A prosperous merchant from Bitola. He is not wearing the thick, warm material woven in the provinces, but a more expensive material from Austria.

**2.2** A *haham-bachi* – a Jewish doctor of religion – from Selanik. His costume is simple: an *entari* made of striped silk; and a dark overcoat, called a *binich*.

**2.3** A peasant from the Ioannina region. The *fistan* no longer figures in this field-worker's costume and gaiters are replaced by *caltchoun*.

**2.4** A Muslim woman from Salonika, wearing the same costume that is seen in Istanbul: a muslin veil, called a *yachmak*, that covers her face and head and only just allows her to see.

**2.5** A *hodja* from Selanik, wearing a white *saryk* over his fez.

**3.1** A poor Arnaout, with a bonnet instead of a fez. The costume is the same as that of the richer people on his right, but is made from a type of felt called *aba*, rather than wool.

**3.2** A well-off Arnaout from Ioannina, wearing a tall fez of red felt with a long *puskul* of blue silk; a wrap-over waistcoat, or *djamadan*, with a straight waistcoat, or *yeleck*, on top; a jacket, or *tchepken*, with long open sleeves; and a leather belt. The toes of his elegant shoes curl up beneath a white *fistan*.

**3.3** An Arnaout woman from Ioannina, wearing a low fez whose red felt and blue *puskul* are decorated with threads of gold attached small golden balls.

**3.4** A middle-class Arnaout, who has discarded the *djamadan*. He is wearing a *yeleck*, a *tchepken* and *dizlik*, or gaiters, all made from fine wool and embroidered with silk.

# ITALY

## THE TRUE DESCENDANTS OF THE ROMANS

**B**ARTOLOMMEO PINELLI, A PROLIFIC ENGRAVER, was one of the most popular artists in lower Italy in the first half of the 19th century. Born in the suburbs of Travestere in Rome, he is still the most exact portraitist and the best historian of his people: the labourers, gardeners and wine growers beyond the Tiber, who believe that only they are the true descendants of the Romans.

The 11 headdresses (1) are from a series of 52 engravings that appeared in 1823, when Pinelli illustrated the Roman poem *Meo Patacca* – a satire dating back to 1695. Pinelli, however, was more concerned with the people of his own time.

*Meo Patacca* is full of wry comments on local society, which is brought vividly to life. This has ensured its lasting popularity among the populace. Written by Giuseppe Bernari in the popular dialect of Rome, it is one of those comic poems in which the characters are sufficiently aware to be able to laugh at their own excesses.

Its subject is the upheaval in Rome caused by the siege of Vienna by the Turks. The news is aggravated by the false rumour that the standard of Mohammed has already been raised over Vienna, and will soon be seen all over Europe.

**1.1** One of the witnesses of the marriage of Patacca, wearing a bonnet that is tied round his hair with a knot of ribbons.

**1.2** A young man with a plaited tress of hair that forms a *chignon*, fixed by a hairpin.

**1.3** Marco Pepe, Patacca's rival, wearing the same beribboned bonnet as **1.1** and also, tipped forward over his forehead, a small cotton cap.

**1.4** Nuccia, Patacca's bride. Some strands of her hair are plaited and others are worn loose. The whole coiffure is piled up on the head

and held in place with a comb and a knot of ribbons.

**1.5** Meo Patacca.

**1.6** A working man, wearing a long hairnet under a hat in the Bolivar style. This hairnet is lengthened by two cords with small tassels that hang down as far as the belt.

**1.7** A working woman, wearing a high *chignon*, secured, as was customary, with a comb, and long pearl earrings.

**1.8** A young man with a flower, placed, not on his open jacket, but at the throat of his waistcoat

**1.9 & 10** Two types of hat.

**1.11** A woman's *chignon*, as seen from behind.

The costumes in **2** and **3** are those of middle- and lower-class women.

**2.1** A woman from the region of Fronsolone.

**2.2** A woman from Naples.

**2.3 & 6** Servants from Naples.

**2.4** A woman from Travestere.

**2.5** A woman of Rome.

**3.1** A woman from Padua.

**3.2** A Venetian working woman.

**3.3 and 5** Servants from Fondi.

**3.4** A woman from Milan.

## PEASANTS IN THE PROVINCES

THE ILLUSTRATIONS OPPOSITE SHOW Italian peasants from the provinces outside Rome. Their costume is partly influenced by that of the Bohemians, with whom they share a superstitious belief in omens and an uncanny ability to foretell the future.

———— • ————

**1** These women are wearing the national costume. Typically, this consists of a stiff headdress, a simple white blouse, a bodice and a coloured skirt. The bodice is a plain piece of cloth that covers the breasts and passes beneath the arms to be laced at the back. Some interesting variations are shown here.

Skirts are nearly always the same in style, varying only in the way their bright colours stand out against the white aprons, or in their embroidery.

Even the poorest women love shiny jewellery, and are rarely seen without gold-coloured chains, necklaces and long earrings called *navicella*. Hair is usually pinned up with a clasp.

**2** Three country girls from the Terra di Lavoro, a fertile area celebrated by the Romans as the richest and prettiest land in the world. The girls from this region are often hauntingly beautiful. They are descendants of the original Lucanians, who rebelled during the Second Punic War and were declared slaves. However, they still hold to the old ways, as can be seen from the names used for their clothes: *vestes*, for example, for skirts, and *scindae* for belts.

**1.1** A woman wearing Cerveran costume, with a small checked shawl over her shoulders and bodice.

**1.2** A woman from Sonnino, wearing a pleated headdress folded several times to form a long strip of material. A small board stiffens the top where it covers the head.

Both this lady and the lady in **1.1** are wearing heavy shoes – useful for trudging through the countryside, but ugly. As a result, those who wore them were known as "cowherds".

**1.3 & 5** The shoes worn by these two Cociare peasants were named after their wearers: *cocie*. They were made by attaching a piece of hide round the ankle with leather laces.

**1.4 & 5** Two women wearing simple headdresses of plain linen, similar in style to those worn by the Vestal Virgins in ancient Rome.

The lady in **1.4** is wearing a blouse with a rounded neck and full sleeves. This is typical of the Agnani region.

**2.1 & 3** The long dress called a *camisa*, with its wide, loose sleeves, was Ionian in origin and entered Italy during Roman times. The girl on the left is wearing a woven apron that she probably made herself. Such was the artistry employed in making these garments, which could also be embroidered or *appliquéd*, that they were known as *scenales*, or "theatre-pieces".

**2.2** In order to stop the wide sleeves from hindering movement, they were often rolled up and held in place with a band of material. Called a *manec*, this band is a distinctive element of Italian dress.

**2.3** This clearly shows a stiff bodice or corset reinforced with whalebone at the front and laced behind.

# SPAIN

BULLFIGHTERS AND LADIES

**B**ULLFIGHTING HAS LONG BEEN ONE of the most popular forms of entertainment in Spain. During the 16th and 17th centuries, it was the sport of the nobility, who faced the bull single-handed with a horse and lance. By the end of the 18th century, though, four types of bullfighter had evolved: picadors, banderillos, chulos, and, finally, the espadas, who tried to kill the bull with a sword. The costumes of these matadors, shown opposite from 1778, are still worn today.

1. All the bullfighters wear a neat jacket with epaulettes, close-fitting breeches and a narrow sash that forms a tight belt. Loose and flapping garments would be a liability in the bullring, where the least hindrance to movement might be fatal.

The red cape, called a *muleta*, with which the matador decoys the bull, is attached to a baton.

1.1 Pierre Romano, a famous matador, with a bull lying dead at his feet. As is customary, the sword is in his left hand, so that he can salute his public with his right hand.

1.2 By 1804, the costume had become simpler and tidier. This matador is the unfortunate Pepe Illo, who – despite his theory that bullfighting was a safe and enjoyable form of entertainment for the family – died horribly in the Madrid plaza, gored by a bull's horns.

1.3 A late 18th-century *torero*.

1.4 The famous matador Joachin Rodriguez, known affectionately as "Costillares", who invented many of the sword movements that became a part of the official "dance" of the bull ring.

2 Ladies from Asturia and Salamanca, part of the Kingdom of Leon, and from Segovia and Avila, part of Castille.

2.1 A woman from Segovia, dressed for a festival. She is wearing a woollen bodice bordered with lace, with matching lacework on her skirt and apron. A long coral necklace is wound several times round her neck, supporting a number of crosses and pendants. The weight of jewellery makes it look as if she is wearing armour plating down to her belt.

2.2 A rich farmer's wife from Salamanca, one of a simple and patriarchal people known as Charras, from the Spanish word for a "plough".

These women are renowned for their beauty, as are the costumes they wear on saints' days. Traditionally, they wear heavy jewellery round their necks and in their hair. This woman has a small silk shawl round her neck, covering a silk bodice. Her scarlet skirt is made of fine linen, and covered by a silk and velvet apron. Both carry designs in velvet that have been picked out in gold thread.

2.3 & 4 Peasant women from Avila. Their hats are made of black straw and are topped with velvet ribbons – sometimes a sprig of cut flowers is used instead. Brightly coloured skirts of coarse material are trimmed with black velvet, allowing the petticoats to peep out.

2.5 A middle-class woman from Asturia, wearing a plain dress covered by a large apron with a velvet border. A *rebozillo*, or cotton shawl, is loosely tied round her shoulders.

**1.1** A Maragato – a member of a self-sufficient, mountain-dwelling race from the province of Leon, many of whom are mule drivers. His jacket is pulled tight at the waist by a belt and his wide knickerbockers reach down to the knee. Typically, his wide-brimmed hat is banded with a cord rather than a ribbon.

**1.2** A peasant from Orense, near Galicia. His clothes are appropriate to this region's warm, humid climate (note the cotton umbrella). His red waistcoat is decorated at the back, and unbuttoned hose shows under-breeches beneath his top breeches. His stiff collar is turned up above the waistcoat collar.

**1.3** A young peasant from Lugo, in Galicia. His *montera*, or hat, has pompons facing the right – a sign that he is still a bachelor.

**1.4** An Asturian woman in the warm woollen clothes necessary for ward off the cold weather of the mountain ranges. Her hair would be tied in a bun underneath the headscarf. The thick shawl, a *denque*, is bordered in rich velvet.

**1.5** A town crier from Aragaon, with an open-necked shirt and jacket, leather breeches and blue stockings pulled up to his knees.

**2.1** Castille's military traditions can be seen in its costumes. Here the peasant's *montera* is similar to a soldier's hat; the cape is like that of a 17th-century soldier; and even the leather gaiters resemble armour.

**2.2** An Asturian woman in her Sunday best. Many such women were servants, and this one has a cotton scarf knotted on her head. Her woollen shawl is embroidered in different colours and the sleeves of her bodice are edged with velvet.

Her short, narrow apron is made of velvet picked out with silver ribbons and her skirt is made of either Indian cotton or of wool.

**2.3** An elderly Galician man, wearing a costume similar to that of the bachelor in **1**: a wide-lapelled jacket with pockets, under which is a traditional red and black waistcoat.

**2.4** An old Galician country-woman, with a large kerchief over her head, an embroidered shawl round her shoulders and a skirt that does not match her bodice. A large apron, or *manteo*, covers her skirt almost entirely.

**2.5** A man from Maragato, showing the back view of the figure in **1.1**.

**3.1** A Catalan woman, with a remarkable long, white cowl.

**3.2** A wealthy farmer wearing a red woollen hat, a short jacket called a *marsille* and blue velvet breeches. His cravat of cotton print is slipped through a silver ring.

**3.3** A woman from Aragon wearing a characteristic headscarf that she has pulled down on to her shoulders. The uncovered hair is often decorated with a single flower.
Her black velvet bodice is trimmed with lace at the front and pulled in at the waist, and her short, flared skirt is made of wool.

**3.4** A village mayor wearing a *gambeto*, or overcoat, and a woollen hat called a *gorro*.

**3.5** An Aragonian, whose *capa de muestra*, made of grey wool and often striped with black, is similar in style to a simple Moorish cape. As here, the shirt is rarely buttoned and the chest is bare. His belt has been unfolded and covers his thighs.

## CATALONIA – ARAGON – GALICIA

THE ILLUSTRATIONS OPPOSITE SHOW costumes from the Catalan region (top); from Aragon (middle); and from Orense, a part of Galicia (bottom). The Galician peasants are performing the traditional *Muyneira*, the Dance of the Miller's Wife, to an accompaniment of a tambourine, drum, castanets and an instrument similar to the bagpipes.

———— • ————

**1.1** A woman from Agramunt, a Catalan market town, with a head-scarf and a gold necklace. The bodice is made of velvet or silk, and is straight-sleeved; there is a gap at the elbow where the upper sleeve ends and the forearm sleeve begins.

**1.2** A Jesuit official, who on more sinister occasions would wear a pointed cap with two eye-holes, when, for example, putting a malefactor to the "question".

**1.3** A rich farmer from the neighbourhood of Barcelona, wearing a hat and belt in matching, violet-coloured wool. His waistcoat and breeches are made of black merino, and his ankle boots are made of black leather.

**1.4** A Catalan woman with a white cowl.

**1.5** A farmer from Tarragon, wearing a brown woollen hat. Underneath the woollen waistcoat is a red belt and a striped blue shirt. He is carrying a linen jacket over his shoulder and wearing cotton socks and espadrilles.

**1.6** A young woman from Tarragon, whose hair is held back by a black hair-net, wearing gold and emerald earrings. Her velvet bodice has similar sleeves to those in **1.1**, behind her. The women of this region tend to have ample bosoms, which, for modesty's sake, are held in with lace shawls, tucked firmly into their belts.

**1.7** Next to the young woman is a young man with a crimson silk waistcoat braided with white. Under his velvet breeches there are blue cotton stockings with leather gaiters. His belt is made of purple wool and his jacket is worn over his shoulder.

**2.1 & 2** Two women wearing dresses of coarse linen, with their hair casually covered with cotton scarves, beneath which hang plaits. Their upright bearing is the result of carrying heavy baskets on their heads.

**2.3** A young girl from the village of Alteca.

**2.4 & 5** A bride and groom. The bride is wearing a silk mantilla bordered with velvet. Whatever the season, the bridegroom always wears a heavy black cape.

**2.6** A man from the Vascongadas region, wearing a beret and a shirt, with a large collar resting on his waistcoat lapels. A large belt holds up embroidered trousers that have strips of velvet *appliquéd* to them.

**3.1, 2 & 3** Galician men wear large hats with triangular fronts, ear-flaps at either side and two pompons, one at the top and one halfway down. The direction of the pompons denotes their marital status. The rest of their dress is casual – sleeveless short waistcoats are worn over high-necked collars and breeches reach below the knee.

**3.4** A woman wearing a *denque*, a piece of red material bordered with velvet that covers her shoulders and crosses over her chest. A cleverly arranged scarf serves to cover her head and a large apron with a wide bow at the back covers the skirt almost entirely.

# THE ISLAND OF MAJORCA

GEORGE SAND REMARKED IN HER *Winter in Majorca, 1837* that the costumes of women and peasants in Majorca still showed the naivety and innocence of the island's inhabitants. Town dwellers, on the other hand, had been corrupted by the rich bourgeoisie, and had changed their dress accordingly. These illustrations show Majorcan costume, as worn by peasants, servants and richer women.

**1** The woman on the left is wearing a *rebozillo*, similar to a hunting hood and made from a double wimple. The top part covers the head to the chin, leaving only the face uncovered; the lower part covers the shoulders.

The two women on the far right are wearing variations on this garment. All are wearing dresses with boned bodices and tight, elbow-length sleeves, as well as necklaces, rings, bracelets, watches and other items of jewellery.

Shoes worn by Majorcan women are always well made, and often high-heeled. Short mid-length skirts reach to their calves, and aprons are only worn by servants and peasant women.

**1.1** Like the women of the mainland, Majorcan women always wear a mantilla out of doors and carry a fan.

**1.2 & 5** Women of a higher class here show in their costume both the influence of tradition and of contemporary fashions of the 1820s.

**2.1** A peasant dressed in his Sunday best in the late 19th century. His costume owes much to Arab influences: he wears a neckerchief and a long belted robe under which can be seen ankle-length trousers and low shoes. A large red cape is draped over his shoulders.

**2.2 & 4** and **3.1** An agricultural labourer, wearing a felt hat, a spotlessly white shirt, a waistcoat and a *sayo* – a short, close-fitting linen jacket. Baggy knickerbockers were sometimes held up by a twisted cord belt (**3.1**) and shoes had no buckles or laces.

**2.3 & 5** Wives of farm labourers with lace *rebozillos*, again made of two pieces of material – one covering the head and passing under the chin like a nun's wimple; the other covering the shoulders. A boned black silk bodice with tight elbow-length sleeves is worn above a skirt of Indian cotton or cambric. Unlike earlier Majorcan women, they carry fans and wear no jewellery.

**3.2** A peasant in his Sunday best, wearing a hat made from the fur of a wild cat with the brim raised at either side. A white tunic beneath the large collar is buttoned down to the belt and cut below into a skirt that covers the top of his breeches. A black cape is thrown over his shoulders.

**3.3** A farmer from Palma, wearing a wide-brimmed hat that shows that his hair is cut in the medieval style and his face is clean-shaven. Under a buttoned cape he is wearing striped knickerbockers, blue hose and open shoes.

**3.4** A farm boy, with a handkerchief wound like a turban round his head.

**3.5** A shepherd, bare-necked and with two different coloured tunics tied at the waist by a large-buckled belt. His legs are protected by leather gaiters and his feet by laced shoes.

# PORTUGAL

## INFLUENCES OF THE INVADERS

THE CELTIC AND IBERIAN TRIBES of the ancient land of Lusitania fought hard against a series of invaders, but eventually succumbed – first to the Romans, then to Muslims. These, together with African influences, left their mark on costume and society. As a result, the style of Portuguese clothes is similar to that of Spain and the South of France. Women wear their short skirts and large felt hats with grace. They do not possess that fierce Spanish beauty, but their thick hair and flashing eyes give them a vivacious appearance.

1, 3 & 6 Peasant women from Minho in feast-day costume. 3 & 6 are wearing black felt hats with upturned brims, decorated with pompons. Under their hats are *lencos*, pieces of material whose pleats spread out over the neck and shoulders.

The sleeves of the chemise worn on feast days are always long, and it is customary to lift up the skirt to show the petticoat. The lady in 3 is wearing a pleated cape, and all three are carrying parasols.

2 A peasant woman from Minho wearing a costume contemporary with the Civil War. She wears a *lenco* under her felt hat and the wide sleeves of her chemise are rolled up. Her bodice is *décolleté* and her short skirt is pleated. She is wearing long earrings and shoes with wooden soles.

4 A herdsman wearing a hat with a brim that sticks out like wings at the sides.

5 A poultry seller whose *lenco* makes a pretty headdress. Her bodice is *décolleté* with a fichu round the neck. Her skirt is protected by a large apron.

7 A shepherd wearing a broad-brimmed hat and a shirt under a waistcoat and jacket.

8 & 12 Fishermongers. Such men play an important role in a society in which their work is vital.

9 & 10 Mussel vendors with gold buttons on their bodices.

11 A piglet seller wearing a small bonnet and an overgarment wrapped round his body. His legs are bare.

13 A prawn seller carrying her wares in a basket on her head, as was customary, and holding a scarf in her hand.

14 A fisherman wearing exactly the same costume as a Neapolitan fisherman: a small bonnet, an open shirt with long rolled-up sleeves, a belt holding up baggy shorts and bare legs and feet.

15 A parish priest with a long cassock, buckled shoes and a *biretta*.

16 A cattle merchant wearing an open shirt, culottes and *alpargatas*.

17 A monk of the Order of Saint Anthony wearing a very large felt hat, commonly worn by most religious orders in Portugal.

18 A Dominican with a three-cornered hat and a black cowl over a white robe.

19 A Carmelite wearing a double black robe and a cape with a capuchin.

20 A Benedictine wearing a black serge over-garment.

# FRANCE

COSTUMES OF THE LANDES

STRICTLY SPEAKING, THE PEOPLE OF LANDES occupy the territory bordered by the Atlantic to the west, Bayonne to the south and Bordeaux to the north. They are given different names in different areas: in Bordeaux they are called *parents*; in Mont-de-Marsan, *cocozates*; in Saint-Sever, *lanusquets*; and in Dax and Bayonne they are known as *maransins*.

**1.1, 2, 3 & 4** *Lanusquets* walking on stilts and carrying long staffs, all of which have pieces of bone attached to their ends.

The shepherd (**1.1**) is using his baton as a seat while he knits. He is wearing winter clothes, including a sheepskin *dolman* and *camauo* on his legs that also cover his otherwise bare feet. His *pelisse*, also known as the "cloak of Charlemagne", has a hood from which bands of material hang down the shoulders in a zig-zag. These are trimmed with horse hair at the lower points. Under his cloak, the shepherd is wearing two waistcoats and culottes. (**1.2** shows the back view of the same shepherd.)

**1.3** shows a woman wearing an under-shirt and a skirt short enough to show the *camauo* covering her feet. She has an apron, and a fichu is crossed over her chest.

**1.4** shows a shepherd in summer costume, with a flat cap of knitted wool, a small sheepskin *dolman* and *camauo*.

**2** Costumes from three regions: Haute-Garonne, including the Languedoc and Guyenne, and the Upper and Lower Pyrenees; all are on the ridges of the Western Pyrenees.

**2.1** A young girl from Bugard in the Upper Pyrenees, wearing a bright red hood that contrasts vividly with her white *cornet*. Her skirt is made of wool and a ribbon with a small silver cross hangs round her neck.

**2.2** A peasant from the Bagnères-de-Luchon area. Throughout the Pyrenees, men's costume is composed of the same elements: a jacket, a wrap-over waistcoat, culottes, high gaiters – the traditional mountain-dweller's garb.

**2.3** A woman from the valley of Louron. Her hood is worn over a ruched bonnet and her shawl is crossed over the bodice of her fustian dress.

**2.5** A young woman from the environs of Bagnères-de-Bigorre. Her hood is made of very fine cashmere and decorated with a strip of velvet. In fact, this woman is dressed in a Parisian style of about 1820.

**2.6** A young woman from the the Aure valley. Her hood is worn over a *cornet* whose ends can be seen hanging down over her bodice. She has a silver cross round her neck, a fichu and a checked apron.

Basque clothing is similar to that of the Pyrenees, consisting of a large linen shirt fastened at the throat and a simple skirt of black fustian.

**1.5** and **2.4** These Basque women are both carrying baskets called *tistets*. **1.5** wears a handkerchief on her head as a hood, with a linen shirt and a woollen skirt. A fringed cape is tied around her waist as is customary when it is not wrapped around the shoulders. **2.4** is wearing a bonnet with its ends tied at the back, a short sleeved chemise and a woollen skirt.

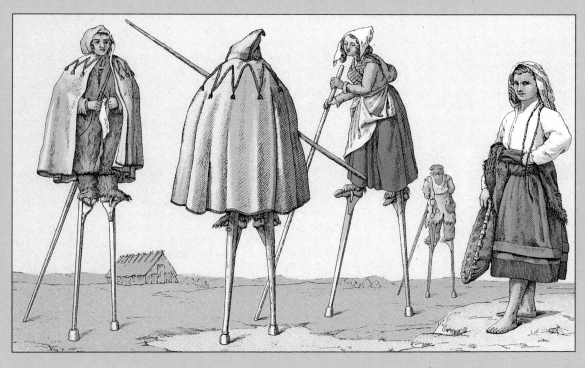

301

## BOURBONNAIS – BOURG – THE SÂONE

THE PEOPLE OF SAÔNE-ET-LOIRE, and of its towns of Autonois, Maconnais, Chalonnais and Charolais, have kept many of their traditions and customs intact. The costume of the women of Maconnais, for example, has hardly been altered by modern infuences, the old-style hood being still worn. It can take two forms: sometimes it is decorated with lace in the shape of a fan; sometimes it is draped with a huge veil in the manner of Bresse. Jewellery is a feature of women's costume, recalling the days of Spanish rule.

**1.9** A woman from the Bourbonnais region, wearing the traditional headdress called the *bourbon nichonne*. This is a straw hat lined with blue silk that curves upwards at the back.

**1.10** A feast-day costume. A lace bonnet is tied under the chin with a silk ribbon, and another long, wide silk ribbon hangs down the back. The hat sits at an angle, and is secured by a ribbon that passes behind the ears.
She is wearing long earrings and a three-roped necklace with ornate medallions. Her pink silk dress has a small silk jacket whose sleeves are decorated with armbands of embroidered white silk.

**1.11 & 13** Traditional costumes from the Bourg region. Typically, dresses here are made either of woollen cloth or of flowered silk. Bodices, also made of woollen cloth, are covered with silver ornaments.

**1.12** A ceremonial costume. The black silk dress is worn under an apron of pale silk with an embroidered bodice and sleeves.

**1.14** A housewife in the early part of the 19th century. Further down the Saône valley, the size of the hat decreases until it becomes a small black felt hat, bedecked with ribbons. The dress is made of pale green wool and has a *décolleté* corsage and a protective apron.

Dieppe and its suburb, Le Pollet, are populated by tough sailors and fishermen. It is thought that in the 12th and 13th centuries the Venetians used Le Pollet as a port of call on their voyages to Holland and the Baltic. Certainly Venetian infuences can be seen in the bright array of colours and jewellery that remain part of the costume of the people of Le Pollet, shown in **2** and **3** opposite.

**18th-century costumes**

**2.2** A group of peasant women.

**2.3** A pedlar of ivory ware.

**2.5** A fisherman from Le Pollet in working clothes.

**19th-century costumes**

**31 & 5** Women in their Sunday best.

**3.2 & 3** A fisherman and child. The 19th-century fisherman's costume is exactly the same as that of the 18th century.

**2.1, 4 & 6** Fishermen and a woman from the second half of the 19th century. The men's costumes are waterproof. The fisherwoman wears a jacket of coarse tarred material, crossed over the chest and tied round the waist with a simple cord.

**3.4 & 6** Men in feast-day costume in Le Pollet, each wearing a velvet hat with wool and silver ornaments and a silk knot that supports a glass plume. Silk jackets embroidered with flowers and baggy woollen culottes are also worn, with silk trimmings.

# ALSACE-LORRAINE

AS A RESULT OF THE TREATY OF WESTPHALIA, Alsace was made part of France in 1648, but the free town of Strasbourg was not united with France until 1681. Some years before this union, a very rigid class structure existed in Alsace society. Laws regulated the quality of silk, velvet, ribbons and fur, and even the value of jewels that could be worn. There were even standards for wigs.

There were six different classes, headed by the rich noblemen of Alsace – the senators, the aldermen and the councillors. Members of this group could dress as they wished, but it was recommended that they should exercise caution in their choice of dress for fear of exciting the envy of the lower orders.

These codes of dress give some idea of the wealth of the society. A headdress called a *bendel* consisted of a sort of tiara that could be simple or elaborate, according to the social standing of the wearer; for the nobility it could be embroidered with silver or gold, and decorated with pearls and fine stones.

When Strasbourg became part of France, men followed French fashion, but women, especially those from the middle classes, remained faithful to their traditional costume. This was changed by the Revolution.

The costume of country folk was very plain during the Middle Ages, but when the laws were relaxed they were allowed to wear some finer garments. The result is a costume that has been preserved and perfected through the generations.

Nowadays, the traditional costume is rarely seen in everyday use, although in the early 19th century some peasants could still be seen sporting small white aprons and silk ribbons on their heads. But long plaits, straw hats, scarlet petticoats and silk aprons belong to the past.

1 A Strasbourg woman of the early 19th century in her garden. She is wearing a pink silk headdress secured with a large ribbon knotted at the front. A *décolleté* bodice reveals an embroidered chemise.

2 A peasant woman from the Colmar region. Her headdress consists of an embroidered bonnet with a ribbon knotted at the nape of the neck and ruched tulle at the front to frame the face. A large fichu crosses over the bodice and over the top of a blue silk apron.

3 & 5 Peasant girls from Kochersberg. The former is a young Catholic, distinguishable by her brightly coloured costume. The latter is a young Lutheran girl. Lutherans wore their green serge skirts with higher hemlines.

4 A silk bonnet with colourful trimmings and silver embroidery.

6 & 7 A circular bonnet of the 17th century seen from two angles. The back is decorated with four cockades and a gold button.

8 A headdress from the latter half of the 19th century, consisting of huge striped-silk ribbons tied in a great bow on the top of the head.

9, 10, 11 & 12 A gold-embroidered bonnet seen from front and back, with details of its decoration.

13 A bonnet entirely covered with gold filigree. The articles shown below are details of ornaments from headdresses.

21 A 17th-century dignitary.

20 Dame Marie-Sabine Krezni, née Kieterin de Kornburg, (1603–1657) wearing a *pelzkappe* hat.

# BRITTANY: A SEPARATE TRADITION

BRITTANY HAS ALWAYS BEEN SEPARATE from the mainstream of French influence. The origins of its unique culture are buried in the past, but they probably derive from the Brythonic Celts, who gave their name, before the advent of the Romans, to both Britain and Brittany. Today, the Brythonic Celts survive as the Welsh in Britain and the Bretons in France. Both have a similar language that is still in use, with many words in common. Many other ancient traditions, including those of costume, are still observed to this day, as the illustrations on these pages show.

———— • ————

**1.1** A woman from Bannalec.

**1.2** A woman from Locmariaquer, in the district of Lorient.

**1.3** A young girl from the "Ile-des-Batz" in the district of Morlaix. With her bonnet tied at the chin and her laced-up bodice she has an almost 15th-century air.

**1.4 & 6** Woman from Pont-l'Abbe', wearing fairly simple outfits, although they still retain the idiosyncratic touches of this ancient traditional costume.

**1.5** A woman from Douarnenez, wearing a similar costume to that seen in Pont-l'Abbé.

**1.7** A woman from Ploudaniel from the district of Chateaulin. Her chemise has a pleated neck-edge and her fringed fichu is crossed over her bodice like a shawl and tucked into her apron – the effect suggests the 16th century.

**2.1** A married woman from the Quimperlé region, wearing a cotton bonnet, a woollen dress and a silk apron. The bodice, belt and apron are embroidered with gold and silver thread.

**2.2** A man from Bannalec, near Quimperlé. His blue wool jacket, a second waistcoat, is worn over a woollen belt.

**2.3** A woman from Pont-l'Abbé, near Quimperlé. The front of her headdress is made of white cotton and is placed on a cap of embroidered silk, so that it only partly covers her hair. Her cotton chemise peeps out at the neck and sleeves from beneath two gowns.

**2.4** A man from Saint-Goazec, in the district of Chateaulin. His wide-collared shirt is made of cotton, and his woollen waistcoat has a double row of brass buttons and is trimmed with velvet.

**2.5** A woman from Melguen, near Quimperlé, wearing a muslin bonnet. Her dress is made of wool and the apron with pockets showing at the front is made of silk.

**3.1** An inhabitant of Faouet, near Morbihan, with a beribboned hat made of felt. His blue and white wool waistcoat is trimmed with black and fastened with brass buttons.

**3.2** A young man from Quimper wearing a short, sailor-style jacket and a double waistcoat.

**3.3** A woman in her Sunday best from the district of Quimperlé. Her woollen dress has a wide opening at the front and shows her bodice beneath.

**3.4** A woman from Pont-l'Abbé, near Quimper, wearing a short, open-fronted blouse, with turned-back sleeves.

**3.5** A man from Ploaré wearing baggy breeches gathered in at the knee with gaiters.

**3.6** An inhabitant of Conbrit, near Quimper, wearing a felt hat, sabots with blackened points.

1.1 An inhabitant of Plouvenez-le-Faou, in the district of Chateaulin.

1.2 A working man from Kerlahan, near Brest. His waistcoat is made of wool and his chemise of cotton. The wide, striped belt is made of wool.

1.3 A hill-dweller from Feuilleé, wearing a jacket lined with long fur. The woollen waistcoat crosses over at the front and is tucked into the belt at the waist.

1.4 A costume from Kerlahan, near Brest. This man is wearing a muslin cravat and a double-breasted waistcoat trimmed with silk embroidery around the neck. His belt is made of silk and his jacket, made with pockets, is woollen with braid around all the edges.

1.5 An inhabitant of Bannalec, in the district of Quimperlé. His short jacket is trimmed with braid and his waistcoat is embroidered with silk at the neck. A belt with a buckle is worn over a cloth belt. In the summer a second waistcoat is worn – this is tucked into the leather belt and cut at the top in the shape of a heart.

2.1 A peasant woman from Plougastel-Daoulas, near Brest. She is wearing a linen headdress with beribboned ends that hang down. Her sleeved under-vest is made of blue cloth, contrasting with her red waistcoat. A brown blouse ends in points at the back and her woollen skirt is tied with a belt of yellow ribbons. Her fichu is made of yellow- and blue-striped cotton.

2.2 A woman from Plonevez-du-Faou in the district of Chateaulin. Her linen headdress is folded over a small red woollen cap and her white linen collar is lightly starched. Her undervest is gathered in at the waist and tucked into a woollen skirt over which she is wearing an apron with a pocket at the front.

2.3 A woman from Douarnenez, near Quimper, wearing a headdress made of either cotton or linen. The skirt is grey and the bodice takes the form of a colourfully trimmed blue waistcoat.

2.4 A woman from Carhaix in the district of Chateaulin, wearing a pale yellow skirt, a linen apron and a headdress.

2.5 A woman from Kerlouan in the district of Chateaulin. Her cotton headdress tumbles down over her shoulders, and her fichu, also made of cotton, is decorated with lace.

2.6 A servant girl from Quimper wearing a costume from Rosporden. Her muslin headdress has a starched wimple and she is wearing a blue bodice with embroidered buttons over a blue *justin*. Her sleeves are false.

3.1 & 4 Working men from Plougastel-Daoulas, near Brest, wearing a costume consisting of a woollen shirt, a woollen cloth waistcoat and jacket, trousers made of coarse cloth and a bonnet and belt made of wool.

3.2 A costume from Saint-Goazec, where styles are similar to those of Chateaulin.

3.3 A man from Pleyben in the district of Chateaulin. This rather severe costume is made of wool and includes long gaiters.

3.5 A man from Pont-Croix in the district of Chateaulin, wearing a sleeveless jerkin over his other clothes.

3.6 An old man from the neighbourhood of Quimper. Baggy cloth leggings meet his long socks just below the knee.

———— • ————

**1.1 & 6** Peasants from the neighbourhood of Chateauneuf-du-Faou in the district of Chateaulin. Their costume consists of a felt hat decorated with multi-coloured chenille; a jacket, called a *corquen*; an embroidered waistcoat or *rokedennon*; and a second waistcoat, worn open down the front with red-trimmed buttonholes. A *bragoubraz* is pleated around a leather belt known as a *gouriz*. **1.6** sports an embroidered shirt collar.

**1.2** A peasant from Carantec, near Morlaix, wearing a felt hat decorated with gaily coloured chenille. His waistcoat is brown, with sky-blue sleeves and buttons made of black horn.

**1.3** A peasant from Landivisian, near Morlaix. His outfit consists of a large hat decorated with velvet, a long jacket and a Basque-style waistcoat with many buttons.

**1.4** A man from Douarnenez, in the district of Quimper. His hat is embellished with a velvet ribbon and gaily coloured chenille and he is wearing a *corquen*, a sleeveless jacket trimmed with brightly coloured braid.

**1.5** and **2.1** *Guenedouriens*, or "whites", from the district of Quimperlé. **1.5** wears a jacket of white linen with red embroidery. The hem of his blue waistcoat is lower than his jacket, and he is wearing baggy linen culottes. **2.1** belongs to an *avant garde* group known as "young Brittany" in the latter half of the 19th century.

**2.2** A man from Quimper wearing a felt hat, an embroidered jacket and a double-breasted waistcoat. The Breton peasants only wear leather shoes on feast days – normally they wear *botou-coad*, literally "wooden shoes".

**2.3** A man from Plonevez-Porzay

in the district of Chateaulin, wearing pleated breeches in the old Léon style.

**2.4** A hill-dweller from the neighbourhood of Scaer near Quimperlé, wearing a round hat with a narrow brim.

**2.5** A man from Plogonnec in the district of Quimper, wearing baggy breeches in the old style.

**2.6** A peasant from Langolen in the district of Quimper, looking exactly like a Cornishman. He is wearing a small hat and a short jacket, two waistcoats, pleated breeches made from coarse material and a leather *gouriz* with a buckle.

**3.1** A woman from Gouezec in the district of Chateaulin, wearing a very starched linen collar and headdress, a pretty blue dress and an apron of paler coloured cotton.

**3.2** A young peasant girl from Ploaré in the district of Quimper. Her headdress is made of lace and embroidered tulle, and her collar of fluted cotton.

**3.3** A peasant from Saint-Yvi in the district of Quimper. His hat is called a *toc*, and his blue waistcoat a *rokedennou*.

**3.4** and **4** A married couple from Kerfeunteun in the district of Quimper. The woman's bodice and skirt are made of red woollen cloth decorated with satin ribbons and her *tavanger* is made of watered silk with dragons embroidered in gold thread.

The man's blue *rokedennou* has a double row of buttons and his jacket, made of blue woollen cloth, is trimmed with black velvet and decorated with pale yellow.

**3.6** A woman from Plonevez-Porzay.

## A BRETON INTERIOR

A TYPICAL BRETON HOUSE CONSISTS of a ground floor with an attic above it. The fireplace is huge and has a large mantleshelf, often pelmetted. On the shelf itself there is a very primitively carved little crucifix made from black wood or a statue of the Virgin Mary in gaudy colours. The hearth is a type of platform, made of large stones on which stand *chipots*, or chairs for the fireplace. This is a place of honour and to ask a guest to sit here is a mark of generosity and respect on the host's part. On dark winter evenings local characters take their places here to recount old tales and tell young girls whether they will be married the following year.

———— • ————

Breton furniture does not seem to date further back than 1600, and one very rarely comes across items made before 1630.

The furniture of this region is not made in the sense that a cabinet-maker would use the term. It is more the work of a *malvunuzein*, a joiner or carpenter of the country. It may appear crude and naive to some tastes, but it does have a certain vigour and individuality.

The furniture most often found in Brittany is made of oak, then blackened and waxed. The bed is always provided by the wife as part of her dowry. Often it is "closed", as here, by panels that slide over one another. When shut, the bed forms a square chest.

All beds in Brittany have a low chest by them, in which clothes are kept – and often bread, butter and milk as well.

The wardrobe, or *armel*, was once used for storing weapons, but nowadays is used for clothes. The second cupboard is a linen chest, placed next to the *armel* and the window. The dining table is nearly always placed in such a way that it receives the full light from the window.

Normally there is a drawer at the end of the table for cutlery and wooden spoons. However, in this example the utensils are kept in a *cliquet*, or spoon-carrier, which hangs from the ceiling.

Besides the three-legged stools benches are the most frequently used seats. *Kadors*, or chairs, have only recently been adopted and many farms only possess two or three of them. They tend to be coarsely stuffed or simply covered with a plank of wood.

The scene opposite shows the preparations for a wedding. While waiting for the bride to leave for the church, a peasant girl is stirring *crêpe* mixture in a huge brass bowl. Her headdress has an embroidered front and the rest of the head is covered by a little bonnet (this shows she is from Pont-l'Abbé).

Meanwhile the man sitting on the hearth, holding a pan, is about to cook a *crêpe*. The man and wife are guests: the former wearing a large felt hat, layers of jackets and a cloak; and the latter carrying a devotional book.

The bridegroom is in front of the table, wearing a red jacket and a hat decorated with multi-coloured chenille. The man next to him is a bagpipe player; his costume shows that he comes from Pleyben.

Next to these two men a kneeling peasant woman from Plougastel-Daoulas puts the final touch to the bride's toilette. The bride wears a lace headdress, a silk bodice with two scapulars, a red skirt embroidered with gold thread, a muslin *tavanger*, or apron, white stockings and slippers with gold buckles.

# INDEX

Maldives 106
*maldroni*, plant 98
Malissor 284
Manchus 76, 78, 82
mandarin 76, 82
Mandoulis 10
*manec* 288
Manissa 118
Manpouri people 104
*mantel d'honneur* 140
*mantelet* 270
*manteo* 292
mantilla 74, 214
Maragato 292
*maransins* 300
Marguerite of France 160
Maria, Empress 130
Maria Theresa of Austria 208
Marie-Antoinette, Queen of France 222, 224
marital status 88, 90, 94, 244, 268
Mark, St 128
Marken 248
*marli* 214
Marmaros 280
marriage 70; *and see* wedding dress
*Marriage à la Mode* (William Hogarth) 234
Mars 30
*marsille* 292
martial arts 86
Mary of England 160
masks 44, 182, 190
Matabele 54
matadors 290
Matheson clan 254
Mathieu de Coussy 144
Maximilian, Archduke of Austria 230
Mazarin, Cardinal 204, 206, 208
Mazovie, Conrad, Duke of 152
Mecca 124
Medes *see* Persia
Medici, Catherine de 162, 178, 180
Medici, Marie de 162
megalithic man 38
*mehil* 18
Melguen 306
Menelaus 28
*Meo Patacca* 286
Mercury 28
Mexico 74
Michelle de Vitry 140
Middle East, The 108–114
Milan 170, 286
military costume 230, 276; *and see* armour; battledress; chain mail; uniform, military
Mina peole 104
Minho 298
Mingrelian, monks 116
Minisoufaux chief 68
minstrels 150
*mintan* 124
mitre 20, 134, 164
*modeste* 202
Moldavians 280
Moguls 96, 98
Mogul, The Empire 98
Mogul, The Grand 98
Mongols, in Russia 268
monks 116
Montagu, Jean de 140, 150
*montera* 292
*moondah* 50

Moors 58, 60, 62, 64, 106
Mora 246
morality, and costume 24
*morion* 176
Morlaix 306, 310
Moses 18
*mouches* 210
mourning 182, 208, 222
*moustache* 188
Movi 10
*mozetta* 200
M'Pongue people 50
muffs 210
*muleta* 290
mummification 26
*munuri Suleiman* 124
Muslim dress, in Malaysia 48
Muslims 96, 114, 118, 120, 122, 124, 284, 298
Mut 10
mutilation 46, 78
*Muyneira* 294

# N

*nankeen* 270
Naples 160, 286
*nartachis* 102
Natal 50
*navicella* 288
Nebraska 68
Negroes 52, 60, 62
Nephertari, Queen 10
Nero, Emperor 32
Nertchinsk 272
Neutraer 280
New Hebrides 44
New Mexico 70
Niams-Niams tribe 52
Nicephore Botoniate, Emperor 128, 130
*niederleibel* 262
*niutze* 274
Nonconformism 200
Norris, Sir Edward 186
Norway 242–6
Notre-Dame de Chartres 150
*Nouroux*, Feast of 114
nuns 116
Nuremberg 166

# O

*obi* 90
*oboukh* 278
Oetzhal 262
Ogilvie clan 254
Oliva, abbey of 152
Oran 60, 64
orator, Roman 32
Oregon 70
*orfray* 134
Orense 292, 294
Orient, The 116
Orsova 280
Osiris 10

Ottoman Empire 118–124, 282
Oustioug-Jelezepolski 272
*oustrough* 284

# P

*paboudj* 118
Padua l60, 286
*pagne* 48
pagoda sleeves 214
Pahouin warrior 50
*Pal* people 104
*palla* 22, 24, 32, 130
Pallas Athena 26
pallium 24, 128, 130
*pallulae* 22
Palma 296
palmata 128
Palou 124
*paludamentum* 22, 32
panniers 182, 214, 216, 220
*panseron* 184
Papuans 44
parasol 82, 90
*parazonium* 36
*parents* 300
Paris (Greek hero) 20
*parma* 36
Parsees 106
Parthamaspare, King of the Parthians 20
Parthians *see* Persia
Passeyer 262
Pathans 100
patriarch 164
*pectoral* 18, 36
*peda* 44
*pelisse* 274, 300
*pelta* 26
peltast 26
*pelzkappe* 198, 260, 304
*pen-bas* 310
perfumes 24
Pericles 26
Persia 110, 112, 114
Peter the Great, Tsar 270
*"perruques à la régence"* 212
Persia 20
Persians, in Assyria 16
Pesello, Francesco 154
*petasus* 28
*pet-en-l'air* 24
Peul tribe 50
*phalangite* 26
*phaleroe* 36
*pharos* 24
Philip of Artois 136
Philippino Indians 46
Philippus Bardane, Emperor 130
*Philomele, à la*, style 238
Phrygian cap 132
Phrygians 20, 30
Picart, Bernard 212
Pierre de Dreux ("Mauclerc") 150
Pierre Repnine, Prince 270
*pileus* 30
*pilum* 36
*pin* 80